Edited by
Thomas T. Smith

. . . .

University of Nebraska Press

Lincoln & London

A
Dose of Frontier
SOLDIERING

. . . .

The Memoirs of Corporal
E. A. Bode,
Frontier Regular Infantry,
1877–1882

© 1994 by the University of Nebraska Press.
All rights reserved.
Manufactured in the
United States of America.

The views expressed herein are those of the author and do not purport to reflect the positions of the United States Military Academy, Department of the Army, or Department of Defense.

⊗

First Bison Books printing: 1999
Most recent printing indicated by the last digit below:
10   9   8   7   6   5   4   3   2   1

Library of Congress Cataloging-in-Publication Data
Bode, E. A. (Emil Adolph), b. 1856.
A dose of frontier soldiering: the memoirs of corporal E. A. Bode, frontier regular infantry, 1877–1882 / edited by Thomas T. Smith.
p.   cm.
Includes bibliographical references and index.
ISBN 0-8032-4232-8 (cl.: alk. paper)
ISBN 0-8032-6160-8 (pa.: alk. paper)
1. Bode, E. A. (Emil Adolph), b. 1856. 2. Soldiers—Southwest, New—Biography. 3. Indians of North America—Southwest, New. 4. Southwest, New—History—1848– 5. Frontier and pioneer life—Southwest, New. I. Smith, Thomas T., 1950–   . II. Title.
E786.B68   1994
978'.02'092—dc20   93-26155
[B]   CIP

Contents

. . . .

Illustrations

MAPS

. . . .

Acknowledgments

As in any project of this nature, there are the contributions
of innumerable persons to acknowledge. Professor Joseph G.
Dawson III, of the History Department at Texas A&M University, served as taskmaster, mentor, and comrade in my
graduate studies of the U.S. Army on the frontier. Dr. Donald
H. Dyal and Ms. Terry Bridges of the Special Collections of
the Sterling C. Evans Library at Texas A&M University not
only introduced me to the Bode manuscript but cheerfully
provided a constant source of background material. Mrs. Judy
Crowder, the archivist of the Fort Sill Museum, took an immediate personal interest in the project, becoming an inval-
uable source of local history, maps, photographs, and a wide
range of archival material. Mr. Towana D. Spivey, director of
the Fort Sill Museum, shared his extensive knowledge of
available photographs and very kindly provided a detailed
orientation of the old fort's geography and architecture.

Robert M. Utley was kind enough to offer his wise counsel
and valuable suggestions toward selecting a methodology for
dealing with the Bode manuscripts. Although she did not agree
with the methodology I had selected Sherry L. Smith of the
History Department of the University of Texas at El Paso
provided keen insight from her perspective as a cultural historian and important advice from her own experience at editing
the diary of another frontier enlisted man. My uncle, Kenn
Smith, not only proved to be a good trail partner, but also
found the key army document entry that verified Emil Bode
was indeed our man.

And heartfelt thanks go once again to my wife, Holly, and

especially to my son, Miles, and daughter, Dustin, who are good natured about having a daddy who, when not gone to the field "playing army," himself, is lost somewhere among the soldiers of the last century.

Introduction

"**A** dose of frontier soldiering" is how Corporal Emil A. Bode neatly summed up his experiences in the West. His recollection of his duty in the post– Civil War frontier army is unique in many respects. The bulk of military memoirs of the frontier are by officers or their wives, yet his is the record of a common enlisted soldier. Of the few accounts of enlisted men from the period the majority were written by the cavalry elite. However, Bode was an ordinary foot soldier, and like all infantrymen, was well aware of the class difference. He wrote, "There is more laboring than soldiering in the U.S. Infantry. In the cavalry companies . . . there are very few on extra or daily duty at the forts."[1]

Many frontier soldiers were at least sympathetic to the situation of the Plains Indian but had limited immediate contact with the tribes. Bode lived directly among the Kiowas and Comanches on their Indian Territory reservation. In the course of his duties he carefully observed and formed opinions on these tribes as well as the Southern Cheyennes, Cherokees, and Apaches. He admired much about the various Indian cultures that faced, as he put it, "incarceration in the gilded cage of civilization." He formed lasting attachments to warriors as individuals and Bode, like any lonely young soldier from any land, had an eye for pretty young women. He admitted that on one occasion an Indian "Cupid" had "sent an arrow clear through the old rusty armor" of his bachelorhood.[2]

Although Bode was often in potentially dangerous situations and confrontations, like the majority of the soldiers on the post–Civil War frontier he never fired his weapon at an Indian, nor did an Indian shoot at him; his life was more frequently threatened by rattlesnakes, prairie fires, raging rivers, angry bulls, and by accidental discharges of rifles than by Native Americans.[3]

Except for a brief stint during the Victorio Campaign, in which he was engaged in chasing Apaches on foot, or, as he put it, "running after shadows," then-Private Bode spent the bulk of his military years in the workaday business of soldiering in Louisiana, the Indian Territory (present Oklahoma), present New Mexico, and Texas. He spent this time on guard duty, on escort, on telegraph repair, and on kitchen or work details.

By and large he enjoyed his adventures as a soldier, particularly the pageantry of military parades, the camaraderie of his peers, and the excitement of exploring new lands. Although he has probably included more than one entertaining tall tale or "war story" in this memoir, his memory is fairly accurate as to sequence of events, dates, and specific details when measured against the available military records of his unit and posts. His chief pleasure, revealed in the stories about wild game in his memoirs, was hunting and fishing. During his constant life outdoors he developed a passion for zoology and botany, traveling with *Line Battany* [Botany] in hand, carefully observing or preserving flora specimens.

With the exception of his marksmanship and hunting skills he seldom took himself, the army, or the world very seriously, modestly playing down his contributions and achievements, always aware of his limitations as a soldier and of the frailty of human nature. It is with a self-deprecating manner and keen sense of humor that he manages the everyday trials of a junior enlisted man in the West.

Typical of Bode's ecological interests as an amateur naturalist, his only moment of rage is expressed in dismay over the sight of rotting animal corpses littering the prairie: "They were slaughtered by the merciless buffalo hunters. . . . If buffalo have no right to live why shall we permit deer, antelope, and other game to exist, why not exterminate them all. . . ."

His narrative is filled with wry comments about junior officers — "Lieutenants are generally good after they have lost their West Point ways," — with well-known frontier army names such as Lt. Henry O. Flipper, Mackenzie, Shafter, Davidson, Hatch, Buell, and Grierson. Bode has equally poignant quips about sergeants, his peers in the ranks, and even green recruits, one of whom he describes as "Darwin's missing link of some backwoods — just fresh from the farm with a frame and walk like a cart horse, back like a camel, with brains to match a monkey."

Bode's account is unusual simply because his experience and focus are on the ordinary. Although the leadership elite and "guns and drums" will always be at the center of military history, it is necessary to have detailed examinations of the more common, or grassroots, level of experience to help complete the picture. Bode's memoirs make a significant contribution to our understanding of the social dynamics of a military unit, and provide new anecdotal insight into better known episodes, places, and personalities of frontier history. For ethnic and cultural historians Bode offers a glimpse into the life of the reservation Comanche society as well as that of other tribes. These statements perhaps reveal more about Bode's own cultural attitudes than about the Indians he observes. However, historical analysis aside, the important characteristic of Bode's memoirs is that they are entertaining, a good story.

Bode probably pronounced his name with a long "o," as in "abode," with an "ie" ending, so that it sounds like "Bodie." While on guard duty at the Fort Sill guardhouse he is sometimes listed in the log book by the Sergeant of the Guard with the phonetic spelling of "Body" or even "Boddy."

Born in Schonhagen, Hanover, on 8 January 1856, Emil Georg Adolph Bode and his three brothers may have had a relatively comfortable middle-class childhood. His father, Georg Heinrich Theodor Bode, was a schoolmaster, as was his grandfather, which may explain why Emil was literate and, for a recent emigrant, had such an excellent command of English. His mother, Charlotte Friederike Emile Forster, was the daughter of a master mirror maker. Their American connection came through the children's godparents, probably uncles, Kaufmann Adolph Forster of Philadelphia, and Heinrich Forster of Baltimore. Bode's father died in 1868, soon followed by his mother in 1869, leaving the thirteen-year-old boy an orphan. Possibly he then came to the United States to live with one of his uncles.

Bode enlisted in Company D, Sixteenth Infantry Regiment in New Orleans on 1 March 1877. Listing his occupation as "laborer" the Register of Enlistments describes him as five-foot, ten inches tall with blue eyes and sandy hair. With the exception of several short periods of detached service he served his entire five-year enlistment in the same rifle company. Discharged at Fort McKavett, Texas, on 28 February 1882, his company commander noted that he was "intelligent, temperate, trustworthy." The captain described Bode's character as "excellent." In a frontier army with as many as one-third of the soldiers deserted and a good number in the guardhouse, Bode's honorable service is well above the norm. He also serves as a good example of a European emigrant in the army. During the post–Civil War period nearly one-half of the soldiers were foreign born. Although he was promoted to sergeant a few weeks before his discharge, these memoirs focus on his duty as a private and corporal; therefore I have titled him at the latter grade, a rank that he took reluctantly but served in admirably.[4]

Little is known of his life after the army. He may have died young, as he never applied for an Indian Wars pension. The memoirs were written sometime between 1884 and 1889, as he mentions that Colonel Ranald S. Mackenzie was at the time in an asylum. Mackenzie was confined in 1884 and died in 1889. The drafts of several letters included within the pages of the manuscript reveal that in the 1880s Bode traveled by railroad in what he calls his "business," spending a great deal of time in both Chicago and Dayton. Although he does not specify precisely, he may have been a surveyor. A journal accompanying the manuscript has several highly detailed hand-drawn topographic maps of New Mexico and of the vicinity of El Paso, all created within a large-scale survey grid. The journal narrative consists primarily of minute topographic descriptions of various mountain ranges, rivers, and roads of the Southwest, and includes annotations of longitude and latitude. The draft letters also reveal his continuing interest in botany, mentioning he had sent to Texas for shipments of various cacti and other plants. He likewise maintained an interest in the activities of his old army comrades, passing gossip and swapping addresses along with last-known locations of friends from the rifle company.

Bode states that he originally enlisted because of "peculiar circumstances," and "without hope of a speedy relief in civil life." This is a reflection of the widespread unemployment and economic depression still lingering four years after the Panic of 1873. The economic situation helped keep the ranks of the army nearly filled during this period, with 10,080 new recruits or reenlistments by late 1876, a 22 percent increase over 1875. Bode's enlistment in 1877 came just before the lack of appropriated funds halted all army general service recruiting.[5]

The U.S. Army that Bode joined in March 1877 conducted such a wide range and diversity of missions that one scholar later dubbed it "the government's obedient handyman." Four months before Bode enlisted for five years in the ranks the secretary of war, James D. Cameron, cataloged in his annual report to Congress the multitudinous tasks undertaken by the army. Soldiers maintained the seventy-eight national cemeteries, ran a military prison at Fort Leavenworth, and were in the processes of publishing the mountain of official records of the War of the Rebellion. The Adjutant General's Office, in addition to its normal duties, was responsible for the Bureau of Refugees, Freedmen and Abandoned Lands, a mission finally winding down after a decade of aiding freed slaves and trying to sort through the political chaos of a defeated Confederacy. The secretary additionally reported on the status of army preparations for an exhibit at the Centennial Exhibition in Philadelphia. Army engineers were supervising the United States Military Academy at West Point, erecting public buildings in Washington, D.C., maintaining and constructing seacoast defenses, supervising public works such as the improvement of rivers and harbors, conducting engineer surveys of the Great Lakes as well as geological explorations, and topographic and hydrographic surveys of the Western territories. The Army Signal

Service was collecting scientific data and issuing meteorological reports and storm warnings to farmers and seaports. The Ordnance branch maintained arsenals and supervised the production of weapons and munitions.[6]

Yet Bode's army was on the verge of a fundamental transformation from a constabulary force concerned with nation-building and police duties to an increasingly professional force with one central peacetime mission – the preparation for war against any adversary. This change in the army's mission paralleled the slow change in national outlook from a continental focus to an internationalist-imperialist stance that would mature with the Spanish-American War.

A subordinate task in which Bode became directly involved was the ongoing installation of a military telegraph in the Southwest. Bode became something of a specialist in the installation and maintenance of telegraph lines, spending so much of his enlistment on this task that he and his fellow infantrymen became "as well acquainted with handling a crowbar as [they] were in the manual of arms or any other military exercises." He was on the detail that completed the Texas and Fort Sill–Fort Reno, Indian Territory telegraph connection, and as a noncommissioned officer led a number of repair crews. He enjoyed this mission for it gave him some degree of independence and took him out of the dull routine of fort life.[7]

Although these were nation-building or ancillary tasks Bode was also directly involved in the army's primary missions. At the time of Bode's enlistment in March of 1877 the U.S. Army's Reconstruction occupation of the old Confederacy had diminished to two artillery regiments and five infantry regiments in the Department of the South and the Department of the Gulf, the two commands embracing most of the Deep South. This represented 2,751 soldiers and officers, or about 10 percent of total authorized army strength. Rather than a general occupation the troops were assigned in 1876 the specific mission "to preserve order in the South," a result of the excitement generated over the disputed election contest between Rutherford B. Hayes and Samuel J. Tilden. Bode joined the Sixteenth Infantry concentrated in New Orleans and seemed unaware, or at least did not mention, the broader political issues, perhaps because the expected violence did not materialize.[8]

While other regiments in the South deployed for strike-breaking duties in Northern cities Bode and his regiment soon departed New Orleans for the Indian Territory. This move involved him directly in a second major task of the U.S. Army, that of being the government's primary instrument of policy concerning the "Indian problem." The secretary reported to Congress that the army would compel the Sioux to "acknowledge the authority of the government," something of an understatement, considering the disaster the previous summer with Custer and the Seventh Cavalry on the Little Bighorn and the campaigns then underway to crush the Sioux. Although Bode was not to be involved with the Sioux he would become a part of the force trying to police the government's reservation system in the Indian Territory. The secretary of war noted that in the recent period there had been no serious outbreaks and by removing the Indians' arms and ammunition and concentrating them on reservations it looked "as if the 'Indian problem' was approaching a solution."[9]

Neither the Secretary nor Bode would anticipate the festering situation in September of 1877 when a group of Mimbres Apaches under Victorio broke from their reservation in Arizona Territory and renewed intermittent warfare in New Mexico and Texas for three years. In May of 1880 Bode and his Sixteenth Infantry Regiment were rushed to New Mexico to participate in the final phase of the campaign to subdue Victorio. Although Bode enjoyed camp life and the hunting opportunities the mission offered he was highly critical of the conduct and leadership of the campaign and saw himself involved in "a useless occupation of chasing Indians from one section of the country to another."

Bode found equally odious the government's Indian reservation policy, and disliked his own role as "game-keeper," depriving the Indians of what was "natural through birth [and] citizenship of America...." However, Bode viewed himself and the army as the protector rather than the persecutor of the Kiowas and Comanches that he lived among at Fort Sill. "The Indians are . . . kept at the mercy of the agent and are driven through his dishonesty on the warpath. Whites infringe on the rights of the Indian and cheat them at every turn." On a number of occasions Bode went with his captain to inspect contract beef "to see if the Indians got their due." After an experience with the ruthless methods of the Texas Rangers, Bode considered the army to be somewhat more humanitarian. ". . . [T]he U.S. troops endeavored to kill as few as possible and to capture alive if possible in order to take them back to the reservation. . . ."

Bode's thoughts about Indian campaigns and reservation duties were shared by many of the professional soldiers of his day and reflect an army uncomfortable with the disagreeable "Indian problem" mission. The army was generally considered a frontier constabulary, a responsibility that was rapidly becoming unneeded, or as the secretary of war had put it, approaching a solution. The army of the 1870s and 1880s, with Reconstruction over and the Indians barely a minor threat, had greatly diminishing constabulary tasks and was ripe for transformation into a professional, modern force.

Some intellectuals within the army had never truly embraced the frontier constabulary concept and as early as Winfield Scott's tenure as general-in-chief in the pre–Civil War era had argued that the army's peacetime purpose should be to prepare for war with another professional army. The impetus toward this concept was even stronger after the Civil War, when military reformers began to reflect on the complex requirements demanded by a modern war in the industrial age. An American army repeating the improvisations experienced in 1861–62 would be unlikely to survive a confrontation against a well-trained European adversary.[10]

This pressure for military reform was in direct opposition to the traditional national policy of maintaining a small peacetime army designed as a constabulary and a defensive force to buy time while citizen volunteers answered the call to arms. That the army leadership treated the frontier mission as a distasteful stepchild is reflected in the fact that although drill manuals were created for linear tactics against another professional force the army did not explore a doctrine or formally study effective tactics for conducting Indian campaigns. Successful methods of warfare against the Indians were worked out by individual commanders and were not transmitted as a body of knowledge to other officers except through informal personal networks or as folkways handed down by frontier veterans. What worked in one military department might never be tried in another. Inconsistent methods used in the field combined with the lack of coherent national policy concerning the "Indian problem" provided decades of frustration for the officers and soldiers such as Bode who were involved in the mission.[11]

To carry out the multitude of tasks cataloged by the secretary of war the U.S. Army had a composition in 1877 of twenty-five regiments of infantry, five of artillery, and ten of cavalry. The army was short about 10 percent of its total authorized force of 27,442. It was near the size of just two of the seven Union corps at Gettysburg and yet was expected to police the West as well as carry out the additional assigned tasks enumerated by the secretary of war. Two cavalry and two infantry regiments were composed of white officers and black enlisted men. The nineteen original infantry regiments of late 1861, with the exception of the Fifth Infantry, had seen extensive service in the Civil War, in either the Eastern or Western Theater.

Bode's regiment of the Sixteenth Infantry, for example, was formed in April 1869 from the consolidation of the Eleventh and Thirty-fourth Infantries. The Civil War battle streamers of the Sixteenth Infantry included the campaign on the Peninsula and the battles of Second Manassas, Antietam, Fredericksburg, Chancellorsville, Gettysburg, the Wilderness, Spotsylvania, Cold Harbor, and Petersburg. The Sixteenth Infantry was very near full strength when he joined in 1877 but its ten companies had been reduced to only 65 percent of authorized strength at the end of his enlistment in 1882.[12]

Bode would probably disagree with one historian's characterization of the soldiers of a post-war regiment as "poor white trash and semiliterate immigrants." About 50 percent of the recruits of this period were foreign born, but did have to undergo, as Bode relates, a medical examination and character determination. Bode was an emigrant but far from semiliterate. Like Bode the majority of recruits were from the unemployed and laboring class. In spite of the high desertion rate and the limited quality of the troops the army of the mid-1870s was probably at least as good as the army of the mid-1970s, with its problems of drug use, racial strife, and lack of discipline.[13]

After Bode had signed his papers he had time to reflect and observe. He later wrote, "I confess after seeing a little deeper under the shining exterior, was not a very brilliant one." He discovered the reality of soldiering in the infantry was hard marching, occasional danger, slow promotion, low pay, and poor rations. Reforms in the 1870s had somewhat improved the quality of the soldier's life, easing the harsh discipline of the antebellum era, providing post schools, sports, libraries, and even encouraging a company garden to improve the diet. That garden, as Bode learned, required a soldier on the end of the hoe. The other luxuries, such as books, came from company funds earned by selling off the company's flour as baked bread. Thus even the well-meaning reforms were not free of a cost to the soldier. Nevertheless, Bode endured and even flourished, coming into his own as a trustworthy soldier and junior leader. At one point on a frozen prairie he spent the night trying to keep warm by a fire, staring into the flames and weighing a civilian's life against the hardships he had endured as a foot soldier. In the end Bode concluded, "I was perfectly satisfied where I was."

I first came across the Bode manuscript in 1991 as a regular army infantry captain (with ten years in the enlisted ranks) engaged in graduate research at Texas A&M, before I began an assignment to teach military history at the United States Military Academy at West Point. I was searching for new material to include in a monograph history of the nineteenth-century U.S. Army in Texas. The head of the Special Collections of the Sterling C. Evans Library, Texas A&M University, Donald H. Dyal, told me of this interesting army memoir. He had purchased the holograph manuscript and journal for the Special Collections in 1986 from the late John H. Jenkins. The Jenkins Company Rare Books and Manuscripts, Austin, Texas, carried the manuscript in its catalog, described as being by an army engineer, "Emil A. Baue." Within the manuscript is part of a letter Bode had written and signed in such a way so the scribbled "o" appears as an "a" and the hasty "d" is unclosed, looking like a "u," thus it was listed and later cataloged as "Baue" instead of "Bode." The company's only record of acquisition is that it was bought from an unnamed book dealer somewhere in Mr. Jenkins' travels. Following his purchase Donald Dyal had a student worker, Lisa Petersen, make a typed transcription of the memoir and journal, a painstaking labor resulting in 448 typed double-spaced pages that required eighteen months and countless ad hoc conferences on the meaning of hastily scribbled, illegible, or abbreviated words.

Being a fortunate student of military history in the right

place at the right time and the grateful beneficiary of the efforts of Dr. Dyal and Mrs. Peterson, I had the opportunity to edit the manuscript for publication. The methodology I selected for this task requires a brief explanation.

The handwritten manuscript has five basic parts. The first two parts are an original draft and a revised version of the period 1877–80, covering Bode's enlistment, the move from New Orleans to Fort Sill, Indian Territory, duty at Fort Sill, and the receipt of orders to Fort Gibson, also in the Indian Territory. Part three covers the period 1880–82 and is the original draft of the period at Fort Gibson, the Victorio Campaign in New Mexico, and of his duty at Fort Davis, Texas. Part four, which I have labeled "Bode's Journal" is a dated journal kept for the period 1880–81. The fifth part consists of various short notations that are labeled as revisions or paragraph insertions to the other parts. I have used these insertions as Bode intended, but without specific notation.

I combined the two-part draft and revision of the period 1877–80 by taking the most interesting or descriptive words and portions of each and fusing them together to form a single narrative. To avoid the endless and distracting use of brackets I have tried to limit their use to only those places where I was required to add a completely new word for clarification. For part three, the period 1880–82, I have cross-dated specific dates or places with Bode's Journal of the same period to make clear the time or location. Bode's Journal is treated more or less as a separate document, but there are a few places where the journal contains insight or interesting narrative not found in the original manuscript memoirs. I have added that narrative to the appropriate place in the memoirs, usually by subject rather than by chronology, using a footnote to indicate the source.

I saw no value in retaining Bode's tortured punctuation, abbreviations, and phonetic spelling, thus "Armee" becomes Army, "sircumstance," circumstance, "enspection," inspection, "co," company, etc. Bode had the habit of mixing present, future, and past tenses in the middle of a sentence. I have taken the liberty to impose the tyranny of the past tense while leaving unchanged the root verb, thereby giving a smoother flow to the narrative. English was Bode's second language and much of his awkward sentence construction makes better sense in his native German. The decision to embellish the very rough original version in this way was not an easy one. In the end I decided to follow the likely policy of any would-be nineteenth-century editor of Bode's manuscript by correcting and regularizing spelling, punctuation, and grammar. For the researcher whose study requires the original of Bode's irregular language usage, the 448 pages of typed transcript is available in Western Box 2, W2, the Special Collections of the Sterling C. Evans Library, Texas A&M University.

1

. . . .

Enlisting in the Infantry,
1877

Finding myself under somewhat peculiar circumstances and my vital powers gradually decreasing without hope of a speedy relief in civil life, I concluded to go under the protecting shield of Mars and join the United States Army, with its well-fed, well-dressed, and citizen-honored sons.[1]

Entering the custom house at New Orleans one chilly day in February 1877, where a regiment of infantry was stationed, I inquired of the sentinel if they wanted any more fighters. The answer being affirmative and directed up a flight of stairs, I passed the main body of the guard from whence another

stairs brought me to the top floor. I found myself in a large
room with iron bunks around the wall, bedsacks folded up
and nicely deposited at the head of the bunks on which were
blankets and clothes displayed for inspection. The bed slats
were scoured white – on which were the haversack and knapsack, the latter filled with rolled up trousers drawers, socks,
and towels. The harness, canteen, and polished tin cup, black-
ened belts, and cartridge boxes [were] ready for inspection. At
the foot of each bunk stood a small box in which was kept
the cleaning kit and rest of the clothes. Back on the walls
were shelves and racks in which covered and uncovered guns
stood ready for use.

The men were variously employed, some sat on their boxes
cleaning equipment, while others were playing cards, or laying
on their bunkboards with their legs dangling over the foot of
the bed, their heads resting against the bedsack, either smoking
or reading books. Addressing myself to one in regard of enlisting I was directed to a cluster of men. Starting in that direction I heard some voice sing out "Attention!" As if by magic
everybody jumped to their feet, standing straight and staring to
the front, heels on line. Almost frightened out of my wits, the
call had also a magic effect on me, it made me stop with hair
standing up. My first thoughts were that this was all for my
special benefit, some initiation performance, an invitation to
ride the goat. But the goat, it seemed, was not yet ready for me.
A "Never mind" from the Captain who had just entered
brought everyone back to their former occupation.

I went to a man with a powerful voice who proved to be
the first sergeant of the company, and inquired of him about
enlistment, which was answered after a criticizing look. Just
then I heard a big cowbell ring and seeing everybody jump
up I expected now the initiation. The sergeant inquired if I
had my dinner. Being answered in the negative he took me
into the dining hall where I saw hundreds of men feasting,

each company having two tables for their men. Here I was given meat, potatoes, bread and gravy which I relished to the great satisfaction of my kind host and future superior, not knowing when and where I had my last meal.

I was soon summoned in the [Captain's] presence for my primary examination. This I fortunately passed. Applications were forwarded for a physical examination by the regimental surgeon. The afternoon came when I and another forlorn individual were taken to a small room where the doctor, a clerk, and the hospital steward were waiting. We were now ordered to dress à la Adam and Eve and put through different maneuvers. The body and mouth were examined, the breast sounded, and the eyes – taking squints with first one then the other eye at charts with different colors and letters. I was declared passed, the other [recruit] rejected.

Every applicant's descriptive list and surgeon certificate was sent to Washington, D.C. for approval before the oath to the flag could be administered. For five days I waited the return of my papers which left me sufficient time to reflect upon the future, which, I confess after seeing a little deeper under the shining exterior, was not a very brilliant one.

On the first day of March [1877] I was again summoned into the presence of the Captain – to take the oath of allegiance to the United States and at the same time to be clothed from Uncle Sam's clothing store. I was now a soldier, subject to orders and compelled to obey them, whatsoever their nature.[2]

A sunrise drum called us to reveille where everybody, in line with the rest, answered to his name, after which bunks were made and the room swept out. The quickest move of the day [was] to the mess hall, answering the cowbell for breakfast – a ration of a little over one-half pound of meat with that indispensable gravy, six ounces of bread, and one pint of coffee. I have heard malicious men say that the coffee was made by boiling the shadow of a coffee bean suspended above the pot. Dinner was about the same quantity of meat and bread with the addition of some vegetables. Supper consisted of a feast of bread and coffee.[3]

After breakfast some prepared for guard mount, others marched to the police sergeant for fatigue duty at the custom house (where they had the opportunity to fill pockets with fine confiscated cigars), the recruits prepared for an hour or two of drill in the forenoon with a repetition in the afternoon. Retreat sounded at sunset, at which time a cannon was fired in the regular forts. Tattoo generally was at eight P.M., another roll call, and taps one-half hour later as a signal to go to bed.

[Retreat] began the time of recreation for the weary warrior. He would get a pass to leave the building, make a race of four bits or a dollar somewhere, meet a soft-hearted civilian, and be shown the town. He would come home either late at night or not at all. When drunk and noisy he would be locked up in the guardhouse under hard labor, taken out to work his headache off. Charges preferred against him with a tail [list] of specifications, he would usually be convicted [sentenced] to a month in the guardhouse with the loss of ten dollars pay. While in the lockup he would use all his ingenuity to obtain liquor, when out at work he would contemplate how to work without doing anything.

Free from the hands of the guard once more he would look to borrow money. When not successful he would examine his box for clothes or new shoes or try to draw some from the company in order to sell them for whiskey. The captain kept enough clothes on hand to meet the immediate wants of the company and would issue every month or fourteen days to every man who was in need, charging it to his clothing allowance varying from $24 to $60 a year. If our gallant soldier should not be successful in the above he would wait until dusk, hook a pair of shoes or blanket unobserved, and throw it out of the window where a pal would catch it on the fly.

Time rolled on and soon I was considered an accomplished

warrior after receiving thorough instruction in drill and the manual of arms. Our Jewish drill sergeant and my superiors seriously contemplated putting me on guard duty, which in a recruit's eyes is the highest accomplishment, a knight's last stakes to a soldier. The day came when I was marched down to guard mount, turned over to the officer of the day and, through one of his subordinates, marched to a sentry in order to relieve him, placing me at his post. A string of orders was turned over to me, but the only thing I recollected was how many prisoners I had to watch. Of these, in five minutes, I did not know how many I ought to have, the affair being more complicated every moment through prisoners being taken out and brought back [to the guardhouse]. Thinking to place myself on the safe side of the bunk I called to one of the petty officers of that day, who, in his turn, thought it advisable for his own good and mine to place me in a less responsible place, posting me in a quiet corner to watch the woodpile. This I did faithfully by marching up and down for two hours, impressing the woodchoppers with my authority.

Men came, enlisted and deserted, and still I was there, apparently to stay. Two months passed and the first payday dawned upon my horizon. Oh what excitement. Long rows of gambling tables were prepared for the event, everything busy and boiling. The afternoon came, everybody was paid. Here were the men standing behind tables shouting "up she comes, down she goes, a one, four and six, and bet there!" The habitual gamblers luring a few suckers and greenies into a chuck-a-luck game; further on a faro and keno game in full blast, while in a corner twenty-one and monte played by an anguished looking crowd with feverish eyes on the card which would make them five or twenty dollars richer or poorer. Groups of fours had blankets spread over the bunkboards, indulging in quiet games of poker. In this way our soldiers passed their payday until all the money was gone, satisfied that their luck was against them.[4]

. . . .

Another class of our heroes paid their debts, twenty-five cents interest on every dollar for two months or less, after which they [would] go out for a spree that meant a beastly drunk, returning to quarters with empty pockets, generally missing one or two roll calls. Put in the guardhouse he would be taken care of by a kindhearted guard and fellow prisoners. The latter would go through him and take all the money the sirens missed. If he had no money left the rest of the prisoners would convey a court. This august tribunal would sentence him to receive so and so lashes, administered to him while held across a chair, or to be "blanketed" – which means the prisoner is put into a blanket which four strong men hold by the corners. A jerk sends the poor victim flying in the air, arms and legs working to all points of the compass, caught and thrown again. These guardhouse courts-martial are more dreadful than the legal military punishments.

The payday pleasures and excitements having died out I was taken to the hospital with a chronic attack of diarrhea, from which a great many of the troops were suffering and dying, attributed principally to the Mississippi River used for drinking purposes. I was placed in a bed which stood next to a man who was there with a vile disease brought on by immoral habits, rotting body and soul. Looking about the ward I saw men suffering from all kinds of ailments – some with sore arms caused through vaccination and made worse by the individual in order to get discharged from the service. Others were lame or crazy, or suffering of consumption, chills and fever, and secret diseases caused through unclean and immoral conduct, which, with shame I confess, existed to a great extent – both officers and men.

Seeing men dying daily and feeling myself a little uneasy I concluded to get out of that place as soon as possible by finding [pretending] strength in the presence of the doctor, [and was] successfully detailed for duty a short time afterward. Thinking that wine would be of great benefit to my shattered system I purchased a bottle of claret and kept it between the folds of my bedsack, in the absence of a cellar. I [soon] found it gone. Every bottle I purchased afterwards went the same way, compelling me to abandon the hope of recreation on this line. I could not find the thief at the time, but hearing the details afterward, the thief being discharged and dead, a friend of his disclosed the fact that the man thought me in such a low state of health that the wine would only be thrown away, consequently of more benefit to a living than to a dead man.

The time drew near when the troops were ordered to more exposed places in the Union and preparations were made to leave New Orleans. Tents were put in good condition, field cooking utensils examined, boxes packed and taken to the railroad cars to be conveyed to our destination. The day came at last when we marched to the depot with the regimental band in the lead.[5]

JOURNEY, NEW ORLEANS TO FORT SILL, JUNE 1877

T. Smith

2

· · · · · · · · · · · · · · · ·

En Route to Fort Sill,
June 1877

The seventh of June 1877 saw us slowly drawing out of the station of New Orleans by special train for St. Louis. Sentries stationed on both sides of the car prevented the men from leaving or from obtaining much liquor, but plenty of New Orleans manufactured ice and whiskey was flowing to produce a marked change in the men: some sang, others defacing or unscrewing everything in the car, as if the devil himself had taken command of the company, no married man or officer being present, they having a separate car for their use.

Past cotton fields and over bayous we sped with a parting

glance at the Crescent City, entering Southern forests. Sky high trees formed a dark roof over the green stagnant water, long strings of moss hung from the branches while trunks were covered with creeping vines. Fan palms and other swamp plants spread their leaves like shields to catch the few rays of light permitted to pass through the roof above.

Night came over us and a deathly sleep soon settled over those who only a few moments [before] were all life. Not so with the ones who had less indulged in the bottle. These unfortunate beings felt the seats – offering a comfortable place for the short man, but by no means to a long one whose legs were in constant misery by putting them in all imaginable positions. Came Morpheus, as grateful to them as he was to the worshipers of Bacchus.

Cairo [Illinois] dawned upon our sight a few days later, where our cars were put on a ferry across the Ohio River to the Illinois side. From here we passed innumerable fields of wheat and corn and the black entrances of coal mines. The same evening brought us to East St. Louis, across the river bridge and into the tunnel of which we found out by the suffocating smoke entering the windows. We left the cars for Jefferson Barracks, a few miles from the city.[1]

The atmosphere stifling hot, it was evident a thunderstorm would soon be on us. Before we had gone [far] the sluices of heaven opened and brought down hail and water on those unfortunate beings who still had some miles to walk. We came to the sheltering roof of the barracks drenched to the skin. In front of the building in rain and a lake was a mountain of knapsacks which had been carried by the wagons. Everybody trampled over his own and others' property to seek only what could been seen with the assistance of a lantern. We soon stumbled with "somebody's" knapsack into a dark room assigned to us as our temporary barracks.

When Aurora showed her blushing face the next morning

on the eastern horizon everybody made a pleasant discovery
– the property he possessed was not his, wet blankets and
clothes, guns rusty and muddy, everything "lovely." We remained four or five days which gave us sufficient time to put
our equipment again in good order. In the meantime our cooks
prepared for the field by cooking the salt out of the pork with
a slight boiling and storing [this] "Cincinnati chicken" in boxes
for immediate wants.[2]

Our marching orders were received in due time and we
found ourselves again imprisoned in nine cars en route to
Caddo, Indian Territory. Immediately west of St. Louis the
train kept to the valley of the Missouri River, bordered on the
south by small grapevine covered hills. Reaching Sedalia,
Kansas [actually Missouri] about dusk we had to exchange for
a south-bound train.

We followed a level country to the south, with German
looking hedges on farms, entering the Indian Territory under
the same landscape, passing no farms, but occasionally a small
Indian village. Within a short distance of the Arkansas River
the country assumed a more hilly appearance. After passing
a fort [Fort Gibson] we reached Caddo and selected a place
five miles west of the railroad as our first camping grounds,
giving us the first sweetness of camp life. Strictly speaking
we were still inside the limits of civilization, although everyone
could not resist the feeling of something foreign, especially
when we were attacked by small insects the size of a red dot,
fastening their sharp pincers into our tender skins, creating a
by no means pleasant sensation.[3]

Caddo, an Indian village of about 2000 on the Missouri,
Kansas, and Texas Railroad, was principally inhabited by the
Choctaw, one of the five tribes brought from Carolina and
Florida. They were further advanced in civilization than a
great many whites and farmers in the states, not to mention
the negroes – but did not enjoy the privileges of citizenship

like the latter. As may be expected the country was overrun with lawless whites, who impressed the Indians with a very low standard of our civilization.[4]

Thousands of cattle grazed in the valley and hillsides where daring cowboys kept watch over them. Who would not envy a cowboy's freedom, but certainly not his lot, which was far from being a bed of roses, night and day on the alert, exposed to weather and wind. Clad in a blue or gray shirt without collar, gray or brown pants in front of which [was worn] a protective leather shield, a pair of boots with large Mexican spurs, a slouch hat, and a cartridge-belt with pistol around his waist, the attire of the Indian Territory cowboy generally different from that of his Texas brother. His horse was either an Indian pony or mustang which he constantly rode with fancy light halter, heavy saddle and stirrups, one blanket under, another blanket or coat at the rear of the saddle, a little frying pan, coffee kettle, and long rawhide lariat comprised his earthly wealth. If [he were] rich there would be coffee, sugar, salt, a few pounds of bacon, and a box of matches tied in small bags, on which he could travel a great many miles. His pony was his home, riding here or there, dashing into the herd with lasso flying around his head, yelling at the top of his voice as he singled a certain animal out of the herd. This set of men were generally good-hearted and jolly, only when they had whiskey on board were they a little too reckless with their pistols.[5]

The company's property and men's private boxes had been transferred from the railroad cars to "prairie schooners" and were on their way to Fort Sill, our destination, 165 miles west of Caddo. The prairie schooner was never found in the more settled country. The four and one-half or five foot high-boarded sides of the wagon were wider at the top than bottom. A smaller wagon was generally attached to the rear, both covered with canvas stretched over bows. This train was drawn by six mules or six to eight yokes of oxen, the latter kept in line by the voice of the driver, while the [mules] were kept in motion with a long whip. From five to twenty such double wagons were frequently seen, crossing the prairie like a huge snake with a white back.

The company started on its first march, walking an hour and resting ten minutes. I, being yet in poor health, was detailed as permanent "kitchen police" or chief cook and bottle washer, in which capacity I had the privilege to ride in the cookwagon, a government vehicle or freight wagon of a straight bed twenty inches high covered with canvas for transporting the company's rations, drawn by a six mule team. My work, very light, consisted principally of gathering enough firewood for a few kettles of coffee and frying a little pork. Dishes – I had none to wash, as every man was compelled to take care of his own tin cup, knife, fork and meat dish of an oval tin plate fitting exactly over a frying pan, the handle of which could be folded over the plate and clasped at the other side, issued to every man as his marching outfit. Our rations on this march were barrels of salt pork, hardtack, coffee, beans, sugar, salt and vinegar. Besides the rations and cooking utensils we had to carry on the cookwagon the four company tents and the men's blankets and knapsacks.

The first day went well, riding on the top of the bows like a broad-backed horse, the wagon not having been scientifically packed owing to our ignorance of camp life. The country spread before us in ever changing scenery, beautiful forests and boundless prairie. The road became very rocky and we held on to the hoops of the wagon for dear life, tossed from side to side. Dismount and trot beside the wagon? – No!, a bad ride was preferable to a bad walk.

[Suddenly at] a high steep bank everybody prepared to jump off, but it was too late, the brake-chain on, the driver held his mules back as we found the hind part of the wagon high above the front, expecting to be hurled to pieces on the rocks. We shot down the embankment as if fired from a cannon,

arriving softly at the bottom of the creek, a cold chill running
through us [from] the danger. In order to prevent future chills
I concluded to walk at such places, descending from my lofty
position. Before us was a steep bank. Eight extra mules were
hitched to our wagon and the black-snake applied to their
hides, a terrible yelling of the drivers, a shower of gravel from
the hooves and the wagon had gone. There was no time to
be lost in silent wonder so I hastily ascended and resumed my
position.[6]

The camp reached and wagons unloaded, tents pitched with
occupants lounging on the outstretched blankets, smoking or
playing cards, while their guns were loosely strapped to one
of the upright poles of the tent. In the evening candles illu-
minated the canvas town, with bayonets doing service as
candlesticks, songs and laughter making the spot an oasis in
the prairie. Soon the scene changed. A cloud, at first small
and insignificant, grew larger and larger until it hung above,
enveloping us with an impenetrable darkness. The lightning
which followed was blinding, the thunder deafening, shaking
the earth to its foundation. The terrible storm drove everything
before it, destroying our whole beautiful village, leaving us at
the mercy of the tempest. Passing as fast as it had come the
damage was soon repaired and everybody slept, except the
guards, who were trying to guard what they could not see.

Long before daybreak the next morning the bugle sounded
reveille, ten or fifteen minutes later the companies were on
the march, the city of canvas folded, nothing [to] be seen
except wagons winding their way across the prairie. By sunrise
we had traveled quite a distance. Fortunately the road got
smoother, the wagon taking pity on my poor soul, softly rocking
side to side, lulling me to sleep. One of the hind wheels
dropped into a deep hole in the road, sending my limber body
heels over head, whirling through the air and landing unceremoniously on the prairie. Being truly awake I mounted my
angry "steed" and stuck there.

From my elevated position I had a splendid view. In every direction a soft rolling prairie covered with rich gamma grass, in the bottoms a height of six feet and over. Along the rivers cottonwoods, elm, oak, and pecan shaded the waters of streams with black bass, catfish, and mussels. Colonies of beaver here built their dams, flocks of wild turkeys roosted on the inclining cottonwoods at night, seeking their food in the sand hills at daytime, preferring a certain red berry the size of a gooseberry to any other. Larger game such as deer, panthers, wild cats, catamounts [mountain lions], coyotes, antelope, and the occasional wolf afforded exciting enough pleasures for the hunter. Wild horses, it was claimed, roamed this prairie, but in all my trips I can not say I ever knowingly saw a real wild horse.

We drew near a farm where the daughter of the house stood in the frame of the cabin door, attired in a bright calico skirt, the picture of Indian perfection. We threw a kiss, receiving a smile in return, the cruel wagon moving too fast.

Entering a forest of dwarf oaks and walnuts interwoven with poisonous vines we gained a clearing where the Indians had constructed a church, schoolhouse, and a shade built of trees and branches for summer service. The children were children; rich, poor, civilized, or wild, they enjoyed the freedom alike when relieved of the strains of school. It did our hearts good to see them chase each other or mount their little ponies and bound off like the wind.

In sight of the Little Blue River we camped. Situated a short distance of the camp was an Indian blockhouse surrounded by a fence to which a couple of magnificent ponies were fastened. Indian maidens, the most bewitching beings I ever beheld, made their appearance, mounted their ponies and were off before I knew that I was head over heels in love with one of them. I really felt sick in the region of my heart and was convinced that Cupid had sent an arrow clear through the old rusty armor of my bachelorhood. I took a good bath in the cold stream and returned to the house to find out more about the unknown, but without success. Many a time I passed afterward on detached service, but never had the good luck of meeting her again. I left camp the next morning with a feeling of loneliness and the knowledge of a lost heart.

Governor Harris' was our next camp, in a rich valley, deriving its name from an ex-chief of the Chickasaw who lived in a neat little farmhouse in the center of a well-kept flower garden. [He] owned, besides a great number of cattle and horses, a store and a flour mill. Two well-educated daughters conducted his house, who had been married to white men but were shamefully deserted by them, after the adventurers had stolen a herd of market cattle from the chief.[7]

After crossing a few more creeks we came to the Washita River and Cherokee Town, an Indian village of about 500 inhabitants on the left bank of the river. A very clever bridge was thrown across the deep muddy stream. The bridge was built entirely of wood. Sections of heavy logs linked together formed six-cornered boxes filled with heavy rocks. These formed the pillars upon which the bridge rested.

While passing over one of the small knolls between towns we saw the frontier stage, drawn by four horses, draw up to a post on which a cigar box was nailed. The driver deposited a letter. Coming closer we saw the unmistakable lettering "Post Office" on the cigar box — but could discover nothing of the postmaster.

The population of these [Washita Valley] towns were generally law abiding people but this valley was infested with a lawless band of thieves who stole horses or cattle in Texas and sold them again in Kansas, New Mexico, or Colorado.

Crossing the Texas and Kansas Cattle Trail [we discovered] a depression where a prairie dog community had built their homes. Our arrival caused quite a sensation. They threw the front of their bodies into the air, giving a long yelp, after which they rushed for their holes, peeping over the edge, barking and keeping time with their tails.[8]

At last we ascended the hill which concealed Fort Sill from our view, passing Cache Creek on its course south to where it empties into the Red River. Above the confluence with Medicine Bluff Creek lay the small elevation of the fort which glittered in the evening sun as the last rays fell upon the blue limestone walls of the buildings. Two miles west the steep walls of Medicine Bluff could be traced running in a half-circle, forming an invincible barrier. It appeared as if forces in the bowels of the earth had split the surface, forcing one section [to] form a bluff where rolling prairie ought to be. The bluff derived its name, according to Indian tradition, from a medicine man who made a leap over the precipice to prove his power over death. What ever the truth of this, it remains a fact that the Indians celebrated their sun dances, their most solemn dance, within sight of these bluffs. Besides [this] they bury their dead on the top.

Six to seven miles southwest of this bluff was a hill of 700 feet. A small stone house erected on the top was formally used as a signal station from where the movements of Indians were signaled to the fort. It was called Signal Mountain.[9]

West and northwest of this hill is the main cluster of the Wichita Mountains, the highest in the territory, about four or five thousand feet. The range covered an area of 200 miles, was well watered and covered with a luxurious growth of timber. The puma, bears, and other wild beasts still held undisputed sway over the rest of the animals. Indians were in former years very hostile in this section and many a battle has been fought by them for their liberty, but they had to gradually submit to their incarceration in the gilded cage of civilization.[10]

One mile southeast of the fort was the Indian agency, partially hidden from our view by the trees along the creek. Indian tepees could be seen in clusters along the bank, while highly colored figures, mounted on light-footed ponies, headed for our wagons, twenty or thirty galloping across the prairie to head us off. Our guns [stored] way down in the bottom of the wagon, to get them out then was too late. Our hair began to rise as we pictured ourselves in hot battle — our small number overpowered, taken prisoner — tortured! The Indians came up rapidly. After a greeting of "How John!" they appealed for tobacco, which we readily gave them, after which our new friends took their departure and left us to continue our way to the fort.[11]

The trip over, we were stationed in very neglected infantry quarters, which unfortunately were the only barracks there built of wood, and got a dose of frontier soldiering.[12]

3

· · · · · · · · · · · · ·

Fort Sill, 1877–1878

Fort Sill, Indian Territory, on the southern extremity of the line of Indian agencies, was first established in 1869 by General Sheridan under the name Camp Sheridan. The Kiowa and Comanche Indians had been brought from their wild haunts in Texas and placed there on a reservation with their agency a short distance from the fort. A vigorous but cautious policy had to be followed to accustom them to their present homes. They were [then] well-pleased with their present situation and most of them had farms or herds of cattle from which they derived a comfortable revenue.[1]

American western forts were not, as their name would indicate, fortresses with breastworks in a zig-zag [with] cannons

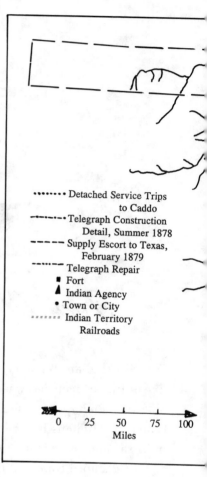

•••••• Detached Service Trips
to Caddo
–•–•–•– Telegraph Construction
Detail, Summer 1878
– – – – Supply Escort to Texas,
February 1879
–––––– Telegraph Repair
■ Fort
▲ Indian Agency
• Town or City
======= Indian Territory
Railroads

0   25   50   75   100
Miles

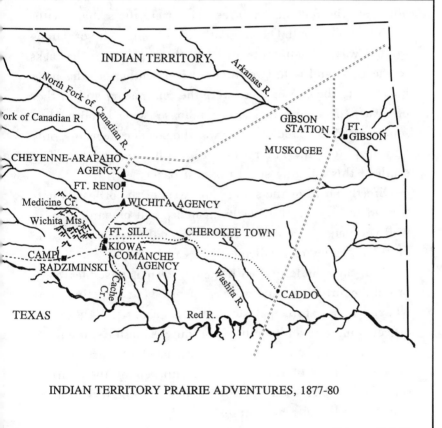

INDIAN TERRITORY PRAIRIE ADVENTURES, 1877-80

T. Smith

planted behind entrenchments. Fort Sill, for instance, had a large square parade of 400 to 500 feet with a flagpole in the center. On the north and east sides were neatly constructed officers' quarters, surrounded by an orchard. On the west side were the cavalry quarters with large dining rooms and kitchens adjoining the rear, and 300 feet west were the stables [with] a ten foot high wall. On the south side of the square or parade ground was the adjutant's office with two infantry barracks to the right and left. Two hundred feet south were the band quarters, to the east of these were the commissary and further on [was] the quartermaster's storehouses. One hundred feet southwest of the band quarters was the powder magazine, only fifty feet from the latter was the guardhouse, and fifty feet south of this building stood the post bakery.

Directly north of the stables and west of the officers' quarters, in the center of a newly created peach orchard, stood a well-ventilated, nicely constructed hospital overlooking to the north the valley of Medicine Bluff Creek.

All of these buildings, with the quartermaster stables, comprised the fort proper and were constructed of a blue limestone which was the principal stone of that country. East of the officers' quarters and south of the quartermaster storehouses were the small picket houses constructed of upright logs, isolated shelters of the wives and children of the married soldiers, quartermaster employees, post interpreters, traders, and a church and schoolhouse.

One-quarter mile northwest of the cavalry stables was the post trader's establishment comprising three or four buildings, one corner of one set apart for the post office with its modern improvement of letter boxes. The post trader was an indispensable evil of the forts. There everything from a collar button to a saddle, and all kinds of hardware and grocery goods could be obtained [by] paying exorbitant prices. Drinks were furnished direct over the bar or through an order signed by an officer of the fort, at the rate of twenty-five cents for one glass of beer and $2.00 a quart for "rot-gut" stuff called whiskey.

A stagecoach ran thrice a week to Caddo connecting with the railroad and the rest of civilization, completing a single [one-way] trip in thirty-six hours.

The municipal power of the fort was vested in one person – the commanding officer, who had as his assistant an adjutant. Next in power to the commanding officer was the "Officer of the Day" selected daily from the officers of the fort, and properly relieved every twenty-four hours by his successor. His duty consisted of quelling any disturbance in the command and seeing that the sanitary rules were properly enforced in the fort and camp. He was always assisted by a sufficient force of guard who were [also] detailed daily and relieved at the same time. The post commissary and quartermaster offices were generally filled from headquarters with either civilian or commissioned appointees belonging to these special branches, as was the post medical staff, ordnance, and telegraph officers. The telegraph office, filled by regular enlisted men or civilians, [was] solely under the surveillance of the signal officer in Washington, and not subject to the orders of the [post] army officers.

The ordnance of every fort was in charge of an ordnance sergeant appointed by the department. The quartermaster at the forts had the power, if permitted by department headquarters, to select clerks and teamster civilians who in [any] other respect would not be permitted on the reservation fort.

A quartermaster had a wide field for dishonesty placed within his reach. He could (and a great many did so) cheat the government in different ways. There were, for instance, 20,000 lbs. of useless corn to be condemned by the commanding officer, where in reality only 5,000 lbs. was presented for inspection, the rest of the sacks filled with sawdust or sand. Or some poor government mule died and was examined by the officer, while a day or two later another mule [dies], and if the weather cold, more mules could die in succession, the body of the first mule representing the other absconded animals. These are only two ways, while there were more than a hundred ways to get rich from Uncle Sam's pockets. The medical head and doctor had the same chances as the quartermaster and commissary, as he was generally the post treasurer and in this had charge of the post bakery where an enlisted man could buy an extra loaf of bread for five cents, and a civilian or Indian had to pay ten cents. From a civilian in need of medical treatment the doctor could slide an unobserved bill into his own pocket.[2]

There were [also] the captains of the companies with their share of easy gains. The day on which the commanding officer of a fort examined and condemned serviceless [unserviceable] property was always considered a day of rejoicing for all parties concerned, except the superior officer [who] did his duty and saw personally that the condemned articles were destroyed, in which case he would find a great many bright faces rather disappointed [and] dark. Nevertheless there were always more bright than dark faces. The commanding officer would go to a company, see an old [canvas] fly of a wall tent, or formerly condemned pieces of tents [that] were again representing a complete tent, [and] with a superficial glance at the pile, condemn the articles to be destroyed immediately as unfit for further service, remaining until preparations are made to burn the old "tents." Presuming that $500 instead of $5 worth of government property lies in ashes, they are checked as [off the records] out of existence. A couple of hundred dollars worth of property and tents may [then be] moved by the captain, afterwards represented as his private property. Officers and men could have tents to the value of $40 to $80 and never pay a cent for them.

[There was] an easy way of making a gun or horse. A man for instance deserts a company without taking anything belonging to the government. If he should be caught he might have found in the company records that he stole a horse, saddle, gun, or pistol, for which he would be charged besides desertion. In this case the first sergeant of the company made an affidavit that such and such article was taken when [the man] deserted. There were very few first sergeants who did not make a false affidavit in the five years of [my] service.

Amongst the captains were some great fellows who deserved to be put on ice instead of being in command of troops. There was one captain who stood at attention when speaking to his first sergeant, while the sergeant suited himself about his own position. Another fine specimen of an officer took a lantern when making his rounds of the guard. That same gentleman ridiculed himself by sending reports of his Indian slaughters to certain newspapers, [events] which had never taken place. Most of the company commanders were of a kicking disposition, delighting in aggravating a weak superior in every possible way, and my captain, H. A. Theaker, was one of the principal.[3]

Lieutenants were generally good, even second lieutenants, after they lost their West Point ideas. Lieutenant Flipper, the first colored man who passed West Point and was commissioned in the regular army, was assigned for duty with the 10th Cavalry (colored) at Fort Sill. He was at first met with contempt by his brother officers, and his tact kept him away from places where he was not wanted, that is, the officers' homes. But his superior knowledge and good tact soon brought him in close commune with his captain who made him his confidential friend and advisor, and entertained him in his private home. Whenever the Captain got into a scrape his lieutenant was sure to get him out. He also proved his courage in a couple of engagements with horse thieves. While he was apparently enjoying the love of this officer and the respect of the men, his enemies were quietly at work laying snares and traps wherever he went. At last they succeeded. It was later at Fort Davis in 1881 where Flipper was made acting commissary officer and accused of intentionally defrauding the government by Colonel Shafter. He was found guilty and dismissed from the service.[4]

Colonel [William R. "Pecos Bill"] Shafter, of the 1st Infantry, was a good and daring leader, but a man without morals or character.[5]

Speaking of officers I would say a few words about a certain colonel, [Lieutenant Colonel John W. Davidson, Tenth Cavalry]. Commanding officers were also at times subject to the weaknesses of mankind. This gentleman was an opium and morphine eater under the strict leadership of his wife. He would walk up to the flagpole on the parade ground in the morning and raise his cap to the flag. He was also seen by the guards at the fort in unworthy and ridiculous places for a commanding officer. He would go up to a sentinel in civil dress and play a suspicious character, or try to enter, unobserved, places under the guard's watch. In which he was, by some sentinels, humored, detained and recognized. But by others he was brought to his senses and treated as a suspicious character, that is he was kept standing in one place with the gun pointed at him, until the arrival of the corporal of the guard. In respect of dignity this colonel could not be beat – a sergeant as orderly had to be at his door, instead of the legal private.[6]

Colonel [Ranald S.] Mackenzie of the 4th Cavalry, the three-fingered Jack (on his right hand) in command of the fort [1875–77], was one of the ablest fighters in the West, in my estimation the only man fit for command of troops amongst Indians. He was strict, but well-liked by all his subordinates, his strong hands kept order, no officer slaves to "kick" like under other camps. The Indians looked to him as their father, they received punishment when they deserved it, but their grievances were also well-considered and investigated. He was not afraid, like his successors, to arrest Indians, put them in ball and chain, and send them out to work in order to obviate an outbreak. This officer is now in Washington, D.C., in an asylum, crazed from drink.[7]

[Colonel Edward] Hatch, commander of the 9th Cavalry and of the District of New Mexico in 1878–80, [was a] perfect gentleman, probably a very clever general in a civilized war, but against hostile Indians the principle objection against him was staying at headquarters at Santa Fe, receiving and giving orders to troops at remote places – where an immediate order and quick execution would have been crowned with success.[8]

Colonel [George P.] Buell, then in command of the 15th Infantry, was ordered to suppress an [Apache] Indian outbreak, but instead of selecting seventy-five or one hundred mounted infantry with twenty-five extra horses and a pack train of about fifty mules, a force sufficiently strong enough to capture any number of hostile Indians, he also went into an extensive scale by taking a long slow tour of government wagons and 800 or so men across trackless plains and mountains, where time was precious.[9]

Colonel [Galusha] Pennypacker [Sixteenth Infantry], having received over thirty wounds during the war, some of which were still running, was most surely unfit for an active service needing a strong hand to rule a lot of contrary and kicking subordinates, where a graceful hand only causes a greater relaxation in obedience and respect.[10]

Colonel [Benjamin H.] Grierson of the 10th Cavalry, preferred the safe side.[11]

Lieutenant Colonel [James] Van Voast of the 16th Infantry had a mania for working the troops.[12]

Major [George W.] Schofield of the 10th Cavalry was a perfect gentleman, but the penny was his god. At one payday while I was orderly for him, I had the pleasure to walk about ten or fifteen times to the different offices, all for thirty-five cents [extra pay]. As major at the fort he had nothing at all to do so he passed his time by experimenting in the improvement on pistols of which he had an interest. [Schofield perfected the automatic ejector for the Smith & Wesson .45-caliber pistol]. Once while at Caddo this same major engaged a negro woman for his servant, brought her up to [Fort] Sill on government transportation and, it was said, made her work for two months free for her fare.[13]

Having partially sifted the commissioned officers in their capacity as officers and gentlemen of the Army, we take a step or two lower and look at the noncommissioned officers and men. We [would] find there the same as with the officers. How could it be otherwise? – So the master, so the servant.

In charge of every kitchen was a corporal [or] sergeant who had to draw the rations every ten days for all the men in the company and supervised their proper cooking and division among the men. In case the company did not use all the rations this man was authorized to dispose of the surplus in the most profitable way and turn the money over to the "company funds," in charge of the captain. The captains generally wish to give the men all they [are] entitled to but they had unfortunately a chief of the kitchen with a hole in his pocket, or [perhaps] one of the cooks would have an Indian sweetheart with a bottomless desire for coffee, especially sugar.[14]

Being still in poor health I concluded to go to the hospital and get well before doing post duty. For two months steady [I was] in the post hospital, swallowing opium pills by the dozens without success. From the early morning until late at night I made lonely trips across the back yard [to the latrine], greeting every breeze as a welcome strength-giving draft from heaven. My feelings were rather depressed at the time and I frequently thought how sad it would be to leave this loveless and cruel, but nevertheless sweet, life and exchange it for an imaginary one. Such were my thoughts when leaning against the deadhouse overlooking from a high bluff the lovely dark green valley [with] the silvery Medicine Bluff Creek passing at my feet. One early summer morning before the sun had taken possession of the day, and while in one of my sentimental moods, lost in meditation, I did not observe the approach of a small white and black animal, until it was almost in reach of my hand. I retreated as fast as my feeble condition would permit, pelting it with stones after learning of the "strong" power of its weapons. Another time I received the full benefit [of] its "cologne" [but] I easily killed the [skunk's] stink by an application of coal oil.

A few nights later at the hospital, while on one of my nightly picnics, I happened to meet with a more dangerous adventure. This time it was a wild cat who had forced an entrance into the chicken coop and played havoc amongst our rooster and his family. I opened the door [and] to my surprise saw [the] beast shoot past me with a tender or tough chicken (I hope it was the latter) in his fangs, soon disappearing into the brush.

We had a little white rooster belonging to the hospital laundress who made his appearance in our [barracks] yard every morning. We had two or three large roosters in our flock but none was equal in strength and endurance to our little stranger. So one day the death sentence was passed over him and he was subsequently captured, beheaded, and put into [an oven] to roost. How our mouths watered for the morsel as we waited for him to bake. At last he was done and a sharp dissecting knife inserted into the body. If our roosters had found their jawbones and spurs too weak and dull to penetrate the tough flesh of that little fellow during his life, we discovered that he still retained his tenacity after death.

Seeing that the [opium] medicine would eventually ruin my system, I concluded to take my case in hand and put myself [on a] light diet in which I so well succeeded to be considered by the doctor, in a short time, fit for duty. Through his kindness I was detailed for extra duty in the hospital, first as a nurse, then as an assistant cook in which capacity I received twenty cents a day extra pay in addition to my soldiers pay.[15]

While thus employed one Sunday morning I received direct

notification from my company commander to attend inspection. Here I was one hour before the time of inspection, without gun or equipment, and if then issued to me – too late to clean properly. The best thing I thought I could do was to stay where I was and not attend. I did most respectfully decline the invitation, in other words I ignored the order. Charges of disobedience were in consequence put against me by my captain and forwarded to the commanding officer of the fort for approval. [These] were returned by Colonel Mackenzie to the former with a copy of an order excusing all extra and daily duty men from roll call and inspections.

One day at the hospital while standing in the kitchen washing dishes and pots I heard a faint yell. In the life on the plains nothing startles a "greeny" more than the war whoop of an Indian so without losing further time I rushed out to see what was going on. To my horror I saw a long line of Indians galloping full speed through the woods, yelling like devils. My first thought was an attack upon the fort, but I was soon convinced of the absurdity of that idea. They soon entered the fort, attired in their best, yelling as if this was their last chance on earth, having a parade with the permission of Colonel Mackenzie. In the front and rear of the line were five chiefs clad in their feather headdresses which reached down to both sides of their horses' flanks. Then came about 150 yelling and whooping Indians. After the parade there was a reception of nations.

After working at the hospital for some time I was taken sick with chills and fever [malaria]. Only a person once afflicted with them can form an idea of what they are. At first a person feels cold, even if it is 105 degrees in the shade, the teeth commence to chatter and hammer together as if a flour mill. When this spell came I would go to bed and cover myself with all the blankets I could find, dozing off as the chills passed over. Awakening two or three hours later was like a dream – a terrible heat in my throat, all my senses were numbed, the evening concert of the regimental band sounding like the strains of fairy harps and music from another world. [With] ten-grain doses of quinine after a week or so I was again considered well and sent to my company for duty under the command of the man I angered by refusing to attend inspection, my place as cook in the meantime being filled by somebody else.[16]

The equipment was issued to me and I mounted my first guard in the Indian land. Night came, the sky clear and bright, not a cloud to disturb the beautiful speckled arch above me, not a sound to be heard as I walked my post around the haystacks on the outskirts of the fort, at least three-quarters of a mile from the guardhouse. I was meditating, building aircastles for the future (the usual occupation of sentinels) [but] was interrupted by a peculiar odor, carried to me on the gentle breeze, followed shortly by an Indian from whom this sweetish odor originated. The Indian was on his way to camp in the bottom near the creek where the others were engaged in preparing for a dance in which the Indians indulged the night before their ration day, once a week.[17]

The broken threads of thoughts were running again when the faint sounds of howling dogs interrupted me once more. The sound came nearer and more distinct. My imagination carried me into the spiritual world, the yells seeming to come from every direction, floating in the air while nothing was visible or any other noise audible to my straining ears. I was almost convinced that there were ghosts or at least the spirits of the "wild hunter" in the air. All my imaginations were cut short by the appearance of the real hunter — not ten feet away I saw burning eyes staring at me like two red coals. A cold chill ran down my back as I saw a pack of wolves throwing hungry glances at this sweet morsel. A few lumps of dirt soon brought them to a greater distance and, as if by command, gave me a parting concert as they took the direction to the Indian camp.

I strained my ears for the welcome footsteps of the relief party but instead heard the click from the sword of the officer of the day making his nightly round of the guard. Mad with disappointment I thought to take all the satisfaction I could out of him. [I] let him go all the way round the haystacks and as [he] turned the last sharp corner I brought my gun down to "charge bayonets" with as much emphasis as possible, challenging "Who comes there!" He stopped as if made of stone, but came to life after receiving the command "advance and be recognized!"

Now it was his turn to crow. "Where have you been, asleep?" "What are your orders?" A great many bewildering questions were asked such as, "What would you do if a steamboat would come up?" Not a very sensible question to ask at a place 500 miles from any navigable stream, in the middle of a prairie amongst uncivilized Indians.

Soon after the officer had left the relief party came, finding me standing at the nearest corner of my post. I was relieved and had four hours to rest before my turn came again for two more hours [of guard]. At the guardhouse [I] rolled in a blanket, asleep without having been permitted to unrobe or take off any equipment. No sooner asleep when there came an order [to] turn out the guard for the officer of the day. Everybody seized his gun and ran outside. I, half asleep, could not find my gun and grasped a broom standing in the corner, appearing with it in the line of the guard. The officer passed down the line in front of the guard and prisoners, the latter in their nightdresses. I was passed without being detected [without a rifle] and punished by the officer. The guard was then dismissed and we returned once more to our bunks to obtain as much sleep as possible in the short time before going on post again. I returned to the room with a much lighter feeling, thanking my lucky star and the darkness to pass inspection undetected with a broom. Next [I] looked for the gun, which I found under my bunk where someone had kicked it.

The clock struck three [A.M.] and we were aroused and posted on our respective places by the corporal of the guard. The Indians had ceased singing, the wolves [ceased] howling. I resumed my duty as sentinel around the haystacks with no other nightly visitors or companions [such] as Mr. and Mrs. Skunk. The morning air [being] chilly I selected a cozy place between the hay for a short rest. Soon heavy lids dropped over my eyes and I was fast asleep.

How long had I slept? Had the relief been there and another sentinel posted? [These] were my first thoughts as I awoke and saw a faint light on the eastern horizon, the cock announcing a new day. A walk and investigation showed I was still king. Slowly the faint shimmer of the coming sun extended along her path, broadened the eastern horizon into the morning, gradually spreading with a beautiful carmine.

A few hours later we were standing on the porch of the guardhouse waiting to be relieved by the new guard at nine A.M. when one of the corporals, in a playful way, brought his gun to his shoulder, pointing it at an old white horse about forty feet away, feeding on the grass around the magazine. Passing the remark that he could hit that horse right in the eye he pulled the trigger of that unloaded gun. How great was his and everyone's astonishment as a sharp report and cloud of smoke issued from the muzzle of the rifle, transforming the corporal almost into stone. All eyes directed to the horse, but he looked unconcerned, continuing his meal to the great relief of the sharpshooter. Strange to say nothing was done to him for his carelessness, which should have been severely punished by the military authorities.

The following morning we, the old guard, reported to the police sergeant for fatigue. The police sergeant was a noncommissioned officer appointed by the commanding officer to attend to the sanitary condition of the fort and had, to this end, the prisoners and fatigue parties under his instructions. Some of our party were sent to the sawmill, where an old

. . . .

boiler, afterwards horses, furnished the moving power for the
circular saw.

Others were sent on the water wagon, a box holding 400
gallons of water drawn by eight strong mules. [After] filling
the wagon with rubber hand-buckets in the creek [the water
detail made] about five trips a day to supply the fort, bringing
water from the creek to the barrels of the troops, laundresses,
and gardens, by a hose on the rear [of the water wagon], or
to wet the roots of orchards and shade trees. We were ordered
to put fifty buckets full on newly planted trees around the
parade ground, drowning every one. Still another party was
furnished with scythes to cut the high weeds in the vicinity
of the fort.[18]

As I previously stated I got the best of my captain, if I may
use that phrase, when refusing to attend inspection while in
the hospital as an attendant. [I], being [again] with the company, my captain did not lose an opportunity to take his revenge
on me and find fault wherever it was in his power to do so,
especially on Sunday morning inspections. I was reprimanded
and checked at every inspection, nothing was clean or neat
enough, although I was selected immediately [after] at guard
mount as the cleanest man for orderly by the adjutant. As
orderly for the commanding officer or officer of the day my
duty being to be always in the presence of the officer, to
transmit any orders by him. [If orderly] in the evening I had
the liberty to enjoy my bed undisturbed.

4

. . . .

Indians and the Indian Territory, 1878-1879

Weeks passed and I was detailed in the kitchen as assistant cook. Each company had two cooks who were detailed from the men of the company and required to attend to that duty for ten successive days, although if they were willing they remained permanently. Their duties were not very inviting for the majority of the men. At three o'clock in the morning they were awakened by the guard [to] boil the coffee [and] get the meat prepared for breakfast.

At reveille the kitchen police put in his appearance, assisting the cooks, washing the dishes and pots, scrubbing the table and floors, chopping wood for the kitchen, also for the dining room in winter, in general the roustabout in the kitchen. Daily inspection was at ten o'clock, when everything had to be clean and shining. There was continual work, with a few hours rest in the afternoon, from morning until seven or eight at night.

One morning the cooks were late, their own fault, in the evening [before] nothing had been prepared – no water in the coffee boiler – out rushed the cook to the water barrel and soon had his kettle full. At reveille breakfast was ready and our coffee stood smoking in our pint bowls as we sat down to our morning mess. Our meat was brought to us and it soon disappeared, but not so the coffee. After blowing at it long enough to bring its temperature down to a lower degree we discovered bones, potato peels, etc. An investigation showed that [in the dark] the cook had filled the coffee boiler from the swill barrel instead of the water barrel which stood near.

My entree in the kitchen as cook took place soon after. We had on the fare for that day beans, regular army beans [that had] been soaking in water overnight. Being late that morning I put them in a boiler without examination. When looking at the beans a half hour later I discovered scorpions floating on the top. Time was precious and something had to be done to give the men their dinner. It was too much of a loss to throw the beans away and I concluded to taste them – should they make me sick the beans would have to be thrown away – if not I concluded to go on and prepare them for dinner. The beans stood on the table that noon – and never had tasted better to the men before. Useless to say I did not eat beans that day, and I examined pots before using [them] in the future.

Being now an expert military cook I was detailed in that capacity to the Indian farm, where I had an opportunity to see and study these beings at their homes.[1]

A band of dissatisfied Comanche Indians had, in the summer of 1876, gone back to their old hunting grounds in the Staked Plains of Texas. They were captured by the 10th Cavalry with great difficulties under extreme hardship and were returned to their agency at Fort Sill. They were first locked up and confined in prison but subsequently two bands numbering about two-hundred were taken to a place five miles from the fort where a farm and houses were built for them by the troops. They worked the farm raising corn, watermelon, muskmelon, and living in their old tepees while their horses were stabled in the houses. They were kept under the supervision of the military for one year, [then] the bands were separated and their camps located in different places.[2]

One band had their camp immediately on the outskirts of the fort and was under the supervision of a soldier. This worthy young man made himself very intimate with the squaws and almost lost his life by the hands of a jealous husband who entered his tent one night and struck him over the head with a tomahawk, inflicting a ghastly cut across the forehead. There was almost an Indian outbreak over this.

The jealous husband of the squaws and would-be murderer was subsequently apprehended and taken to Fort Smith, Arkansas for trial. A U.S. marshal was sent to Fort Sill to procure the witnesses in the case. He was accompanied by soldiers and the post interpreter to make the Indians understand the nature of the mission. Through some blunder of the interpreter the Indians thought that the man [witness] was to be arrested and they naturally resisted the authorities. The consequence was that a couple of Indians were shot and two or three wounded. The Indians began the fight by feigning friendship, shaking hands with every white man. Soon a shot was fired, the Indians driven back, and the dead and wounded [soldiers] thrown into the wagon [and] sped back to the fort.

Cavalry was immediately ordered to the Indian camp and the infantry kept under arms at the fort. The Indians saw their mistake and kept quiet while we put their wounded into the hospital and the dead in the guardhouse, from [which] they were buried in the military graveyard. Strange as it may seem the [dead] Indians had been scalped in the guardhouse by some guards or prisoners overnight, and had naturally, in that state, [been] kept from the sight of the other Indians or there might have been some more "fun."[3]

Notable during this excitement was the display of courage amongst the "old soldiers." One claimed to be in charge of the kitchen, the others had passes – but they had to go along!

At the beginning of the year [1878] there were at least fifteen guards at the camp, but shortly before the excitement took place I was the only one, besides a corporal with another band one-half mile from mine, who guarded the Indians or at least camped with them. There were from twenty to twenty-five tepees in my section [which] stood in the shade of high trees on the banks of a clear cool stream, Cache Creek. The rations were issued to them daily by the corporal who drew them at the fort. My abode was a picket house on the lower corner of the camp where the farming tools were kept with the tents for some of the homeless Indians.

A young Indian by the name of Tasstaouy who was the most good-hearted fellow I ever met out West, lived, with his mother, two wives, brother and sister, in a tepee next to my picket house. The oldest [wife] was about eighteen years of age and of exceptional beauty with very pretty eyes, but the youngest squaw [was] the reverse of the first, in fact a mere child of eleven or twelve, I think kept in reserve for future marriage.[4]

We were naturally on good terms and mutual exchanges were frequent. I could enter their tepee at any time in the day or evening without running the risk of my modesty being shocked by the display of nude squaws lounging about, or the sight of seeing [them] eating their own vermin, or nursing young dogs, as I have seen others do. They took their baths every day, dressed neat, and kept themselves very clean and tidy. They also used paint, like their civilized sister, only they used red instead of black paint for the lids of their eyes.

The red paint was very artistically applied to their cheeks and eyelids, making the oldest [wife] the most bewitching soft eyed and innocent looking woman in the camp, especially when dressed up [for] visiting. In spite of her beauty, innocent eyes, and good behavior she was not exempt from the weakness of women. She knew she had control over her husband through her beauty, that is as far as a squaw is [able] of getting control, and she kept him there. He would not permit her to work in the field where he worked with the hoe and spade from morning to night, although she would do a little work around the wigwam such as cooking, making moccasins, tanning hides. She had to follow the custom of the tribe, for which the long scars on her arm above the wire bracelet gave sufficient proof.[5]

They [the women] frequently paid me a visit at my house where they offered me a splendid opportunity to study their language and pass the time pleasantly playing casino while the "old man" was at work on the farm. Although always hungry like the rest of the Indians they never made themselves disagreeable with their behavior and I never had occasion to check them with a "vamoose."

Strange sights were seen in [the] Indian camp. A talisman was always to be found in the center of a camp, consisting of a shield, weapons, feathers, and various other articles fastened to a pyramid shaped arrangement formed by three sticks meeting at the top. In front of the chief's tent stood a leather shield, a quiver with bows and arrows, scalps and other articles suspended by three sticks. There a lot of [the] men sat upon their heels around a fire diving with their hands into an iron meat pot — if the piece was not satisfactory it was thrown back and exchanged for another — smoking and discussing the news of the day.

Squaws entered the camp with loads of wood heavier than

themselves. In one of the tents an Indian practiced on a homemade clarinet, a hollow tube with holes in it and dough [clay] used as the mouthpiece. Others amused themselves with gambling, for which [was] used a number of marked sticks. An old man beyond the age of fighting made arrows, straightening the shafts with his still sound teeth. There we [could] see a squaw scraping a buffalo robe with a bone, while others softened [one] by working it to and fro over a rope between two trees, again others had a robe on the ground, scraping and painting it with battle scenes. [Some were] making ropes of rawhide or threads of sinew.

The squaws did all the work in or out of camp and even saddled the horses for the men. The latter hunted and fought, but generally did nothing, or attended to the duties of the family. The girls were brought up to work and were mothers before they were women. The boys were given all the liberties of the race, were early instructed in archery and hunting, and taught the secrets of warfare. They used a stick with different marks as a geographic map.

The [Comanche] men were well proportioned, with an awkward walk, being Plains Indians and always on horseback. They had projecting cheekbones and rather flat noses. Their dress, as may be expected, was original. It consisted, for the men, of a breechcloth kept in place by a string or leather, held around the waist, while the ends fell below the knees. A pair of tight leggings with fringe on the seam, nicely painted, were supported like the breechcloth and elegantly ornamented with beads. [A] buckskin or calico shirt and a red blanket [went] around their waist when on horseback, but covered the upper body and head when on foot. The feet were covered, by the Plains Indians, with a pair of beaded moccasins the style of which differed with the tribes. A leather sock with a heavy sole which curved in front to protect the toes [was worn] by the Mountain Indians.

The hair, parted in the middle and braided with cloth and

scalps, ornamented with bear claws, eagle feathers, and panther teeth, was kept hanging over the left shoulder. Their cheeks, noses, eyelids, and tops of heads were painted with red, yellow, blue, and black circles and lines. As ornaments they wore five or six large earrings. An ornament made of bones or bear claws was frequently seen on the chest, running in four rows, each two inches wide, from throat to waist.

The bows and arrows were made of strong and elastic wood, the two ends of the bows connected with a string made of sinew. There were four different kinds of arrows, one with an iron or stone head, and others with a three or four-cornered painted wooden head, the third [type] with a kind of ball on the top, and the fourth was only worked into a point. Bows and arrows were kept in a quiver made of deer or beaver skin and embellished with beads. Sometimes an Indian didn't consider it beneath his dignity to fish. Their fishhooks were made of bone, and a fish catches himself sometimes on them. The "bucks" were sure with an arrow. I have seen them hit a five cent piece at a distance of forty feet. They [had] also shot their arrows in the air and struck a six inch circle [at] about ten feet.

The Comanche squaw was small and clumsy in shape and by no means a beauty (except some). The women were clad in calico gowns reaching a little below their knees, a pair of leather hose with heavy soles on the lower limbs, and at times a cloak over their shoulders. A nicely made pocket with colors in [it], needles, and other nic-nacs, accompanied [their] dress. Their ornaments were fewer than the men's. Feathers were not worn by them, neither were earrings, and red the only paint which they used. Their hair very seldom reached below their shoulders and was kept loose. They wore wire bracelets on their arms and tin fringe belts with beaded painting, needle cases, besides other tingling articles attached to them.

Remarkable was the squaw's constitution in pregnancy. There was no suspension from her daily labor, no rest on the

road. Should her hour come when traveling she leaves the
pony for about ten or fifteen minutes, rolls the baby in a cloth,
and mounts her pony as before, proceeding on the journey.
Squaws carried the baby in a nicely decorated case made of
buckskin and a board, covering the baby completely, except
the face.

At an Indian death [a] great demonstration was prepared
for his burial. Under considerable crying and singing the body
was put in the grave, with his arms and other property at his
side, then covered with stones and a monument erected to
indicate the place. After this his favorite horse was killed.

The ponies were indispensable to the comfort of the Plains
Indian and [he] would not walk one step if he could ride.
Both sexes rode the same way and mount from the right side
of the horse. Indians were great gamblers and would bet their
last on a horse race.

The tepees were [then] mostly made of canvas stretched
over poles. The height was fifteen feet, the diameter of the
tent twelve feet. However, the old buffalo [hide] tepee was
frequently seen in winter. A flap with a pole attached to one
corner regulated ventilation. Bunks were arranged around the
sides and a place for fire in the center. The opening or door
was four by two feet, with a door of cloth or skin. These tents
were in [a] permanent camp, which were always on top of a
hill, surrounded with shade under which were elevated bunks,
affording a pleasant resting place for the weary hunter.[6]

Small dog-tents, thirty inches high, four feet in diameter
were frequently used on long trips, which in cold weather
were heated with hot stones. The sweat tents were similar to
this, only hide was used for covering the half-moon tent. The
man was then placed in the tent and water poured over hot
stones to generate steam. A good while elapsed and the man
[then] rushed out, plunging in the coolest water he could find.

The agencies issued the rations every week to the Indian,

while [he] had to report in person and present his paper [census record] with the name and number of his family. Clothes were issued every year by the agencies, but were generally disposed of again, with the exception of red blankets, to civilians and [to] soldiers who wished to desert.

On dances they had [four]. The medicine dance [was] kept in a small tent by the medicine man who dances with a knife in his hand around an iron pot, singing and accompanied by a tom-tom drum. The medicine was then given to a sick person or to the warriors to make them bullet proof. A buffalo dance was a representation of a buffalo hunt with a subsequent smoke and dance for the hunters. A scalp dance [was] celebrated after a successful raid where the scalps were put on a pole while the warriors danced around it and "blow" [brag about] what they did do and might have done. The sun dance [was] most important of all. It was the time when the new warriors were initiated and chiefs elected.

The Indians were generally cruel when on the warpath and nothing would soften their hearts. At a raid in Mexico by the Comanche Indians a woman fought to the last but was eventually overpowered and killed, her heart eaten by one of the raiders who assumed the name of Woman Heart [Woman's Heart], afterwards a well-known person at the fort. The Indians believed that by eating a brave person's heart the bravery is transferred to them.[7]

I used to be acquainted with an Indian chief who delighted in telling me his career. At his first raid into Mexico he was given a stick by his father with a serrated mark for each hill, river, or particular formation of the country as his map, to guide him to a certain village or farm. The raid was successful and they returned with one prisoner who had fought like a tiger, to Texas, where the prisoner, after riding for days with his face to the sun, was buried alive with his upper body above the ground and deep gashes in flesh, left to the mercy of the flies and wolves. Another ghastly curiosity of his was the skin with full beard of a white man's face from Kansas who had been killed in a raid.

He also gave many tales about hunting. One evening when his tribe was on a buffalo hunt he took his well trained buffalo pony and ascended a knoll to view the country. His eyes detected a dark spot on the horizon and he was soon in the presence of a negro who was frantic with thirst. The chief said that the negro's horse was half dead but he possessed a fine rifle, pistol, and a belt full of ammunition. He thought to do away with him but in which way he did not know as he did not take any weapon besides a knife when leaving camp. A puddle of water was shown to the negro, who stooped to drink. Quick as lightening the Indian was upon his back and pressed the negro's head under water but the latter was up to the situation. [He] got the Indian in his clutches and made him swap horses, after which he hastily departed. The negro was pursued for two or three days by the Indian but never overtaken.

Indians, even the most cruel, have a soft spot in their hearts. I knew an old war chief, a devoted friend of mine, who loved his children more than anything else. Our friendship sprang up through the sickness of one of his children I had under treatment and cured of malaria fever.

These sons of the forest only had traditional laws and such rules as the chiefs saw fit to apply. In only exceptional cases the government took them to Fort Smith, Arkansas for punishment. There were also Indian police, endowed by the agent with some authority, to keep order and report any disturbance amongst the tribes.[8]

During my stay at the Indian farm, which to my sorrow was only a short time, I took frequent hunts, either alone or in company with an Indian. At one hunt along the creek [we] kept well in the woods, following a drove of wild turkeys. They run as fast as horses and we were unable to get a shot.

At last we came to an open space where the creek made a large bend, giving us a splendid opportunity to cut the turkeys off, getting ahead of them. The grass was about six or seven feet high and in our eagerness to make the cutoff we came almost on top of a cow and calf before we knew it. The mother, angered by the sight of man and maddened by the flash of color in the Indian's breechcloth, lowered her head and came for us. There was never made any faster time as we made that day through the grass – Indian and soldier alike took a beeline for the creek, leaping over the steep bank into the water where our enemy declined from following.

Another day when out hunting alone along the bank of a creek I heard the pitiful wail of a woman. There is nothing which affects a man more than the cry of a female and I thought at first that some jealous Indian was cutting the nose off [of] his unfaithful wife. After crawling to a place from whence I could observe without being seen I saw the woman.

Before me, on the bank of the river, sat a naked Indian squaw. In her right hand she held a large knife with which she was cutting herself across arms, legs, and breasts, causing the blood to flow in streams from gashing wounds while she was singing an Indian deadsong, making other frantic movements with her arms and body.

My curiosity satisfied, I left the squaw to mourn her dead and took a shorter route to camp. My path led me past an abandoned Indian camp with the sticks of their small half-round shaped tents still standing, [with] the formerly heated rocks in the center. I was met in camp by the corporal who had done me the never forgiven trick to get me relieved and a favorite of his put into my place on the Indian farm.

While at Fort Sill I made frequent trips on detached service to Caddo and other points. [On] one of my first trips to Caddo our party consisted of one corporal and three or four men. Our duty consisted [of] escorting a quartermaster to the railroad station. While there we had the misfortune to meet a certain major [George W. Schofield] of our fort on his return from a leave of absence. He naturally took our accommodation instead of the stage to convey him there.[9]

This gentleman had nothing whatsoever to occupy his mind in the fort and had no duties, except [when] the commanding officer was absent, in which case he took the command for the time being. He generally passed his time with improvements of the pistol on which he already had a patent. While on this Caddo trip he engaged a colored woman as a servant and took her to Sill on government transportation, but subsequently made her work two months without compensation as the price of that trip. This gentleman took also the liberty to take freight, belonging to the post sutler, on government transportation, and without doubt received his share for it.

[On] our first day out [from Caddo] a hole got into one of the above mentioned sutler's freight boxes which gradually became longer and longer as soon as it was discovered that there were oranges in it. If the major did not get his share of them, we surely did, and it was not our fault that any reached the fort.

We were traveling through the woods when the corporal's gun, [which was] standing in the front part of the wagon, caught between two trees and bent almost forty-five degrees. Fortunately the gun was a supernumerary one issued to him for the trip to save his own from wear and exposure of the weather. That evening the gun was straightened again between some trees and given to a [visiting] civilian, who claimed to be a good shot, for practice. As might be expected the ball went way off its mark and somewhere around the corner.

At one of our camps a friend and I took a walk to the different Indian houses in quest of butter and eggs. This by-the-way was mostly an excuse to introduce ourselves into the families and get a chance to speak to the young folks and pass the evening at their houses. [We] happened to strike it rich this time. Our way led us to a secluded farmhouse where we were invited and entertained with singing and music by the [Indian] daughters of the house, and where we spent one of our [most] pleasant evenings of our trips, in something for us unusual — ladies' society.

These blockhouses stood generally in a clearing surrounded by a rail fence. They were constructed of horizontal logs, with mud to fill the cracks. The floor was constructed of logs, [as] was the chimney. The roof was covered with homemade shingles, but the doors and windows were an importation of civilization if the owner was not too poor to buy glass. All the logs were straightened and beveled with the ax, and some skill was required to make the furniture and wooden utensils for the kitchen.

We had successfully dodged the barn dogs as we left our pretty girls that evening and were soon comfortably rolled in our buffalo robes and sleeping the sleep of the just. We were awakened during the night by the major who fired his revolver to frighten cows out of the camp. The next night the major [ordered] the corporal to put a guard over camp. I was selected as the first relief. The mules had been picketed in the grass around the camp to give them plenty of room to feed during the night. How faithfully I executed that order may be seen by the fact that I took my blanket in the prairie and slept on the outskirts of the camp, beyond the reach of the mules, until the sun awoke me the next morning to my duty as guard.

We entered the Washita Valley where in one of the stores I invested [in] twelve to fifteen dozen eggs, packing them in salt as an, I thought, profitable investment, [by] paying ten cents a dozen and making one hundred-fifty percent, transportation not costing anything, thus following the major's example in making money. That evening I discovered the bottom of my egg box yellow and slimy from the broken eggs within, which caused a repacking of my investment. Keeping the broken articles aside for immediate use we had nothing but eggs for the balance of our trip.

The next day we discovered smoke on the horizon and coming nearer [realized] that the prairie which we had to cross was on fire. Prairie fires are not as dangerous as they are represented to be. A person with a cool head can easily place himself out of danger. [In] this instance the fire was raging in grass of two to three feet. The road proved too narrow to check the fire so we had to drive through a sea of smoke and flame for one-half mile or more, almost suffocating us and the stock.

A day or two later we returned to the fort. Our corporal returned his gun as if nothing had happened to it. With the investment in eggs I made only what [I] paid by selling the good ones at twenty-five cents a dozen.

How [does] a soldier's time pass at a frontier fort? Payday was always a holiday and duly celebrated by all concerned. Buying necessary articles, spending foolishly, or on whiskey and gambling, the money was generally invested and nothing left for most, [other] than the hope of another payday. If one or more were unlucky enough to have their pay taken by a court-martial there was always a dollar or so left to gamble with, trusting their luck for drinks.

[If] the commanding officer had issued orders to the officer of the day to enforce the military rules in regards to the lights being extinguished after taps the gamblers were up to the emergency. The windows of outhouses darkened with blankets, the tailor shop filled with men anxiously awaiting their luck at monte, others took possession of the post bakery or butcher shop, and others went into the woods. The gamblers were especially persistent, selecting all unknown places as their dens. [Sometimes] about ten or eleven o'clock the guard [would] quietly surround the houses and arrest all the players, taking them to the mill [guardhouse] for that night. The next morning their vessel of sorrow was filled to the rim by walking the Bull Ring all day, walking continually without stops in a circle, one behind the other. This would only temporarily check them, they would be as bad as ever after their long march in the "ring."[10]

During our stay at [Fort] Sill I had got into my possession six or eight wolf skins which the squaws refused to tan on account of the animals being poisoned, for fear of getting the poison on their hands. Having no use for the skins as they were I accepted the offer of my first sergeant who put one dollar against each wolf skin [to] play poker. At first his dollars were rolling into my pockets, but luck changed – the dollars went back into his pockets and my wolf skins soon followed.

A year or two later a man gave me five dollars to bet at his "twenty-one" game in order to call suckers [as a shill]. I bet until all the money was lost, but it left me in a very excited state and I declined the next time to play decoy.

Theatrical entertainments were occasionally gotten up by the men, or dances given to wile away the monotonous time of frontier life. The only thing a soldier hates to do is what he is compelled to do as a soldier.

The guard at [Fort] Sill consisted of fifteen men. During the daytime only two sentinels were walking posts, while the rest were supernumerous [or] taking the prisoners out to work. Poor fellows those prisoners, chained in shackles, not able to take a full step, taken daily to do all kinds of dirty hard work, until their departure to the military prison in Fort Leavenworth, Kansas. Early after breakfast they went out to gather garbage in the fort, in the afternoon they chopped wood, and in the evening the sinks were cleaned – not a sweet chore.[11]

Guard was always a treat in peach season when one could take, in the middle of the night, an undisturbed feast in the officers' gardens. The guard also had a good time when taking prisoners out to chop wood for the laundresses, in which case the sentinels were fed on pies and homemade cakes. But guard was not always so pleasant, especially in winter when walking post at twenty below zero, [or] in such weather when one was taken out by the officer of the day to make a grand round of the fort and visit all the sentinels, with the probable chances of getting lost on the prairie. This was where the funny line ends and time of hardship commences.

Parades were the military display of strength and power and were very interesting and pretty to look at. There were lots of fun in them for the soldiers when dressed in their glittering uniforms, marching up to the parade ground for inspection with their gallant officers in front and rear. [With] the troops all in a line the band played a lively tune while marching and counter-marching in front of the line. The band of the 4th Cavalry, while at Fort Sill, was always accompanied by a tame deer who followed them like a dog through all their maneuvers. The troops were marched in review and brought back into line, with a couple of repetitions of the same. During all this marching we had to keep our eight-pound guns at a "carry," that is, the hammer resting over the middle finger, for at least fifteen or twenty minutes, causing something like a cramp to the muscles of that finger.

Apart from these kinds of fun we had foot and handball games, or we could go to the post library, where we found a great variety of weekly and monthly papers, besides useful books to enrich the mind a thousand different directions. For those who wished to be educated [there] was a provision made by the government. Schoolteachers were stationed at every fort to teach the men in the evening and the children during daytime. Great attention was especially directed to the education of officers' children at these post schools.[12]

Some men in the army were favored with the doubtful honor of [being] an officer's servant, striker, or "dog-robber."

What would a soldier be without drill? – No order, nor discipline, nor anything which makes an army effective. As a rule the regulars did not take much interest in anything they were compelled to do – except fighting. They went through the motions in drilling like a machine. Every man would take pride in drill so long as it was useful skirmish drill accompanied by the manual of arms. But when it came to the bayonet and saber exercise – the infantry not using the bayonet and the cavalry [not using] the saber in the field – then a man [would] lose interest.

We want to follow the infantry on their skirmish drills across ditches, creeks, and rocks, or the cavalry jumping fences on their bare-back horses, but let us turn to the more sullied duties of the enlisted man. Take an [infantry] company of thirty-seven men and see how many really did garrison duty – that is guard duty and general fatigue. Subtract from these thirty-seven men: five sergeants, four corporals, two cooks, one or two servants (dog-robbers), two gardeners, one tailor and shoemaker, one clerk, about eight on extra duty detailed in the quartermaster department receiving thirty-five to fifty cents a day extra, add four or eight for daily duty in the fort and we have two or six men left to do the military work for the company and fort.

There is more laboring than soldiering in the U.S. Infantry. In the cavalry companies, besides being stronger at seventy to eighty men per company, there are very few on extra or daily duty in the forts.[13]

Extra work in the company [included] work at the Captain's quarters, or wood hauling in case our allowance for the month ran short (each man was entitled to one-sixth a cord of wood per month), or work at the lime kiln burning lime, or having the pleasure to try muscle in the rock quarry. In the winter there might be work on the ice pond, to cut and pack ice for the summer.

But as hard as it was, there came a time in the evening when everything was forgotten and we lived a life like Adam and Eve, not [only] mentally, but also by outward appearance. In the summer evenings, when the day's work was done and the shadows of the trees got longer, troops with towels under their arms wound their way down the steep banks of the creek [to] take a plunge in the clear waters. A happy and jolly lot of men diving and playing like so many dolphins, not caring if immediate death may lurk in the shape of a hostile Indian behind the trees and bushes on the bank. [We] lived a true life of "today" – live so long as you can, the next instant you may be dead.

When a company was stationed at a fort they usually had a small garden [of] from one to five acres where a couple of members of the company raised enough vegetables to keep their table well supplied for the summer. In our company at Fort Sill the gardeners had the care of a dozen or so hogs and fed them on garden produce and weeds, in addition to the slop from the company kitchen – which gave us a profitable addition to our mess in winter.[14]

One summer I [worked] there with another one [soldier] as assistant to the gardener, cultivating five acres in a field of twenty-five where the other companies had also their garden sections assigned. The water was brought the same as to the company quarters, by the water wagon. Our head man, who lived in the garden under the large roof of a wall tent, was a German by birth. He was naturally inclined to weariness, not to say lazy, and made us do all the necessary and unnecessary work. But there is not a rock too hard that cannot be cut. He was very fond of drink. If there were days we did not feel like working – and there were some – all we had to do was to give him a couple of drinks of rotgut whiskey and work was done for that day. The hoes were put aside and a small meal prepared for us – the best the house could afford. [One] time an Indian and a couple of squaws put in their appearance and the fun commenced. Our hero [was] put on a horse with a squaw while the latter was instructed to give full reins. There was [not] anything more laughable on earth [than] to see our superior behind a squaw on horseback hanging on for dear life, seeking protection from an insignificant little girl in front of him.

In the fall when the sweet potatoes and onions were dug

up and stored for the winter we were always welcome guests at his tent. Our entry was celebrated with a bottle of homemade wine and a possum feast prepared worthy for the table of a king. We generally would help him gather fox grapes and hunt a possum in the evening, of which there were an unlimited number in the garden and the adjoining woods.

[When] the autumn weather fairly set in the leaves began to wither and fall to the ground. Innumerable wild geese passed over our heads day and night on their southerly flight. The smaller animals and reptiles sought their warm burrows and wintering places. Here and there we could see curls of smoke from distant prairie fires as flame danced in the high grass of the bottom land, or dashed across the treeless hills, leaving in its path a black smoldering surface. Our time [then] was principally occupied with watching and counter-burning the prairie to protect the fort from that destructive element as the fire approached the combustible material in the vicinity of the post.

How the cold northerly wind howled, bringing with it a shower of gravel and sand, while a cloud of grasshoppers darkened the sky, how the tumbling weed broke from its roots, fleeing with spirit wing across the plains to seek shelter in a nook or hollow. We gathered around the warm stove in the quarters, throwing piece after piece of wood into the fiery bowels, trying to console ourselves with the skunks beneath and the scorpions and centipedes above – that there was warm weather coming.

It made us feel so much colder to think of summer with its beautiful green trees, plums and berries, and the hot dry southerly wind, even if it did carry fine sand through all the cracks in the room and transformed our lungs into a bank of quicksand – it was still preferable to twenty degrees below zero in a building where the wind had free access from all sides, as well as from below through cracks in the floor large enough to admit a hand. Let us not think of the horned toads

we carried in our pockets [in] summer, and [of] the pleasures
we had while fishing for bass and catfish, nor the fun we had
when sleeping in our bunks and a scorpion dropped down on
us, nor receiving a visit from a tarantula. We would also forget
the flies we swallowed with our meal and the acquaintance
we made with the colonies of big red ants when standing [at]
rest during drill hour.

Most of the men drew their beds together and "doubled
up" to keep warm, sleeping as well as circumstances would
permit. [One night] I did not rest snugly in the arms of a
loving wife nor in the arms of Morpheus, but tossed restlessly
with intense pain from side to side, chewing tobacco, paper,
straw, and everything else to stop the aching in my tooth. Old
Sol the next morning threw his light on a very pitiful looking
individual and my first walk was to the hospital steward. I
was soon resting with my head upon the back of a chair while
this worthy man of quinine pills and medicine stood over me
with a pair of tongs, having a hold on my sick molar. Our
combined efforts could only bring [it] half-way out and I was
dismissed, unable to speak or close my jaws. A little shake and
pressure brought the tooth back to its place, permitted to
reoccupy its former position, which it held without giving
further annoyance.

The thunderstorms which I experienced in summer were
very short but destructive. I remember during one of these
storms lightning struck one of the cavalry quarters, demolished
a gun, destroyed the headpiece of an iron bunk, and split the
floor on its way to the ground. Fortunately for the man [of
the bunk] it occurred in the daytime or he might have gotten
his transfer papers without his knowledge.

Sometimes the monotony of the fort was interrupted by the
funeral of a soldier. A long line of men, while the flag of the
fort was at half-mast, wound their way down the hillside to
a lonely spot in the prairie, keeping step to the solemn music
of a funeral march. At the head of the procession was the

band playing the dead march and in whose footsteps the firing party was following. [The firing party] consisted of eight men and a noncommissioned officer if a [dead] private, and sixteen if a sergeant. All officers according to their command in ranks − a major was entitled to four companies. Next came the hearse with six pall-bearers walking along the sides, then followed, if the deceased was a cavalryman, by the horse of the [man] saddled and bridled, the reversed boots of the dead man in the stirrups, led by two men. At the grave the men were drawn in one line, the coffin, covered with the U.S. flag, was carried and placed on cross-trees over the grave, while the firing party [was at] "present" arms. They came to "rest" arms during the reading of the funeral service by an officer or the doctor. Three shots were fired across the grave, the band played a lively march, and the men marched off back to the fort − the man just buried a thing of the past.

[In the] fall guard duty came quite often, [and] I will give a few occurrences connected with sentinel duty at the guard-house. I [often] walked in front of the guardhouse, executing my duty to keep the Indians out of the fort and [away] from the powder magazine, seeing that no prisoners left the guard-house unaccompanied by a member of the guard, and kept watch over all the government property in view.

[Once] on the porch of the guardhouse I saw a prisoner in the shape of an Indian who had a chain and iron ball attached to one of his legs, judging from his pallid face [he] was very sick. Next to him sat a sacrificing squaw who went willingly into prison with her husband. Every morning for guard mount his face was carefully and artfully painted by his wife. She followed him every step, nursed him, and carried the chain and ball. At the beginning of his incarceration, when taken to the parade ground to work, which was on the account of sickness discontinued, she also did the work there. I can see them now, setting on the bench side-by-side, conversing in their Indian tongue. She appeared to be happy in her knowledge of duty, and seemed to see a heaven in the face beside her. Happy man who can call such a devoted being his own I thought [then] as the green monster of envy slowly entered my heart.[15]

Behind those gray [guardhouse] walls have been confined sons of poor and rich parents, intelligent and imbecile, murderers and innocent – all were there to await or receive their just or unjust punishment. A man [for example], poor fellow, who deserted but got caught – awaited his trial while both his legs were connected with a twenty or twenty-four inch chain. More than one young man had surely repented there for having ever left his mother's apron strings. There [were] also confined behind those walls the outcasts of civilization in the shape of horse thieves. Those birds were kept there after their capture by the troops, until they could be transferred into the hands of civil authorities and taken to Fort Smith for trial.

It may [have] happened that the civil authorities were saved the trouble of trying them. Legally they could not be executed without a just trial, but the military had a right to shoot if they should attempt to escape. The rumor was of some thieves who had been captured in Texas, were taken fifteen or more miles from [Fort] Sill and there shot dead, acting under the verbal instructions from the commanding officer of the fort. The detachment of soldiers returned with the report that the thieves attempted a break for liberty and were all killed, five in number, buried on the spot.

Besides horse thieves there were proud Indian chiefs with ball and chain attached to their legs, who have graced at different times the hard stone lower floor of the guardhouse. [Also] an unruly civilian negro who refused to leave the military reservation, or work for his board when in the lock up, was tied with his thumbs on the posts of the porch.

Leaving the gloomy walls of the guardhouse [I recall] Indians passing on the way to the post butcher shop [to] buy meat or [to] stop at the post bakery for bread. It [was] on

ration day [that] whoever had a little money bought food at
the fort and repaired to the creek [Indian camp] for a nights
jollyfication, as ration day was a kind of Christmas day for
them. The ones who were less fortunate directed their steps
to the company kitchens and laundresses where they would
enter (if permitted) into everything that is private, and appropriate anything in the line of eatables and other desirable
things – or they would stay in the kitchen with a tenacity
worthy of a traveling agent, saying "no savy" to all questions.
They could only be dislodged by a savage "vamoose" or a
bucket full of water.

While watching from my [guard] post the passing Indians
who frequently nodded to my Indian [prisoner] on the porch
I saw an Indian damsel and, presumably, her beau returning
from the butcher shop, stopping at the bakery. He did [a] very
unusual thing for an Indian – carried the meat for her. The
woman soon returned with the bread in a sack and fastened
it on the saddle of her pony. She mounted, waiting for her
Adonis to do the same. We found there again human nature
having the same tendency as in a civilized man – he liked to
display and be graceful, but instead was awkward under the
admiring eyes of his sweetheart and made a misstep. Loosing
his hold upon the horse brought his posterior in a rather
uncomfortable connection with the ground. We sympathized
with him in his calamity and hoped he had not hurt himself
but it is human nature to laugh over others' misfortunes. In
this case soldiers and Indians joined to make the situation a
very embarrassing one for the unfortunate lover who, after a
savage look at the guard, mounted unceremoniously and was
soon lost to sight, with his Juliet at his heels to console him
with a good meal.

The girl was still in sight when another Indian beauty with
three or four others passed the guardhouse on [their] way to
the butcher shop. How different was this girl from the first
one – she didn't ride "à la man," [rather, she rode sidesaddle],

her hair instead of black [was] a beautiful veil of nice soft brown enveloping her shoulders — how erect she rode and how willingly the pony followed the guidance of her delicate hand — I had to see her again [after] my two hours were up and I was relieved [of duty]. The butcher shop was not far and I soon found myself in the presence of my admired. She had her beautiful liquid eyes not on me but on the butcher's scale, waiting for the meat. Next to her stood her brother eating, with apparent relish, a raw kidney. Further on another relative or friend of hers had just commenced at one end of a gut, gulping it gradually down his throat. This was enough of an acquaintance for me and I returned to the guard without having received a smile from the object of my admiration.

In front of the guardhouse stood the powder magazine. Upon my return I found most of the members of the guard congregated, examining a large snake which had been caught by the ordnance sergeant in his chicken coop. It was a rattlesnake-pilot measuring seven-feet one-inch. They were longer and thinner [than] a rattlesnake, but have the same color and are considered as poisonous.[16]

That same afternoon we saw a fight between a wolf and a pack of hounds. The wolf, caught by an officer of the fort when young and tamed, had broken his chain and took a ramble around the fort. In this he was opposed by about eight or ten dogs who, frightened of the sharp white teeth of the wolf, contented themselves with giving him an occasional nip in the hindquarters and by making a hideous noise. The wolf was recaptured and chained before any damage was done to some of the valuable hounds. Wolves, as a rule, are never truly tamed, like deer or other wild animals, but always keep their wild nature which, sooner or later, would sprout out again — with increased fury.

The sun was on that day nearing the horizon and I prepared to load the cannon to fire the evening salute. The powder was rammed into the muzzle and, intending to create a louder report, a round rock and wet gunny sack [I] hammered down on top of it. Everything was ready, the cannon pointed to the trees of an old dry creek one-half mile off, while the musicians were beating retreat – at the last note of which I had to fire. To my consternation I saw the major of our fort on his evening drive coming up the road which passed between me and my target. My blood changed from hot to cold to hot again as I pictured to myself the punishment in store for me if the major should hear a stone whiz over his head. To my relief he was passed and over the hill by the time of firing. I heard the stone rattling in the trees as it left my cannon and went straight to its mark, striking a hill on the other side. So much about my experience as an artilleryman. Nothing is easier for a soldier as to get [in] an escapade.[17]

My post at the guardhouse that night [was] a dark one, I had to depend more on my ears than eyes. I was startled by the sensational brightness of the sky. The prairie had been fired by the Indians. The fires were generally created by the Indians in fall and spring to get fresh grass for their stock. Miles of the grassy sea was laid waste [in] one night, the ashes forming the manure for the new crop. The nights were made bright as day by the burning country. In time of war and peace the Indians employed the prairie fires to communicate news to their far off friends. An idea [of] how fast the Indians communicate the news may be taken from the fact that the news of General Custer's massacre in Dakota was received by the Indians at Fort Sill before the soldiers received theirs by telegraph.

During the rest of the winter we were marched to the creek to cut ice, and had at times a very rough time on guard, with the only difference [that] in the first [former] there was plenty of whiskey and hot coffee to keep us warm, in the latter case we were well treated with pies etc. by the laundresses.

5

· · · · · · · · · · · · · ·

*Frontier Duties in
the Indian Territory,
1878-1879*

The winter with the cold weather was a thing of the past and
the hot wind of the summer months was again bringing us a
shower of sand and gravel [when] we prepared to build a
telegraph line between Fort Sill and Fort Reno. Owing to the
annual destruction of the [Fort Sill to Fort Richardson] southerly line by prairie fires it was decided to construct this line,
the northerly, with iron poles.

About sixteen men were detached from the two infantry

companies and provided with crowbars and shovels, starting one day in June 1878 to sink three-foot holes for the poles, shortly followed on [our] heels by about eight or ten civilian wire stretchers.[1]

Our hands were sore and blistered from handling the tools and hot iron telegraph poles for the first few days, but soon got accustomed to the work and burning sun. We moved along in pairs to the designated spots for the holes, here digging in loose sand, there in solid sandstone or gravel, or trying our muscles and temper on the sticky black sod of rich bottom lands. It was altogether a very dry and tiresome piece of work for our unaccustomed backs. But this lasted only a few days and we were soon as well acquainted with handling a crowbar as we were in the manual of arms or any other military exercises.

Five miles from the fort we passed the Indian farm, this was a branch [of the farm] on the west side of a creek. A stone throw from there, situated on the top of a small hill overlooking the farm, stood a vacated Indian village. The inhabitants had vacated their winter habitations and departed for a summer hunt, leaving nothing but their surplus property well protected upon a platform and covered by canvas against the weather. In charge [were] a few old bucks and squaws who cast their inquisitive eyes at our work.

Eight miles further [was] another Indian town, also situated on an elevation, away from the fever region of the creek and swarms of mosquitoes of the bottom land. Here the curiosity was on both sides equally strong, especially with some of our men who had never seen Indians butcher and prepare meat for winter. An Indian drove a plump heifer up the hill to a convenient spot near the town where a well directed bullet brought the animal to the ground. Before life was fairly extinct a number of squaws went to work at it with butcher knives, taking the hide off the carcass. The belly being cut, it was discovered that there was an unborn and still living calf. A rush was made for it. Torn from its innocence [it was] carried in triumph to a hut where it was later consumed as the choice tid-bit of the animal. In the meantime the internals were taken from the heifer and the kidneys and other morsels were consumed by the men and children. The rest of the meat was cut in thin slices and hung up in the sun, in other words being jerked.

We soon left the disgusting feast, returning to our camp satisfied with our tour of investigation, determined never to kiss an Indian squaw again.

We progressed with our telegraph line at the rate of four and one-half miles a day and were gradually leaving the town behind us, passing a prairie dog town. It was at the prairie dog town where I had my first opportunity to see the poison of a rattlesnake. We were compelled at one place to walk quite a distance for the telegraph pole which had been previously, rather irregularly, distributed along the line of construction. We discovered a large rattlesnake sleeping under its coils near the pole.

Disturbed by our arrival it attempted to make off but was checked by the heavy iron post brought down on its back. Like a flash the head of the reptile turned and struck with full force at the iron pole, sending streams of yellow poison from the broken fangs. The snake was soon dispatched and we resumed our work with another rattle added to our collection of frontier curiosities.

Our provision wagon had proceeded us and prepared a camp at the upper branch of a stream which, after many bends and windings, passed Fort Sill to the south. The banks of the stream were very steep, formed of a bluish soft clay apparently of a limestone origin.[2]

There was little timber at this place and a Comanche chief had a considerable portion of the bottom under cultivation, but like the rest of his kind only raised watermelons and a little corn. He only varied in one respect from his fellow warriors, that is in physical proportion. His squaw was also as fat as himself and both, when seen together, were a picture of happiness and good nature. She was also considered chief of all the Comanche squaws in the territory.

This country was rolling prairie. The water courses could readily be traced for many miles, their tributaries and smaller valleys conveniently used as guides to travel by, especially if one kept on top of a divide or the reach of hills which divides two water courses. A person with a little frontier experience can follow [them] with the same accuracy as if traveling by the numbered streets of a large city.

Our [next] camp was near the top of one of these divides, at a small spring shaded by high cedar trees – hence the name "Cedar Spring." The water flowed from under heavy sandstone rocks and formed, with other small springs after their consolidation, a nice clear creek. The valley gradually assumed the fertile timbered appearance of the main valley of the Washita River. Upon the rocks above the spring were engraved the names of white men who had camped and passed at a time when the Indian[s] were still in undisputed possession of the country and tall in the shape of scalps. Cattle in great numbers roamed over the country and had possession of the water. Our appearance at the spring was unexpected and [the cattle] had no other exit except the steep rocks which they climbed without hesitation and with the grace of a goat.

The place had a good location for larger game. I made a proposition to one of the men for an evening hunt, which was gleefully accepted. A few minutes later we followed the border of the timber for whatever might come within reach of our guns, from a squirrel to a bear. Nothing of any account turned up worth shooting. Darkness overtook us and we crossed the valley to return to camp along the opposite side of the timber. Our direction was due west but after walking for a considerable length of time and no light of the campfire yet in sight we discovered by the brightly shining stars that we were walking in a southerly direction, consequently at right angles to the camp. The realization of our position may better be imagined than described as we stood there. Strong feelings run through a man when he realizes the greatness of the world and his own insignificance. Our minds were soon made up to go due west where we knew we would strike the road or our telegraph line, which ran almost due north and south, after which we would have no difficulty of finding the camp.

After walking a few steps we made the unpleasant discovery that there were obstacles in our way which might compel us to remain and wait until daylight before venturing further. Our path was hemmed by a steep deep gully at the bottom of which I could hear the sound of running water. After striking a match to discover the possible depth and nature of the bottom I concluded to venture a slide. Taking the gun in one hand and guiding myself with the other I sat down on the brim and made my descent faster than expected, but landed softly on a pile of dry twigs at the foot of the rocks. My companion soon followed and by the sparse light of a match and after considerable crawling we managed to cross the bottom. Here we were confronted by a steeper, higher wall as the [one] we descended.

We were well nigh at the end of our wits, realizing the possibility of making this our sleeping place for the night with the probability of a storm and subsequent washout [flash flood], not to speak of wild beast, rattlesnakes, or other unwelcome visitors. But nature lent us her helping hand in our misfortune. There stood a tree close by with one branch reaching to a pro- jecting rock which we in safety reached. From here we gained the top by one standing on the other's shoulders and [then] drawing the other up after. Our hearts beat free as we had the open prairie once more under our feet and saw, not over one- quarter mile away, the welcome lights of our campfires.

Our next day's work on the line brought us into view of the Washita River. The country gradually sloped down [to] the river and after leaving a very rich valley of about one-half mile on each side made an abrupt ascent to the north. Immediately at our feet was a well cultivated field and a farmhouse surrounded by a large garden. Here lived an old Indian chieftain whose daughters were married to white men and who was considered an authority, not alone in his own tribe, but with all the smaller tribes in this section. His name was Black Beaver, chief of the Delaware Indians and [he] traced his lineage back to the same Delaware who concluded a treaty with William Penn in 1682. The walls of his rooms were adorned with pictures representing the signing of the treaty. He had in former years [been] employed as a scout and interpreter by the government, but [then] enjoyed the comforts of a nice home in the midst of his family and kin.[3]

Across this old chief's farm on the other side of the river [was] the main agency, of the Comanche, Kiowa, and Apache Indians, including a dozen or so smaller tribes, numbering probably 10,000 all told.[4]

[We] descended and crossed the yellow river by a well beaten ford, about one hundred feet [below a] falls of two or three feet, following the road through a half-mile field of wild sunflowers. In the midst of the weed, surrounded by the large drooping discs of the flowers, we met an object too pretty to pass without mention. It was in the shape of an Indian lady from the half-civilized Wichita Indians who passed us on horseback. [She wore] her calico dress, red jacket with large silver buttons, headdress in a crown of diamond, silver, tin or some other reflecting material which glittered in the strong light of the sun. Her attitude was commanding and we bowed in homage and admiration as she passed us as proud as a queen. My heart was rolled at this occasion. It was some time before we could get over this meeting and straighten our faces again to an everyday mask.

From time immemorial the Indians have been considered a roaming class of people but there is nothing more absurd than this assumption, as an Indian loves his home as dearly as a civilized man. Each nation had its distinct territory with a division for the different tribes and under these again there were the different bands who had their permanent homes at some convenient hill. From there the young men took their annual hunting tours in some part of the territory belonging to their nation, while the old men and squaws remained at home.

The U.S. government had most of the Indians removed from their own territory and given or assigned them to a smaller border, with an agent to civilize them. The Indians were allowed by the government a sufficient amount of rations and clothing for support until they [became] self sustaining.

There was one great mistake of the government in civilizing the Indians and this was to give them a school education, to train the children at places far from their homes, surround them with the luxury of the white man, and then cast them back again to their former obscurity. It was not alone unjust, but cruel in the highest degree to condemn them to their former mode of living after teaching them the wrong of it.[5]

In order to civilize the Indians they ought to be elevated step after step. Teach them the value of cattle raising. Enlist them in the army instead of whites, and teach the young only in schools at home. In five and twenty years we would have no more "wild" Indians in the country.

As the Indians are at present [1884–89] they are at the mercy of the agent and are driven through his dishonesty on the warpath. Whites infringe on the rights of the Indians and cheat them at every turn. Some colonel of the army, anguished to better his record, assists in a general kick and drives them on the warpath.

The Kiowa-Comanche agency at Wichita, I must confess, was conducted in a very honorable way by Mr. Hunt. I have on several occasions accompanied an army officer to that place to inspect the meat to see if the Indians got their due and found them, to my knowledge, to receive enough meat for a week to live on.[6]

The Indians there were also given the contract to haul the Indian stores from the railroad to the agency. The army gave them the wood contract.[7]

Passing this place [we] took a glance at a schoolhouse under construction, the old one having been burned down by the Indians two years [before]. We ascended the small reach of hill bordering the valley on the north side and found a valley richer than the last. From there to the South Fork of the Canadian River the country was a continual change of wood-covered sand hills and rich valleys where isolated Indian farms gave life to the scene.[8]

While at camp on the Canadian River we started out for a bear hunt, having seen a bear and two cubs during the day in one of the small valleys. Our luck was against us and we only brought home a raccoon for our supper where I had the first taste of the strong dark meat. The water of the river was very brackish, flowing in thin sheets over the quicksand covered bottom. We dug a small well into the quicksand of the bank of the river, using old barrels for walling, in order to obtain cooler water for our canteens. We found the well water too much saturated with alkaline which was useless for drinking after it becomes warm.

From there we had only a short distance of ten or twelve miles and had the pleasure to complete our work to Fort Reno a few days later. At last fourteen or fifteen days hard work were at end. Facing the hot sun day after day, Sunday is an unknown thing with soldiers, we were permitted a few days rest. Our first walk, after we had established ourselves near the fort, was down to the North Fork of the Canadian River for a bath and a thoroughly general cleaning.

The current in the river was too swift for bathing so we concluded to take a swim in one of the small ponds formed

by high water in the bed of the broad river and kept fresh
by the flow of the water through the quicksand. There was a
little hesitation at first about bathing there as we saw black
water moccasin snakes leaving their comfortable places along
the edge and getting back into the pond at our approach. But
it was agreed to count "three" and then take a dive together.
The jump was made with feelings as if jumping amongst
alligators or sharks and we naturally made haste to return to
the bank while a lively movement was kept up with our arms
and legs to frighten the snakes.

It was either the strange sight or the accumulated dirt from
our bodies which paralyzed the quiet inhabitants of the pond.
We saw the edge of the water lined with apparently dead fish,
but who came to life again when taken up to be examined.
Unfortunately the fish were not good to eat, as we were
informed, and we had to content ourselves with a usual supper
of biscuit, coffee, bacon, and one-half [an] onion – the last
was an allowance for the good of our health.

The fort [Fort Reno] was established somewhat later than
Fort Sill, [and] was located on the right bank of the North
Fork of the Canadian River. The plan was similar to Fort Sill
but the buildings were constructed of wood and, with few
exceptions, were frame houses. The country was more level
than further south, and the river, a brackish yellow stream,
flowed between low banks. There was no timber or shade trees
within view.[9]

Across the river two miles northwest of the fort the Cheyenne Agency had about 4,000 Cheyennes and Arapahoes on
the reservation. The [former], a very courageous tribe, made
a daring break for the north through Kansas in 1877 but
succumbed, returned to the agency by the troops after a long
and tenacious resistance.[10]

This tribe had, in average, the best looking men and women
of the Plains Indians. The women frequently marry whites,
especially soldiers, or the better young and pretty squaws were

sold by their mothers to soldiers at a price of $20 per year. The mother kept the money and the soldier provided his young wife with shelter and provisions and, if soft-hearted, for the whole family.

This way of buying squaws was in fact legal marriage among the Indians. A young Indian woos his "Juliet" as ardently as a white "Romeo." If the young wooer succeeds he would go to her parents to barter and pay the price which varied according to the beauty of the girl. The girls were bought as young as ten years and generally lived happy, although they had a hard road to travel through life. Elopements were more frequent than in civilized countries and were accompanied with a great deal more danger. She may lose her nose by it, or both their lives, when apprehended.

After a few days stay at Fort Reno we received orders to return to Fort Sill, which was accomplished with only the following mishap. We were all riding in our mess wagon when the team halted in the middle of a river, on apparently sound bottom which gave way with alarming rapidity to the weight of the animals and wagon. The words barely left the driver that the wagon was sinking into the quicksand when everybody made quick time from under the shady covering of the wagon and got hold of the spokes and wheels. A moment longer and it would have been too late. The wagons and animals were saved, through our quick action and combined strength, from a dreadful grave.

At last we were back at Fort Sill after an absence of fifteen days, within the comfortable walls of our barracks among friends. To my great sorrow I learned the bad news of the death of a little pet I had left in the care of a friend when starting on my trip. At the beginning of the spring I received as a present from an Indian a young prairie dog. He was very young but as he grew up he became the pet of the garrison on account of his fondness for sugar and cakes, [and] was fed by everyone who had money enough to treat him. The hounds in the fort were afraid to go near him for fear of a lashing. I never saw him real angry except once when a young raccoon was brought to our place. The hair stood up on his back, his eyes shot fire and he made a rush for that unfortunate animal. Thanks to the young age or sickness of the latter our prairie dog was not made acquainted with the sharp teeth of the coon.

He answered to the name of "Dick" and would come and play when called. A small box was provided for him as his abode but he preferred to live in his burrow which he had dug in the yard. At one time he had a fondness to go between the boxes in the rear [of the barracks] and I was compelled to use stringent means to break him of it. Scolding was useless, he would lay quiet in the forbidden place when called. One day, after peeping around the corner to see if the coast was clear he was trying to sneak back to the yard. But it was too late − I had him by the back of the neck and gave him a couple of dunkings in an old water barrel. When liberated he gave a squeal or two and went to his burrow to think over the philosophy of obeying orders. The next day he was back at his place again and I concluded to give him a good sound lashing. He tried his old antics again to evade me, but with the same success as the first time. He received his punishment [and] never left the yard again after that lesson, remaining a wiser prairie dog than before. The friend in whose care I had left my pet overfed him gingerbread or snaps and the consequence was diarrhea [from] which he subsequently died.

A few days after our return from the telegraph line I took my gun and fishing line for a days sport. [I] killed a beaver in the forenoon who, by all probability, had been expelled from his colony and was seeking another further up the creek, as beaver never move in the daytime. Beavers only work at night. Trees near a stream to a thickness of ten to fifteen inches [they] fell across the water in order to get a strong hold for their dam. Smaller trees, branches, and stones, the latter carried upon their tails, are placed between the branches of the large tree in such a manner as to form a network. Leaves and grass are then used to check the water to the desired height. The entrances to their burrows are under the level of the water to which regular paths may be seen to lead from different directions on the bottom of the stream. Their burrows are generally about six or eight feet from the water and from one to three feet above it. A beaver is very cautious when leaving his hiding place after dark and a trap has to be well hid and all traces of a man's presence removed before one may [be] expected to be caught, especially so if placing a trap in front of a hole which is above the water line.

Meeting no other game I concluded to pass the afternoon with fishing. While in this way occupied I saw an Indian and a squaw advancing. The man was dressed in breechcloth, leggings, and beaded moccasins. The upper body was covered with a clean white shirt and a red blanket with a large U.S. thrown around his waist. His breast was covered with a shield of bones and his ears decorated with rings on the border, the face and hair parting line was painted, and an eagle feather fastened in his scalp lock. Over his shoulder was thrown a beaded quiver with bow and arrows.

The squaw wore painted buckskin hose, a calico gown fastened around her waist from where the paint stick case and other Indian trinkets were dangling, her whole face painted red. I was wondering what their object may be of paying a visit. After the usual greeting of "How John" it was insinuated by the young man that his blushing innocent sister was still free. I naturally declined this Leap Year offer and they turned their horses and left me with my fishing hooks and thoughts of their decaying race. As Cortez in the sixteenth century conquered the Aztec, disease was unknown to the Americans, but it soon made its hideous appearance in their midst and carried from parent to children, unable to check its progress with herbs of the forest and sand of the prairie, [and] killed more of their number than all the wars of extermination with the whites.

Moving from one place to another and trying quiet places with my line I experienced the usual end of a fisherman's luck. It was well nigh disgusted when I struck a place where my fishing thermometer rose to one hundred-twenty. The recent high water had brought down large trees and left them at a bend in the creek in about eight feet of water. Here on one of the trees floating in the water the fishing spirit had tempted me to go. It was only a short time, that is a fisherman's "short time," when I had three fine catfish fastened on my extra line.

I was already thinking of going home and cooking what I had caught when my cork went without warning clear out of sight. A gentle pull on my pole convinced me that a larger fish than any of the former had got himself into trouble. The fish made a dash to the full length of the line while his head was drawn to the surface. How great was my surprise when I saw the head of a garfish four or five feet long with a mouth as large as an alligator. Feeling that he was captured he turned and made in a straight line for me and struck the log where I was standing. The log gave a turn and for only a timely quick jump to the bank I would have been the captured instead of the captor in this contest.

My fishing line was now gone and also my fishing spirit. I went down to the water to get my extra line with the catfish. I found the line still in the same place where I had fastened it, but no catfish. The heads were still on the line, but the bodies had been eaten in the meantime by some water snakes who, by the way, delight in playing such tricks on an ardent fisherman [in] any of the western rivers. I took my rifle and beaver, following one of the cow trails along the river, returning home a wiser man.

The 4th of July drew near and preparation had been made

to celebrate this national holiday in as grand a style as was possible in a frontier post. In the morning at sunrise thirteen guns were fired in commemory of the Declaration of Independence by the thirteen original states of the Union. At noon thirty-eight shots were fired in honor of the present states. The day was celebrated throughout very pleasantly. [A] blindfolded wheelbarrow race, sack race, and other laughable games were played in the forenoon, while in the afternoon a horse race took place between the Comanche and Kiowa Indians. In the evening the day was concluded with fireworks. The horse race of the Indians was very interesting, with a saddle as first prize and a carriage whip for the second (a carriage whip for an Indian!). Horse racing was one of the principal amusements of the Indians and they would wager their last penny on their favorite horse. I saw handfuls of paper money exchanging hands during a race at the Wichita Agency when I was at that place as an escort for an inspecting officer.

Although they were very excited, they never gave way to such ridiculous exhibitions as we frequently see on our civilized racetrack, but [they] patiently waited and paid their money over to the winner as quietly as if paying for a box of matches. They rode their horses bareback with nothing but a bridle to guide the horse. When racing amongst themselves they generally had their track in a straight line.

Hearing that the race was going to be an Indian horse race a friend and I started to the track to see it. We went first to the Indian Agency where a few Indians were lounging around on the porch while some squaws received their rations and [were] packing them on one of their pack horses. [In a nearby] level valley we saw a cluster of soldiers and Indians preparing for the race at the starting post. The long grass was mowed off and a round one mile track made on the short dry turf.

As we were thus engaged in viewing the scene an Indian mounted on a magnificent pony came up and greeted us. On his right side was a rusty cavalry saber suspended, which he probably captured from one of the cavalrymen in some fort. Being curious how the Indian would handle such a machine of war in an engagement I asked him to show me. No sooner said than done. I made a jump to get beyond the reach of that dangerous weapon as he brandished the blade over his head and made a plunge at me. We all laughed as he put the saber back in his place and took the direction of the racetrack.

The racing was quite exciting for us whites. On dashed the small muscular ponies, urged to the highest speed by their nude riders. We may say nude, as the Indians had selected very light men or boys for their riders, who relieved themselves of all their clothing except the breechcloth. With their horses bareback the riders gave as little as possible weight to the horses and resistance to the air.

A short time after or before the 4th of July race we [were] starting on our usual Monday morning target practice when an order came from the adjutant's office for four or five men to report immediately with one day's ration. I was one of the selected and we reported to the office for further orders. Here we met a detail of the same number from another infantry company and were placed under charge of a corporal, put in an ambulance [wagon], and driven to the Indian Agency.

Our corporal was reticent in regards of the orders he had received and we were kept in ignorance until we gained the agency and our mission [made] clear to us. The Indian agent had ordered the arrest of Big Bow, the head chief of the Kiowa, for some irregularities committed by the latter. On the chief's appearance at the agency for rations, five or six cavalrymen were ordered to execute the order of the agent, but finding themselves impeded by about fifty of the chief's followers eight infantrymen were ordered to their assistance. We were ordered to "load" which singularly enough was also executed by the Indians surrounding us, with the only difference that they put sixteen cartridges into their guns against our one.

The chief was leaning against the fence around the agency

as our corporal ordered him to a seat in the ambulance. Seeing that he would be the first one to bite the grass if one shot was fired by his men he did the wisest thing under the circumstances following the orders of the corporal, entering the wagon. The door was closed behind him, the driver gave whips to the mules and the chief went to his prison under charge of the cavalry while a few Indians set up a howl and followed them close on their heels.

He was taken to the office of the commanding officer where another demonstration of the chief and his few followers (as I was informed afterwards) caused that officer to leave their presence, while a captain equally as frightened as his superior called the assistance of the post guard. The chief was at last placed in the guardhouse and subsequently informed by the commanding officer that the order directing his arrest was not from him but from the Indian agent, clearing in this rather singular way the responsibility of the arrest from his own shoulders. The chief was detained in the guardhouse only a few days and received, by order of the commanding officer, all the attention and comfort possible in such a place.

During all the excitement at the fort over the chief's arrest we, the infantry, remained at the agency and stood the pressure of the greatly increased and excited Indians. Five or six of our number were stationed on the porch of the agency while the rest were intended to guard the rear doors, with orders to keep the Indians bearing weapons outside. The excitement grew with every new arrival and we saw ourselves surrounded by at least one hundred-fifty Indians while the hills and trails were lined with squaws and children.

Speeches were made by some old chiefs to pacify and quiet the crowd but with no apparent effect. I expected every moment to hear the report of a gun or see one of our number stabbed. Hot and cold chills ran up and down my back as I thought of the possible consequence of such a fiddle to dance by. But the cold feeling in me at last got the upper hand and

I selected one end of the porch as the best place to fight – if fight we must. I was sitting on the [porch] rail with my right leg extended along the top and had my rifle resting in my hands, ready to use it at every moment. To the left of me stood a civilian employee while the nearest Indian to me was sitting on the rail at my foot so I considered myself comparably safe from any Indian Bowie knife. The porch stood about two feet above the ground, with a little garden and a fence to keep the main body of the Indians about fifteen feet from our throats. The rest of our men were taking it easy on the porch and permitted Indians to stand to the right and left of their chairs. My eyes were continually kept on these Indians and I noticed one of them pushing one end of the blanket back which he wore around his lower body. I expected to see the knife plunged into its victim and I took a glance at the young Indian at my foot to see what he was doing or intended to do, but he was quiet and not a muscle in his face indicated a murderish thought. It was different with me, I had selected him as the first one to introduce to my "Long Tom" and had kept her in such a position as to get him in front of the gun in the shortest possible time.

Lucky for our precious scalps the excitement subsided and some old bucks who had kept at a safe distance during the excitement now made their appearance at the agency and begged tobacco from us to smoke the pipe of peace. I was heartily glad to see the old men with their pipes appear on the porch. [I then noticed] the removing of a .50 caliber buffalo gun by an Indian who had put his big rifle in position on the garden fence to the right of me. [He had] hid behind some bush in the garden and had evidently a bead drawn on me and intended me as the most convenient one on the porch to let the daylight shine through in case it should be found necessary to stop me from harming the Indian perched on the railing of the porch at my right foot. He smiled as he saw me looking at him removing the gun and I must have cut a rather saner face as I fully realized the danger I had been in. How foolish I was to consider myself comparatively safe so long as I kept my eyes to the front and on the porch.[11]

The number of Indians grew smaller and smaller [as] the sun neared the horizon and we were permitted to return to the fort. Our rations were still untouched in our haversacks but we felt after the excitement was over that we could stand any kind from a Delmonico dinner down to a bacon and hardtack supper. Our tastes were for anything to fill up while the quality was not necessarily considered. Our cook had, in expectation of our return, done justice to our stomachs and prepared a large dish of hash which disappeared so fast that it frightened him out of his wits. It requires some extra fast eating to frighten an army cook.

The above occurrence had long passed [when] we received news of an Indian dance to take place on the parade ground at the fort. The war dance was given by the Indians to satisfy the curiosity of the commanding officer. The Indians formed in platoons outside of the fort and marched eight abreast. They kept time by the sound of a drum, entering the fort with long measured steps. Presumably they had the formation of military marching adapted from us. In making a wheel their marching was excellent and could not be surpassed by a company of soldiers. The dance was performed by the men walking in a circle and singing while the squaws kept up a dance on the outside.

Companies on the frontier were generally stationed at one fort for two years but frequently stay less and then are transferred to another post in the department, or exchange quarters with another regiment from another department. In the latter case the whole regiment was ordered either to the north or south as the case may be. While companies are stationed at a certain fort they were frequently ordered in the field, establishing a temporary camp for a month or two during the summer, thirty to three hundred miles from their station. The cavalry companies might be absent for months or longer at a time — according to the feelings of the Indians and their disposition to go on the warpath, or the state the country was kept in by the horse thieves and lawless characters.

The infantry generally remained at the fort and did all the escort duty or work connected with that place and were only sent to the field when short of cavalry. [At times] the infantry, mounted on ponies or mules, were employed as cavalry.

My [company] and a cavalry (colored) company were ordered to select and establish a camp at Boulder Creek camp thirty miles west of Fort Sill, the uneasiness of the Indians having made it necessary to have troops at a place near the line to their old hunting grounds in order to intercept them in case of an outbreak. My company was one of the lucky ones selected for that camp and we started with wagons and pack mules one hot summer day.

I, for some reason, had the privilege to ride that day with a half-dozen others. [We] crawled under the canvas covering [of the supply wagon] and made ourselves easy while the rest of the company hoofed it across the prairie. We passed the time sleeping and smoking. Little was thought of the men in front and pack mules behind, until the wagon descended a steep rocky bank and aroused us from our dreams of idleness. Here we discovered that one of the pack saddles had sprung a leak, the coffee sack open and our fine Java beans strewn along the trail for a considerable distance. The joke was now on us. [We] had to leave our comfortable places and gather them. Our work kept us about an hour back and there was considerable growling as we came into camp. We were well starved and many a walk was taken to the cook fire to see how supper was progressing.

At last the bacon was fried and one of the cooks cut fresh bread. A yell from the cook found us all on time with our tin cups and plates. We received our ration of coffee and bacon and were permitted to help ourselves to bread. There was too much unbaked dough in the center but it went all the same.

The next day we left the trail and took across the country. Everything went well until we attempted to cross a small gully. By some mishap the wagon upset and we had a narrow escape of being buried under a load of corn sacks. At last we got into camp and selected a place at the bend of the creek near a nice fresh spring.

The tents were soon pitched in a line with large ditches in front and rear and smaller ones between the tents as a drainage in case of rain. Two men were assigned to each tent and they went to work to make their little home as comfortable as possible, dirt being thrown on the ground flaps to keep out the draft. Four wooden forks [were] driven into the ground with crosspieces for the foot and headboards to our beds. Willow pieces [were] placed on top of this and fastened lengthways to the crossbars. We then cut enough dry prairie grass with our knives to make a good foundation on which to spread our buffalo robes and blankets. Our bed was completed with overcoat for a pillow, where we slept as warm and comfortable as in a brownstone house. A [rope] line was drawn between the upright poles of our tent for our surplus clothes, and the gun fastened to the reach pole. The bed was lengthways and we had plenty of room to pass in and out of our little abode.

Guard duty was light and we had plenty of time to play cards, fish, and hunt. Game was plentiful in the vicinity, pumas even ventured so far as the cook tent for the offal, making, in company with the wolves, the night hideous with their roaring and howling. When in the field the men had to do their own washing using, if obtainable, a rock for a washboard.

Passing Indians frequently gave variety to our lives while couriers kept us in connection with the fort, bringing us old papers and other reading material. The state of health of the troops at this place was excellent and, with the exception of a couple of chills and fever cases, we only had one sick man. This one undressed himself to wrench out his clothing after falling into water and was poisoned by the fumes of poisonous vines. He lay in his tent with nothing but a mosquito net around his swollen body, looking like a boiled crab.

There was a notable occurrence which brought the whole camp to their legs and threw everything in confusion. Separated and isolated from the rest of the tents stood the wall tents of officers and their mess tent with a soldier as cook. This cook, while busy preparing a meal set fire to the grass, the wind carrying it with [the] speed of a bird in a straight line over a small knoll, but [it] fortunately died when reaching a prairie dog town. The flame was soon extinguished, making a track of only about thirty feet, but it was just broad enough to fire one officer's tent. Men came running with buckets full of water but it was too late – the burning canvas roof fell and set fire to everything inside. Now the fun commenced. Inside the tent were stored about 5,000 rounds of ball cartridges packed in wooden boxes. These boxes were ablaze and the heat began to explode the cartridges within. Shells and bells went whizzing past our heads, sounding as if the Indians had attacked and were giving us a shower of blue-beans. We succeeded at last by throwing enough water on them to save most of the cartridges, putting a stop to the unwelcome "whizzers" who, in not a small degree, endangered our precious lives for a while.[12]

Unhappily we were ordered back to the fort before our thirty days were up, exchanging our happy camp life for the drudgery of fort life. A very important change soon took place in my military career which relieved me of all the labor and work which a private soldier is compelled to do in the army. I was promoted to corporal in the place of a man who was reduced to ranks for incapability and various other reasons.[13]

My first duty as corporal consisted [of] taking charge of an escort party for a paymaster trip. On the evening before our trip we were standing in line to answer retreat roll call as the first sergeant read the detail for detached service. To the surprise of the company and myself [he] read my name as the corporal of the detail and the corporal's name as a private for that detail. There was surely a mistake somewhere I thought – as a man when promoted or reduced to ranks is published to the company or regiment when drawn up in a line so as to acquaint the command with the fact, which in our case had been neglected. Nevertheless, we went on with our preparations for the trip.

The next morning about one hour before the start the company was ordered to assemble and the privilege given me to put stripes on the seams of my pants while the corporal was ordered to take his off. Now I was a corporal, the leaf had turned and I was given the first chance at a man who was hated by everyone in the company. It was a pleasure to order him at the heaviest and dirtiest work connected with the preparation. Fortunately for him he was selected as the cook for the officer in command and in this way got beyond my official reach for the balance of that trip. He subsequently got into favor with the paymaster and [was] selected by the latter for his cook on the return to the railroad where our man, disgraced as he was, availed himself of the opportunity and took "French leave," in other words deserted.

Orders had been received from headquarters that the paymaster would be at Caddo at such and such a time and to have a sufficient guard at that place to receive him. Our second lieutenant was quite green. The young officer was placed in command of our little party and [was] on his initiation of prairie life. He was just fresh from West Point, still chockfull with book learnings and thoroughly saturated with an idea of superiority above enlisted men. He ridiculed the advice of the old timers about the men pulling the "horns" off of him and laying snares, or in other ways trying to get an unfavorable officer into a court-martial.[14]

Before he left the fort on this journey some mischievous brother lieutenant advised him to put in a requisition to the quartermaster for knives, forks, and spoons for his private use. It was returned with a severe answer from that official, stating that the quartermaster department did not furnish such articles to officers. He was thoroughly ridiculed, the quartermaster department supplying only tents, axes, [and] transportation to traveling parties. Another of his city importations was a number of beautiful clean white blankets which he gave to one of the men to pack up for the tour besides a bunk and mattress. There can not be much care taking with such fine articles on detached service. The bundles were thrown with our blankets between the greasy and dirty pans in the wagon. There wasn't much color in them after fourteen days traveling, while our blankets were protected by a rubber blanket or old canvas sheet.

We left the fort with one ambulance and two escort wagons, traveling at a rate of forty to forty-five miles a day. We usually broke camp long before sunrise and got into camp about three o'clock in the afternoon. The time passed with spinning yarns and smoking. Flirting with pretty girls along the road gave us occasionally a variety and spice to our lives.

Hunting was also indulged in after getting into camp or if game happened to be near the road of our travel. It was, I think, on our second day out when one of our party made such an excellent hit on a prairie chicken that he was constantly reminded of it for the whole trip. One of the men sighted a prairie chicken and dismounted to get a good shot. He was all excitement as he cautiously walked within twenty yards of the fowl, steadily kneeled down and aimed. Bang went the shot and we saw the bird jump and drop dead on the spot. Our mouths were watering as we imagined eating a juicy supper, but all our happy thoughts came to naught as our hunter returned without the bird, keeping a dead silence about his game. Another man was sent to the spot to investigate. He had shot and killed a buffalo chip. A war whoop went up as the fact became known to all. The hunter was made the target of jokes for the balance of that day.

When going into camp near a village or farm house we were generally annoyed by hogs and pigs, who paid their respects as soon as we had the tents up. They busy themselves around the mules and wagons to pick up the loose grain and other eatables, they [would] even carry off the rations, especially our bacon, when placed by their reach. [One] memorable night the mules, after having been fed, were fastened to the tongue and wheels of our cook wagon with long halters and were thought to be beyond the reach of our rations. The next morning we were looking for the bacon to prepare breakfast. It was gone – nobody knew what had become of it until we saw one of the mules chewing at the gunnysack in which we carried the bacon.

Our only recourse was to fall back on the livestock and kill the pigs when they were picking up the grain. We became quite expert in knocking them over with an ax and skinning them by the light of the moon. All went well until we were in a camp near the railroad when our sins were forcibly brought to light. [We] narrowly escaped paying a high price for our fun. One of our men made [a] purchase of bacon in town and had just returned, placing it upon our table in camp when a hog made a dash, grabbed it, and ran off. There was a lively tune for possession for the bacon as the thief dodged axes and other missiles [while] running for the woods. One or two bullets were sent after it and it let go its hold and rolled down an embankment, badly wounded. A man soon engaged with the work of butchering the animal, so busy that he did not observe the appearance of the owner who had been attracted by the shots. The man claimed and proved his property by the marks in the hog's ears, demanding $20 as his share of the fun. We naturally objected, claiming a right to protect ourselves against loss and damage of our rations.

Our grievance was carried before the officer in charge who satisfied the owner with $15, to which he himself contributed $5 of his own purse, we paying the other $10, which cleaned us out. We swore revenge for this outrageous price as the real value of the hog was about six dollars. We killed and supplied our mess with fresh pork at every subsequent trip to the railroad from this man's herd.

The paymaster and money box were in the ambulance and we kept close on his heels as we traveled back to the fort. At night the money was kept in [a] tent while a guard stood watch. After a few days of travel we were camping one evening near a nice springs a short distance from the road. I took my gun and went to the officer to get permission for a hunt when the paymaster signified his willingness to go along. He had a beautiful breech-loading shotgun and a complete modern hunting outfit. Unfortunately he never had the luck of hitting anything. He would pop away at every real or imaginary animal he saw and naturally frightened all the game in the country, besides endangering my life to no small degree.

I concluded to keep him continually on the alert so as to draw his attention to a certain spot. [Then] I would tell him that there was a deer in front and to be cautious. Down we went on our knees and commenced to crawl through briars and thorns, or dodge behind trees — only to find the deer gone. The breakage of a dry branch would start a rabbit and, the deer forgotten, both barrels were emptied. I also drew his attention occasionally to a squirrel. At such occasions everything else was forgotten. He'd run around the tree to get a full view of the animal, stumble over trees, get entangled in vines, tear his hands and face bloody, only to find that he missed his mark and the squirrel still alive. We returned in the evening from that hunt with only one or two squirrels and birds.

That night about one o'clock, when everything was asleep, I was standing at the fire to warm myself. I saw our worthy paymaster make his appearance from behind the folds of his tent and direct his step in my direction. He was hatless, coatless, and shoeless, his step cautious and uncertain, his eyes had the appearance of weariness. After a talk about our hunt I was invited to a drink of whiskey, which of course was accepted, also with a drink for the sentry on guard. He tried to call the stagecoach which was passing about a half-mile away, but this was rather unceremoniously interrupted by a curse from one of the men in the tents who thought that the guards were neglectful of their duty permitting such noise at night. This brought the paymaster to his senses and he returned to sleep the balance of the night.[15]

The following evening we were camping about two miles from a farmhouse and I took a walk over to buy eggs and butter. I was compelled to pass some cattle on the open prairie. The bull of the herd confronted [me], my passage questioned. He seemed very angry, and in a great hurry about it. He tore the ground with his horns and hoofs, lowered his head, and came thundering towards me. I was not willing to make his bovine lordship's acquaintance so I turned in short order, taking to my heels. I can not state the exact speed with which I flew across the prairie but I know that I lowered my own record by many seconds. I gained the woods before I had a chance to get that bull by the horns – or it might have been the last of him if I did.

[The next] evening I started again for a hunt, this time unaccompanied by the paymaster. Squirrels were very numerous, as I was in quest of turkeys they were left unmolested to play in the shadow of the evening, but they gave me great annoyance with their playing in the dry leaves. I soon returned to camp without having seen any game worth shooting at with a rifle. Supper was over and I went on a tour of inspection around the different camping utensils where I found that my absence had not been overlooked. A pot full of sweet potatoes, bacon, fresh pork, biscuits, and a kettle of coffee [were] still near the fire. I did justice to all. After a hearty meal I went to our tent where my junior "bunky" had already rolled in and was fast asleep.

I followed suit, soon comfortably sleeping under warm blankets after I had relieved myself of unnecessary clothing, that is cap, blouse, and shoes. I was awakened by the crashing of thunder and splashing of water. We heard the voices of men and [the] tramping of feet past our tent. We ventured with one corner of our eye outside of the tent to see what was going on. It was nothing serious – only a tent or two down and its occupants hunting in the dark for an ax to fix the tent pins. A terrible gust of wind struck our tent and shook it as if it must tear it to pieces while the rain beat against the walls and sent a fine spray of water through the canvas [onto] our shivering bodies. One corner of the tent became loose and the storm came in upon us with increased force. The wind found free access, threatening to raise our little house bodily from over us. I grasped the dangerous corner with both hands while my bunky had to do the dirty work going out in the storm to fasten the pins.

We retired once more and the rain lulled us to sleep. How long we enjoyed the sweetness of this slumber I do not know but we were again aroused by the falling of the tent poles and the dropping of wet canvas on our heads. What mischievous spirit or soldier raised our tent pins and exposed us to the fury of the tempest? Were they jealous of our comfortable shelter after their own was destroyed by the angry gods? They [did] not have the satisfaction of seeing us in the rain – we remained where we were, covered partly by the fallen canvas. Slowly the water took possession of our beds and gradually came higher and higher until at last we could not draw our legs up any higher. We grabbed our caps and ran feet into our shoes [which] had, in the mean time, become water tanks, emptying up our pants legs like two streams from a fountain.

There is nothing miserable in the life of a soldier. That

was the idea we were trying to impress upon our minds as we stood shivering around a big fire, endeavoring to get warm. What fools we mortals were — to imagine ourselves safe against a storm and laugh at others in their apparent misfortune. It took two days to dry our buffalo robes by exposure to the direct rays of the sun from the back part of our wagons while traveling home. We returned to the fort in due time, got paid, and experienced the usual excitement of a payday.

6

. . . .

Prairie Adventures,
1879–1880

The following winter, to a place over one hundred miles west of [Fort] Sill, our company was detailed as a guard for a supply train to the cavalry in Texas. It was February and a heavy layer of snow covered the ground as we started our march. The train consisted of about eight or ten civilian wagons – prairie schooners and trail wagon, or double wagons, conducted by their wagon master. For a guard they had a herder who took the stock of the train out to graze overnight and enjoyed whatever rest or sleep he could get during the day in one of the moving wagons. We also had an Indian to guide the train across the trackless prairie to a place where we were to meet government teams with an escort of cavalry to take the rations and grain to their command, some fifty to one hundred miles further into the Staked Plains of Texas.[1]

Unlike our government teams who generally made three to four miles per hour, the civilian train moved at the rate of one and one-half miles in one hour, and we hardly knew what to do with ourselves as we rode, [then] walked with the wagons. We made our first camp near a little creek which most part of the year was dry, but at [that time] could easily float a ship of a size between a rowboat and a nut shell, according to the melting of the snow in the mountains. There our Indian guide met all of his relatives, taking his [issue of] his thirty-days rations to their camp. They celebrated a pow-wow and left our Indian without food. We were consequently compelled to mess him from our own kitchen or else do without his service for the trip.

We retired early that night as we thought bed the most comfortable place in cold weather. We could not sleep as the cold was excessive. [We] four who slept in one tent were huddled so closely together that if one of the outsiders would take a turnover the rest had to follow. We were trying all imaginable ways to get as much space as possible between our hips and the ground. We were laying on top of our guns, rolled the overcoat up like a rope and slept on it, some even tried to sleep on top of the others while they were asleep.

In this way we passed the first night, thanking the bugler as he called us to reveille at one or two o'clock in the morning. A warm cup of coffee and breakfast gave us a chance to walk ourselves warm. Before I left the fort I had provided myself with a couple of quarts of whiskey which I kept secreted in a bundle of clothes, taking a two-ounce bottle full for my daily use. To this I gave my frequent attention. I was soon rid of

the chill and bad effect of the last night's rest and could sit
on one of the wagons, smoke, and enjoy a ride while waiting
for the sun to thaw us up.

We came within view of an Indian village where the governor of the Kiowa and Comanche resided. He was a Comanche
half-breed, Quinine [Quanah Parker] by name, made the head
chief of the Comanche Indians by the U.S. government. The
Indians respected his authority so long as they saw fit, but
did not dare to openly oppose him as that would be a breach
with the government. The chief lived like the rest of the Indians in a tepee and had two or three of the prettiest young girls
for his squaws. He was very wealthy and had a large herd of
cattle and ponies grazing in the adjoining valleys. There was in
the vicinity of the village a field of about fifteen to twenty-five
acres under cultivation. The Indians were also provided with
wagons which they used when coming to the fort.[2]

We sat on top of the wagons, carefully keeping a blanket
around our shoulders and heads as a protection against the
"norther." We crossed rich fertile valleys heavily timbered,
keeping along the southern borders of a range of mountains.
We came to a prairie dog town where nothing but fine buffalo
grass was permitted to grow, apparently to bite, for the little
rodent. Mesquite trees gave the town the appearance of a
peach orchard. There we saw a herd of antelope, a flock of
turkeys, or a wolf run for their lives as they were made
acquainted with some bullets from the rifles of our hunters.

We met an Indian packtrain driven by squaws while little
papooses clung like monkeys to the back of a pony and were
decorated with red cloth and small bells. The caravan slowly
disappeared between the trees, leaving nothing of their passage
but their trail, furrowed by the dragging tent poles.

We crossed a river or creek and went into camp. In consid-
eration of the atmospheric changes and heavy storms, in the
western territories creeks were always crossed by the teams in
the evening, so as not to be detained by unexpected floods in

the morning. Freezing at night we rolled up the frozen tents at one in the morning and continued to move. [We] camped at old Camp Radziminski and left the section of good water and rich valleys. The mountains to our right bent to the north and we entered the sand hills and sandy valley of the North Fork of the Red River.[3]

We had great difficulty in crossing this stream with our heavily loaded wagons. The banks were steep and we were compelled to travel for a mile in the sand of the dry portion of the river to get to a suitable crossing, having to double the teams to prevent the sinking of the wagons in the quicksand. At last safely across [we went] into camp on the high banks, preparing our supper with brackish yellow water, and [got] to bed early. I was detailed on guard for that night and brought in a good supply of logs for the fire.

Everything in the camp was quiet, the men asleep, the animals at rest, as I sat near the fire and sought consolation in my clay pipe. The usual building of air castles was this night suspended and more solid thoughts crossed my mind. Happy days of my youth passed before my gaze. I saw the long past, but not forgotten, kindness of a friend and loving kindred appear in the warm flame. How could I forget those good old times when, through with my day work in an unhealthy dusty shop, I could seek recreation in theaters [or] concerts. I was thinking of the difference of a civilian and a soldier. The first – in the midst of a loving family and intelligent friends, surrounded by the comforts of civilization, enjoyed his existence at the fireside at home. The latter – far from any home, thrown in company with all classes of mankind, exposed to all kinds of weather, not knowing at what instance a bullet or arrow may pierce his heart and end his unhappy existence. These pictures are surely in favor of civil life.

But look at them a little deeper [and] see if there is nothing desirable in the life of a soldier, in preference to the first. We have an intelligent civilian, willing and worthy. He arises early and goes to his place of business in order to make his existence. He remains there all day and uses all his physical and mental power at his work in an unhealthy place, returning in the evening too tired to enjoy the few hours which are left to him before he retires to repeat the same the next day. Or he has a family, [and] an extravagant wife who scolds him when he is in need of rest. Business is dull. He fails, disgraced, and can not get enough money to buy bread for his crying children. [If] he is doing well [he] has to listen to the senseless conversation of the so-called society fops. He is deceived, his daughter seduced and wife disgraced, and he is laughed at by the heartless friends of civilization's production. He goes out in the evening to take a little exercise and fresh air. He is sandbagged, robbed, killed and his body found the next day. A coroner's inquest follows with a burial, the grave is robbed, the body taken to some medical college, butchered, and dissected in pieces — if there were any left — put into alcohol for preservation. This is the last of him.

A soldier supposes to do nothing else but to obey orders and do what he is told. If he has hard times for a while there are surely ninety percent sunny days coming. He is permitted to hunt and follow any pleasure he is inclined to. He can read books and papers, study all branches of science, and cultivate himself when in [the] fort. He has concerts, dances, and theaters, and selects his own companions. He does not need to worry his brains about the next meal, and if sick there is somebody to nurse him. There is no smiling and deceiving society to contend, but the pure virgin of nature's creation daily before him, within his own grasp. If he should die, no matter what place or time, he is buried with military honors and there are no hands to disturb his sacred grave. There are surely good sides in all stages, [but] I was perfectly satisfied where I was.

My thoughts, as I was setting near the campfire, were rather abruptly interrupted by the cry of an owl from a tree overhead.

I started to my feet and to my intense surprise saw I was not alone. Two or three large timber wolves were standing on the other side of the fire, staring at me with their burning eyes. I took a piece of wood from the fire and made for them. They were not so easily frightened away, slow to abandon their hope of getting one of the turkeys in the tree near the fire. They only ran about ten yards, stopped and clattered their teeth at me. These wolves were accompanied by a large number of coyotes who set up a terrific howl and ran between the tents and wagons. The whole camp was awake before I could drive these beasts to flight and restore order and peace.

The night passed without another invasion from wolves. In the morning we took our tin cups to get our ration of coffee for breakfast and prepared to cross a plateau. Little we could drink and enjoy, the alkaline of the river made it salty, the yellow mud and sand made it appear as if we had the unusual treat of milk in our coffee. We started on our day's journey half-choked with thirst.

We ascended a small rise and gained a plateau which we had to cross on a trackless road. Our Indian guide was far in advance of the wagons as he rode ahead to find and avoid impossible cuts. Only occasionally we could see him stop to wait for us to come up, while he drew his red blanket closer around his bony body. The wind was cutting and the cold intense. Only with difficulty could we keep ourselves warm with walking as the wagons moved very slowly. The sun soon made her appearance and took control of the day, thawed the snow, disclosing a fine growth of grass under our feet.

We had a fine day before us and before evening set in we were drawing near to the Salt Fork of the Red River. The atmosphere was warm and the ground dry. Within view of the river, and of the beautiful growth of trees on its banks, our hearts were longing for camp and a good hearty meal. What do we see ahead? Smoke – the prairie was on fire at the very place where we intended to camp and rest. Large clouds of smoke enveloped the trees and the flame rose playing between the branches, slowly traveling before the gentle breeze.

We crossed the river and circumscribed a circle to get beyond the fire, soon in camp beyond, on the safe side of the destructive element. We provided ourselves with wet gunny sacks and long sticks to fight the fire and prevent it from turning with a change of wind and delay or imprison us with nothing but the black barren soil to feed our stock upon. Our task was not an easy one as the grass was eight to ten feet high and the heat intense, so much so that it was impossible for us to reach the seat of the fire with our sacks. We were compelled to abandon all hope of checking its progress, leaving it to continue its destructive work unmolested. What a change! Only a short time before we saw a beautiful forest, now black smoldering arms, shadows of their former beauty.

Traveling westward we came to places where the buffalo, only six months [before], wallowed in the loose ground, making round holes to roll in the mud and enjoy their free existence. Nothing was seen of them but their bones and skulls. They were slaughtered by the merciless buffalo hunters for the sake of their hides, their bodies left to the wolves and buzzards. We found the carcass of an old buffalo bull with his torn and ragged hide still clinging to his bones, [dying] alone as one of the last of his race. It may be justly stated that cattle raised upon the same ground are more profitable to man and consequently there is no loss for us if they were extinct. But if buffalo have no right to live why shall we permit deer, antelope, and other game to exist – why not exterminate them all and live entirely upon the meat of domestic animals. Formerly the buffalo furnished everything the Indian required for his living: clothes, tents, needles, thread, and meat. Now he is thrown on the hands of the government for a living, besides the few antelope and deer he may kill.

The number of animals had been reduced to such a small figure that in all my travels in the Indian Territory, Texas, and Kansas I never, to my knowledge, saw a genuine wild buffalo. Had it not been for the cavalry who killed a few in Texas and brought some of the meat home I never would have had an opportunity to taste buffalo meat.

After passing the buffalo wallows, where the snow water formed miniature lakes, we came to a large prairie dog town ten to fifteen miles long. The surface of the ground was almost bare of any vegetation, no trees or grass patches to relieve the monotory vision. We were at a loss [as to] how a great many of them managed to live. They probably followed the example of a superior race and lived like people in some overcrowded city.

Turning from the prairie dog town we came to a valley and a creek called Turkey Creek. Innumerable flocks of wild turkey there went to roost in the trees overnight. There was no difficulty of hunting these birds as they were seldom disturbed by a hunter and consequently [were] easily shot down at night. Here we had the misfortune of losing our Indian guide who absconded during the night after learning from some passing Indians that his brother had been shot in Texas.

We only had twenty-five miles more to travel to get to our destination, which we happily reached, and found the government teams already waiting for us. The transfer was soon accomplished. This place was about two miles north of the Red River, where the 100th meridian forms the boundary line between Texas and the Indian Territory.

We remained a few days to give our teams a short rest before starting upon our return. I [took] the opportunity to scout and hunt a little in this section, especially to take a view of the Red River which I had never seen before at this longitude. I found the river, what there was of it, a small creek flowing in the middle of a broad red plain. The plain was about three-quarters of a mile wide, bordered by a two foot high bank. The red plain constituted the bed of the river. Through the red sand, or quicksand – at some places packed

solid, at others quivering pockets — the main portion of the
river water was flowing until, at some distance further down
where the hills compressed the bed, the water was forced to
the surface and continued to flow above ground.

Being naturally curious to place my foot on Texas soil I
took a walk across. I found the water clear as crystal, too salty
to drink. My life was more than once endangered by the
quivering sand [when] I stepped unconsciously on places where
I was sinking with every step and my shoes held fast by the
sand. I accomplished my task and returned to the Indian
Territory completely exhausted. I took a seat to watch the
setting sun and rest before returning to camp. The change of
the light was magnificent. The sun slowly sinking behind the
western horizon transformed the sky to a beautiful red. The
air was quiet, no sound to disturb the death of the parting
day. I took my gun to give a parting shot to Texas and the
valley, the report almost startled me. I could hear the ball
whizzing across the river while the echo reverberated between
the hills and made the plain ring with thunder. Darkness
surrounded me, the stars twinkling overhead, the timid rabbits
ventured out of their hiding places in search of food, while
the wolves were howling in the distance.

I found the camp in safety. [There were] a few peculiarities
of that place. The water was altogether alkaline and had a
salty taste. The wood was small and we were compelled, in
order to get good coals to bake with, to dig for mesquite roots.
An old Indian mound or monument was said to exist in this
vicinity, but I was unable to find it.

[Upon the] start for our return three men were sent a day
in advance to hunt turkeys for the company at Turkey Creek.
We found them waiting with sixty some-odd birds at our
arrival. We preserved them with salt and charcoal filling. In
spite of this precaution we lost twelve to fifteen birds by the
prevailing warm days before reaching the fort.

One more incident remains to be mentioned in connection

with this trip. This was the temporary loss on one Frenchman, an old warrior of many battles and travels under the French flag, [whom] we had the honor of calling one of our members of the company. Although an old soldier who had been in campaigns before – the Franco-Prussian War, Algeria, and under Maximilian in Mexico, he always had the misfortune of getting lost from the company if we undertook a trip. He was considered the most useless man in camp for work, and consequently was promoted to Camp Fool, of which a camp always had a couple. This time he made no exception to the general rule. It was, I think, on our third day [en route] back when he had occasion to leave the wagons early in the morning. He got lost in the dark but struck our trail at daylight. He followed but later left it to follow the trail of a buffalo hunter's wagon and was entirely lost.

He spent the first night in the wilderness [by] shooting at wolves, keeping them at bay. At daylight he started to find our camp or trail. After crossing a river three or four times he was fortunate enough to find – not us – but a buffalo hunters' camp. He was fed and directed in the right direction by them, but instead of finding us he got lost once more and ran half-starved into an Indian camp. Here he was detained and nursed. A squaw eventually put him on [a] pony behind her and turned him over to the commanding officer of a cavalry company at Camp Radziminski, thus ending his exploits amongst the wolves and wild beasts in the prairie. He subsequently returned to us with the return of the cavalry after leaving word for the squaw to visit him when coming in for rations. She soon put in her appearance at the fort and was duly honored with $5 in money and a sack full of rations.

While staying at Fort Sill I took walks in the woods and hills for botanical and mineralogical researches which brought me often a variety of new things, [and] into some strong places and adventures. All of the plants and fine specimens of stones, by the way, I was compelled to leave behind at the fort as we were ordered to another place afterwards, not having a chance to store them away for transportation in one of our company boxes or wagons.

Of cactus there were only three varieties [in] this section of the country, while of other plants I had a whole box full, nicely pressed and dried specimens. We had also two kinds of wild plums, strawberries, raspberries, and gooseberries growing at the bluffs a few miles from the fort, to where I frequently took my walks.

One time when descending [Medicine Bluff] from a good feast of berries and crossing a trail at the creek, I passed a couple of mounted Indians who stopped to greet me. My vocabulary of their language was very limited, and so was theirs of English. Our conversation was consequently confined to a few signs added by the little Indian I knew. There was really nothing strange in this meeting and I would have thought no more of it, had it not been for the suspicious glances they threw at me, which seem to say more than words. They were evidently sizing me up to see if I was armed or if it was worthwhile to go into details about my further existence. I was far from being at ease after that discovery and the knowledge that I had nothing for a defense, except the rocks at my feet − with the possible chances I stood with the quickness of my legs.

I always had traveled unarmed when not out hunting and had met Indians in more isolated places than this, but never had a reason to wish for a pistol until then. It was too late to think over that so I put on a bold face and acted as cool as if I were laying behind breastworks, not caring if there were two or three hundred of them there. [Either] my confidence in my lucky star and my action, or the Indians suspected more soldiers in the vicinity − whatever it may have been which kept them from executing their unspoken desire − they said "Goodbye John," and resumed the trail, while I took to the hill to see where they were going, before venturing home.

I recall a walk to the top of Medicine Bluff in company with a friend, where we went to pick raspberries and gooseberries. After the inspection of an old fortified camp halfway between the fort and the bluffs, once the headquarters of General Sheridan before the fort was constructed, we ascended the hills above the bluff. They were about one and one-half miles from the fort and faced to the north, with a creek of the same name passing at the foot. At some places the walls were perpendicular and consequently inaccessible to any human foot, while at another place we found a platform midways, strewn with smaller rocks. There the vines of the berries had found a foothold and were thriving well, bringing forth delicious fruit.

To this platform we descended. After encountering a couple of rattlesnakes and maneuvering past dangerous places we were fairly installed in the midst of berries and picking with both hands. But there is no rose without a thorn. We soon found that the place was anything but comfortable. The south wind could not strike us and the sun overhead made the rocks as hot as a bake oven. A burning thirst aided our pleasures, which even the juicy berries could not satisfy. We were standing on an old cedar tree picking to our heart's content when we heard a rattling noise under our feet in the vines. A sickly feeling crept over me as I thought of the possible chances of going to heaven on a rattlesnake route. It would have been sure death for us to jump and fall over the bluff, so we were compelled to remain and await developments, not long in coming. A large panther or puma had selected this place for a bed and left it to look for a quieter one [to] continue his disturbed nap. The look he gave us before disappearing was enough to show his displeasure – we took the hint as we had no gun to attack him.

A few days later I came again, provided with a rifle to get the hide of the panther. After climbing, crawling, and hunting all accessible places on the bluff I had to return without it and leave the king of the felines of the U.S. in full possession of his pelt.

Another time a party of us borrowed ponies from some of the men in the fort and started to a place for blackberries. On our return somebody suggested a race and was immediately accepted by all. The ponies went off at full speed across the prairie and we had fair chances to break our necks or turn somersaults at some of the water cuts. My pony especially seemed to select all breakneck places and bound upon having a little extra fun for himself and me. I lost all control of him. Instead of keeping straight ahead with the rest of the horses he persisted upon describing a circle to the left and taking me to a large ditch which I surely thought would be our halting place. He cleared it with one jump and continued his mad race until he was completely exhausted.

I had lost my foothold on the stirrups in the jump but managed to stick to him. There could be no chance of winning a race under such difficulties so I slowly followed the rest to the end of the designated course, where I had to stand the ridicule of the winners.

Fort Sill was connected with the civilized world with a telegraph line, making a connection at some point in Texas. The line was constructed of wood poles between the fort and the border, consequently easily damaged by prairie fires and storms, which had to be repaired by details of troops sent by the military. I had about three or four trips of this kind [and] will give a detailed description of one.[4]

Our party consisted of myself and two men, besides a civilian teamster and a six-mule team to carry a number of poles and the necessary tools and rations. The weather was bad and a steady rain set in and continued all day, drenching us from head to foot before we left the fort. Our progress under such circumstances — very slow. We concluded before we had traveled five miles, to go into camp and await a better day.

The tent was soon up and the rations securely stored under

shelter, while a fire, after considerable difficulties of building it, returned some of our bodily warmth and brought the blood again into circulation. The following morning broke with the indication of a nice day, and so it was. The sun had full control and made the effects of the foregoing day fast disappear. We were following the road with the wagon while one man walked along the telegraph line to see where repairs were needed. The damage was comparatively small and we accomplished our task sooner than expected, one and one-half days making forty-five miles, leaving us two and one-half days out of the four to return to the fort.

We were naturally adverse of returning so soon, so we concluded to go into camp at a convenient place and pass the balance of our time with hunting. The place selected was about six miles from the road, situated at a bend of a creek in the beautiful valley of Cache Creek. The grass was high and rich, the woods hid us from view of any curious eyes. Game was plentiful, venison and antelope meat our principal diet. To this life of plenty was added the hind-quarter of a heifer, presented to us by some cowboys who were herding upon forbidden ground.[5]

We made our regular meals on game meat while between time we cut off a hang from the heifer, broiling it on a stick over the fire, eating the delicious steak with a little salt. If our time was not occupied with hunting or eating we could walk a couple of miles up the creek and pay a visit to an Indian hunting camp, or go about the same distance down [the creek] and play cards with the cowboys.

One of my hunts in the afternoon took me past the Indian camp and I stopped at one of the tepees for a little rest. On my way home I crossed the creek where I met a number of squaws digging for some kind of eatable roots, and I stopped there for a short time to watch and try to get some of that delicacy. The sight was similar to one we see in civilized countries where women dig potatoes, with the only exception the dress, which had a little more color and was more picturesque.

I stood there for some time listening to their talk and laughter. One little plump thing turned her laughing face to me and made some inquiry, an unintelligible question. Not caring to admit my ignorance of their language I wobbled out my "Kim e heights" – "Come here." Down went the digging tools and everything came running towards me. Dumfounded and paralyzed from the unexpected rush I soon found myself surrounded by old and young, homely and pretty squaws who gibbered and chattered like parrots. Enough of it I could understand – they wanted tobacco. [I was] undecided if I should kiss some of the pretty lips or go down into my pocket and distribute tobacco.

There was not the least bit of difference of these simple creatures as they stood with smiling faces and laughing eyes asking for a gift [as] from a scene we [would] meet at our fairs where their civilized sisters with their sweetest smiles and tongues tug at strangers for the favor of ten cents. It is hard to resist the pleading of female eyes. The siege to my heart being at last successful, and my tobacco bag empty, I pursued my way along the creek. I found our camp still in its place at my return, and a warm supper waiting for me.

It was altogether a life too good for any ordinary man, but not so for Uncle Sam's children, who could have stood this for some time, and we were naturally loath to leave it. But everything has an end, and so our pleasure. We were at the eve of our return to the fort and were preparing the surplus game to take home to the company. A little before dark the mules, knowing their feeding time near, came in from the pasture to be tied up for the night and receive their corn. But it was yet a little too soon, and they were driven back, no further notice taken of the way they were going. A half hour passed and we started to bring them in, but to our greatest consternation they were nowhere to be found, as if some mischievous spirit had carried them from the surface of the earth.

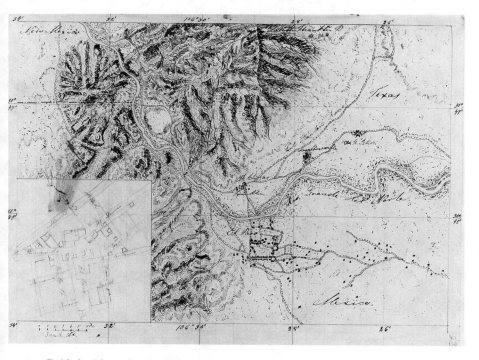

Published here for the first time is a detailed map of El Paso and vicinity, drawn by Emil A. Bode in the early 1880s. In his journal Bode included several carefully drawn topographic maps of New Mexico and Texas. Although they are not signed, the labeling on the maps matches the handwriting of the Bode manuscripts. Map by Emil A. Bode. Courtesy Special Collections of the Sterling C. Evans Library, Texas A&M University.

Birds-eye View
of
FORT SILL, I. T.
from G.T.C.

"Above the confluence with Medicine Bluff Creek lay the small elevation of the fort which glittered in the evening sun as the last rays fell upon the blue limestone walls of the buildings." Looking west, this painting offers a bird's-eye view of Fort Sill, Indian Territory, in 1877, the year Bode arrived for duty with the Sixteenth Infantry Regiment. The large building on the upper right is the post hospital, the right-hand border is Medicine Creek. Lining the left of the parade ground are the enlisted infantry barracks, directly opposite are officers' quarters. On the upper side of the parade ground are the cavalry barracks and stables. Water color by Brigadier General S. B. Holabird. Courtesy Fort Sill Museum, photo number P527.

Looking north from the guardhouse, a panoramic view of the Fort Sill parade ground in 1873. Bode's infantry barracks, in the center foreground, he described as being "very neglected ... [and] unfortunately ... the only barracks there built of wood." Courtesy Fort Sill Museum, photo number P1406.

The "well-ventilated, nicely constructed hospital" at Fort Sill, where Bode lay as a malaria patient for two months, "swallowing opium pills by the dozens without success." Bode also served temporarily on extra duty as a nurse and cook at the hospital for a month in 1877. The hospital stewards' quarters are on the right. Post Hospital, ca. 1890s. Courtesy Fort Sill Museum, photo number 8729.

THE OLD GUARD HOUSE FORT SILL OKLA.   BUILT A.D. 1868.

"Behind those gray [guardhouse] walls have been confined sons of poor and rich parents, intelligent and imbecile, murderers and innocent." The Fort Sill guardhouse where Bode often served as guard. Although the date on the front of the photo indicates the building was constructed in 1868, it was actually built in 1873. The photo was made in 1918 but the building had remained unchanged since its construction. Courtesy Fort Sill Museum, photo number 8079.

Big Bow, Kiowa, ca. 1870. This chief's temporary arrest in 1878 caused a minor sensation on the reservation, leading Bode and his comrades into a confrontation with one hundred angry Indians on the front porch of the Kiowa-Comanche Agency building at Fort Sill. Courtesy Fort Sill Museum, photo number P1774.

"The tepees were [then] mostly made of canvas stretched over poles. . . . However, the old buffalo [hide] tepee was frequently seen in winter." An Arapaho family camp near Fort Sill, 1870, similar to the Comanche camp at which Bode was detailed as a guard in 1878. Courtesy Fort Sill Museum, photo number 3042.

Woman's Heart, Kiowa, ca. 1875. "The Indians were generally cruel when on the warpath and nothing would soften their hearts. At a raid in Mexico by the Comanche Indians a woman fought to the last but was eventually overpowered and killed, her heart eaten by one of the raiders who assumed the name Woman Heart [Woman's Heart], afterwards a well-known person at the fort. . . . By eating a brave person's heart the bravery is transferred to them." Photo by W. S. Soule. Courtesy Fort Sill Museum, photo number P1780.

"His name was Black Beaver, chief of the Delaware Indians and [he] traced his lineage back to the same Delaware who concluded a treaty with William Penn in 1682." Black Beaver–fur trapper, commander of a volunteer company in the Mexican War, and highly respected friend and guide of the explorer Captain Randolph B. Marcy. Photo ca. 1874–75. Courtesy Fort Sill Museum, photo number P4026.

"Her attitude was commanding and we bowed in homage and admiration as she passed us proud as a queen. My heart rolled at this occasion." Arapaho sisters Zah-e-cha and Har-ke-i in a regal pose for photographer W. S. Soule in 1874 or 1875. Courtesy Fort Sill Museum, photo number 3046.

Medicine Bluffs, Fort Sill, Colonel B. H. Grierson and party, 1869. Bode
relates, "The bluff derived its name, according to Indian tradition, from a
medicine man who made a leap over the precipice to prove his power over
death. . . . The Indians celebrated their sun dances, their most solemn dance,
within sight of these bluffs." Bode had several unexpected adventures while
hunting for blackberries on the face of the bluff. Courtesy Fort Sill Museum,
photo number 1812.

A somewhat blurred but rarely published panoramic view of Garrison Hill, Fort Gibson, Indian Territory, about 1909, looking much the same as Bode would have seen it when stationed there in 1880. From left to right are the commissary, blacksmith shop, west officers' quarters, armory, south half of barracks, Presbyterian Church, and hospital. Published by J. C. Bert, Fort Gibson, Okla., postmarked 7 October 1909. Courtesy Oklahoma Historical Society, photo number 13380.

"The Prairie Schooner . . . a smaller wagon was generally attached to the rear, both covered with canvas stretched over bows . . . drawn by six mules or six to eight yoke of oxen. . . . From five to twenty such wagons were frequently seen, crossing the prairie like a huge snake with a white back." The type of wagon Bode escorted to Texas in the winter of 1879, shown here in 1877 in front of John Becker, Co., in Belen, New Mexico, through which Bode passed on the way to the Victorio Campaign in 1880. Courtesy Museum of New Mexico, negative number 66013.

The closest town to Bode's Victorio Campaign camp at Knight's Ranch was the mining town of Silver City, which he reported had "hotels and saloons fitted up in grand style. One of the latter even went so far as to bring a piano to these wild regions. . . . " Silver City, New Mexico ca., 1882. Courtesy Museum of New Mexico, negative number 11428.

"Fort Cummings ... had a wall twelve feet high ... with one arched entrance.... [It] had been made the headquarters for the troops in the field. We saw long rows of cavalry and infantry tents in the rear of the dilapidated fort." Fort Cummings, New Mexico, in 1882. Courtesy National Archives and Records Service, Washington, D.C., negative number 111SC-82937.

Our anxiety increased with every minute as the shadows of the evening were getting longer and longer. No sign or sound from the [mules'] shackles struck our ears. At last we were compelled to give up the hunt and wait for daylight to track them to their hiding place. The following morning we found their tracks and followed their trail so far as the road. Here they had taken the direction of the fort. We [then] knew that after driving them away from the wagon the foregoing evening they took a beeline for the fort, twenty-five miles [away].

There was one animal still in our possession who had been kept in camp as a herding mule. This one [was ridden] to the fort to bring the other five back. We also borrowed a pony from the Indians, giving a blanket for the privilege, to assist the first one.

We who remained in camp made the best of the situation and in the meantime enjoyed ourselves [but] were compelled to live almost entirely on meat, as the flour and coffee had been all used up. The following evening, after hunting all day for antelope, we were around the fire conversing as good as we could with an Indian who had come down for a visit to await the arrival and return of his [borrowed] pony.

The air was quiet [without] a sound to disturb the motionless surroundings of our little camp when the Indian raised his hand and, pointing in the direction of the fort, said that our animals were coming. They were still one-quarter mile away and nothing was audible to our untrained ears, but we soon discovered them turning the corner and coming down for the camp, to deliver us from our imprisonment. The animals, immediately after their arrival, were taken to the creek to water and, as misfortune once set in never comes alone, we almost lost one of them by drowning. The banks of the river were steep where one of the mules while drinking lost his foothold and fell into the water. Although the water was not one and one-half foot deep the animal seemed to lose all control of his limbs in the swift flowing current and could not rise to his feet. [He] always fell back after every attempt, with his head under water. [He] would have soon joined his ancestors on their happy roaming ground where there are no blacksnakes and pack saddles if he had not been saved by a man jumping into the river for his assistance, bringing him to his feet again. He was at last brought back to the wagon and chained for the night while our Indian friend returned to his camp with the pony.

The night passed without an interruption and we were aroused on the morning of our departure by the bellowing of a cow. It was yet too early and we took another turn. We were once more aroused by the lowing of a calf. It was after daybreak and we got up to prepare breakfast, brought face to face with the disturbance of our morning slumber and saw at once the connecting links of a drama and probable tragedy between some quadruped mammals.

A cow had lost her calf and following the valley for her offspring was probably a good distance [away]. The little one, presumably alone, was standing a short distance from our camp and eyeing us as we emerged from the tent. It was a sight, [this] young creature just starting in this world. But our minds were adverse to philosophical thoughts, the desire of our stomachs had the upper hand. We took the gun to exchange the dry tough turkey breakfast for that of a juicy veal omelet and were preparing to shoot the calf. Providence put her protecting hand over the defenseless being in the shape of another enemy, neutralized two destructive elements, and saved the weak. We saw three or four large wolves following, keeping intervals of about forty yards, endeavoring to encircle the calf and preparing to throw themselves upon their intended victim. It would have been murder to take advantage of the situation and kill the calf, our guns were therefore used for its protection and those wolves killed and scattered by a few bullets from our rifles. The calf, frightened by the reports of our guns, was permitted to continue in its search for its mother and enjoy a little longer the pleasures of its existence before furnishing food and nourishment for some ravenous animal.

Although it was against the law of the country and the order of the military to kill the stock of a citizen, it could not prevent the occasional slaughtering of cattle for private use. Soldiers would kill stock whenever they have an opportunity of doing so without being caught, cowboys whenever they felt hungry and have a chance of stealing a heifer from another man's herd.

After this early episode [we] continued to prepare our meal, broke camp, and started on our return to the fort. Nothing of note came within our vision until we passed a small hill near the road where the brown tepees of an Indian village looked down on us from their lofty position. We saw an Indian squaw descending, carrying a bundle in her arms, going to a smaller hill to the left of the road. The bundle contained the body of a child and the mother was taking it there for burial. She cried continually as she covered the little body with rocks to protect it against the wolves, singing a dead-song before taking the final parting. She turned to leave after her sorrowful duty to her departed beloved and returned to the care of the living in her tepee.

Here was a mother – a wild mother, but was there ever a mother's heart in a civilized race more sorrowful in parting from her beloved treasure than this simple woman? Although there were no carriages and magnificent displays to convey the body to its last resting place. There were no flowers or other visible tokens of love placed upon this little departed being's grave, it nevertheless received a token, insignificant in appearance, but more valuable than all colored and sweet scented offerings. It was a tear, a mother's tear, which fell and pressed the last seal of love on the eyes of the dead child.

Continuing our traveling we were soon within the lines of the fort. After reporting to the commanding officer and notifying him in person of my return I retired to the company barracks to clean my equipment and put them in good order again. This naturally included the airing of the blankets. The blankets were put together by two or three men and one bed made of them. A rubber blanket or piece of canvas with a buffalo robe and some woolen blankets were used for the bedding, while one to three blankets, according to the atmosphere outside, were used as covering. These latter were straightened a little in the morning and the whole rolled into a bundle for convenient transportation. In the evening the bundle was thrown into the tent and the blankets put down as they were taken up in the morning without disturbing the original bed. It so happens that snakes and other animals may seek a rest between the warm folds and are not discovered until the shaking and cleaning process [which] takes place at the fort after the return, which may be two months after starting out.

I found, as I took my blankets on the parade ground for an airing, between their folds a nest of snakes who seemed to be rather indisposed to give up their claim for the possession of the blankets, which they had probably shared with me in peaceful harmony for the last four or five days.

Thanksgiving Day was drawing near and hunting parties of four men each from every company were sent out to furnish the garrison with the customary turkey dinner. Our party started independently from the rest and were consequently compelled to furnish [our] own transportation, which consisted of some borrowed rickety buckboard drawn by two ponies belonging to some men in the company and an extra pony for riding. We started for a five day hunt and selected a place about thirty miles west of Fort Sill as the most suitable for an operation.

We pitched our tent in the middle of a large forest on the banks of a dry stream where the water could only be obtained by digging a little into the sand of the bed of the stream. Turkeys were numerous, but very shy, and we experienced some difficulty of hunting them. Nevertheless we were fortunate enough to kill about fifteen of their number before we returned to the fort.

To successfully hunt these birds a man ought to have a shotgun and start to walk shortly before or after sunset along the banks of some creek where turkeys are known to have their roost. They can easily be heard flying up in the trees. They generally select a high cottonwood tree overhanging the water for their resting place. Their bodies are distinctly visible against the starry heaven, easily shot after dark. Where the leaves are off the trees in the fall [they can] be hunted all night. In the morning before daybreak their presence is brought to notice by the morning call of the gobbler who begins to chuckle.

After daybreak the game leaves the roost to feed and wallow in adjoining sand hills, and only return about one o'clock for a short time to water. They are in the daytime best hunted with a small dog who barks and drives them in the trees and draws the attention of the birds from the hunter. The hollow bone from the leg of a turkey is also used to imitate the call of a hen and draw his turkeyship within the jaws of death. They are also deceived at night, in country where there are pigs roaming in the woods, by crawling on all fours and imitating the grunt of a hog. Hunting with a rifle affords undoubtedly more sport to a pleasure seeker, but for a living I prefer a shotgun, even when hunting for deer, as there are more chances of hitting some vital spot.

On the first evening after our arrival at the camp two men went down to the river and killed about eight turkeys, but they were too heavy to carry home that night. I started the next morning after receiving a description of their location, to bring them in with our pony. I had no difficulty finding the place where the turkeys were hanging in a tree. After tying their legs together and throwing them across the saddle in front of me I took a shortcut through the woods for camp.

According to my calculation I was about one-quarter mile

from camp, where I expected to strike the river again. At that moment I was thrown into confusion by the voice of the man I had left in camp. The voice came from my right and the man seemed to be in great agony and in need of speedy relief. I hesitated, as I had thought the man to be in camp, and that I had lost my bearings. I concluded to keep on my course for a short distance to see if I was wrong. The horse was urged to full speed and I saw that I had not been mistaken in regards to the location of the camp. But the man was not there, nor anywhere near.

The voice was now stronger and two shots were fired in quick succession. My turkeys were thrown to the ground in camp and the pony given full rein in the new direction. The possible fate of Absalom stared me in the face at every jump as the pony passed under branches and through bush and thickets. I came to the man with the full expectation of seeing him combat with a bear or puma. He welcomed me with a sickly smile and claimed to be very tired, but would not admit that he was lost and went through all this vocal exercise to attract somebody's attention in order to get back to camp. I let him mount the pony and took him back to camp which, by the way, he never left again for another hunt, preferring rather to tend to the camp duties than go through the same ordeal.

The same afternoon I kept on hunting until way after dark when I started for camp with two turkeys hanging over my shoulder. The night was clear but it was impossible for me to see the north star on account of the trees. My compass had been borrowed by some of the other men and I was consequently left without a guide. My only means of telling the north was by the moss covered side of the trees, which I examined every couple of hundred yards by the light of a match. In this manner I came to the [dry] bed of the river and here found the [downstream] direction I had to take by the leaves and branches which a flood had washed down the stream and deposited at projecting points near the bank. [Near camp] was the feeling of a warm current of air originating from our campfire which I struck when yet a good distance away.

The next morning we arose early to get a last chance at the turkeys but they were now so wild that we met with little or no success and returned to camp empty-handed to prepare for the home trip. Our return from the hunt was accompanied with only one or two breakdowns. We found at our arrival that the other parties had been comparatively less fortunate [with] only six or seven turkeys to the company to our eleven.

I recall another of our Caddo trips where a detachment of soldiers were sent to receive a number of recruits destined for the different companies at the fort. Those trips generally lasted fifteen days and were mostly in charge of a commissioned officer. We had on this trip, shortly after Thanksgiving day, the most delightful weather, while the hunting was excellent.

Wild geese of great numbers were found in the Washita Valley, we killed more than we could eat. This was also the time for pecan nuts and we found the trees so full we could gather enough from a small tree to last us for the balance of the trip and to give to every man in the company after our return. The nuts on the trees in the vicinity of Fort Sill were all worm eaten and consequently useless.

We found our recruits already awaiting us at the railroad station and we took them to a convenient place to camp. Oh what a variety of humanity, from a very intelligent society man, to Darwin's missing link of some backwoods – just fresh from the farm, with a frame and walk like a cart horse, back like a camel, with brains to match a monkey. Another was from the Puritan City in the Bay State, a real Yankee "by gosh." He read too many dime novels, poor boy, and wanted to go west to kill Injuns, and wished he'd never left home. There stood a young man, apparently from a better class and more intelligent than the general run. He had both hands in his pockets and a languid look about him as he gazed over the camp or stared into the fire, apparently dreaming of the

nice home he had so recklessly thrown away, where his wish
was law, and where he never knew any other will but his
own, a loving mother and sisters left behind. We hoped he
would do better when his time of service was expired – if he
didn't leave before.

We found men without the least knowledge of the English
language who had enlisted after unsuccessful attempts to obtain work. [One] said he wanted to join "soldier boys," a very
dubious honor, another had to leave on account of a girl. We
found men of intellect and stupidity, sons of congressmen and
sons of farmers, rich and poor, men who are willing to work
and can not find it in civil life, men who are looking for work
and hope that they never may find any: gamblers, thieves,
cutthroats, drunkards, men who were formally commissioned
officers. There was a combination and variety of stock which,
under careful training, had produced some of the best soldiers
on the frontier.

The recruits in camp had their own mess and we took a
walk to their fire to see how they progressed with baking.
They had built a large fire with enough coals to roast an ox.
The ovens were completely covered [with coals] and their
burning bread filled the air with smoke. We naturally gave
them all instruction required.

That evening some of the most timid recruits came over to
our camp. They wanted to know all about Indians and the
dangers of prairie life. A couple of our best yarn-spinners made
the poor fellows think that their hair wasn't their own when
outside of the camp. This might have been wrong, but it surely
served as a check for those who had any inclination of deserting
or leaving camp to go to town.

We remained at the camp for a few days longer to give
men and beasts a rest before starting home. The home trip
was made without any hindrance or special occurrence, except
with one remarkable case of losing. I was returning from a
hunt and could hear the voices of the men when I met our

officer in charge who asked for directions to the camp. He
was apparently lost and was skylarking on the outskirts, in
search of the camp. A nice officer to command soldiers on the
plains, I thought, as I escorted him back to his tent.

The recruits were assigned to the different companies by
the commanding officer after our return to the fort. The
noncommissioned officers had not an easy task to drill and
instruct them in the science of military tactics to make soldiers
of them. It required more than public school teacher's patience
to do this, as I have myself experienced it.

Fires were seldom at the fort and we only had two while I
was there, both in the winter. One was at the post hospital and
originated from an overheated stovepipe, but was timely extinguished [with] very little damage. The second one took place
at the haystack and destroyed hundreds of dollars worth of hay.

The night was bitter cold and we were comfortably sleeping
between the folds of our buffalo robes when the bugler on
duty sounded the fire call. In less time than it takes to write
we were in line in front of the quarters, awaiting orders. They
were not long in coming and we started for the seat of the
fire at the double-time. The haystacks were over one-half mile
from the barracks. Although a well-beaten road led there we
stumbled over rocks and tumbled into ditches at a very lively
rate as we had nothing but the glare of the fire to guide us.
We found all the hay on fire and nothing for us to save but
the fence. We stood with shivering bodies before the fire while
a norther blew through our thin clothes and shook the marrow
in our bones. The thermometer, inspected while working,
[showed] twenty below zero.

The fires lasted four days and nothing remained of the hay.
Nobody knew how the fire started. The sentry claimed to have
seen a man running away and fired at him, but it might have
been himself, seeking shelter behind one of the stacks and
attempting to smoke. One curious sight connected with the
fire was a stampede of skunks. Hundreds of these animals had

made their winter quarters under the hay and were driven out by the heat and smoke. They were rushing madly between the burning stacks from where the heat drove them back to their burning nests again, to perish in the flames.

In the first part of February a dozen of us, accompanied by the post interpreter, under the charge of an officer, started in the mountains to exercise our muscles in chopping oak trees and splitting fence rails for a new garden at the fort. We all started in good spirits. Sun Bow's camp, a Kiowa chief who had a contract to furnish wood for the fort, was passed on our way to the "picket camp" in the mountains. The place was in the heart of the mountains to the west of Fort Sill, at the foot of one of its highest peaks, surrounded by a forest of post oaks. The peak was called Sheridan's Roost and was one of the most abrupt mountains in the range. Its summit is accessible from only one side and was about 1200 to 1500 feet above the camp. The stream passing at its base was Medicine Bluff Creek and formed a junction with Cache Creek at the fort.[6]

Our work was comparatively light and we had plenty of time to hunt and roam around. One day a friend and I concluded to make an ascent of the mountain and we gained the summit after a long circuit and difficult climbing. We stood on the brim of a couple of hundred feet high precipice. A few cedar trees had found a foot-hold between the rocks of the cliff while the slope below was covered with bush and small scrub trees. A couple of flocks of turkeys were seeking food while bear slept in the caves between the rocks. Pumas were the masters of the rocks to our rear and kept a small round valley clear of any game, while deer selected the rich grassy slopes of the larger valleys for their home.

To our right, past the highest mountain in the range, Mount Scott, we [could] see, eighteen miles [away] the bright buildings of Fort Sill with an endless rolling prairie beyond — a magnificent view! Hostile Indians had, in former years, their strongholds in these mountains and many a battle had been

fought in the narrow ravines. We frequently met places where
the troops had their fortified camps, or where fights took place
with the Indians, [finding] equipment of soldiers and Indians
scattered over the battlefield.

Although the work was hard the time passed pleasantly and
I had every opportunity to pass my time hunting along the
creek after turkey, or in the valleys after deer. Traveling Indians
frequently paid us a visit, asking for tobacco and "chuck away."
The latter appeal was made more plain by cutting across their
stomachs with their hands which generally produced the desired effect and they were furnished with what ever there was
left of the last meal.

I remember one young Indian who came to our camp
claimed to be a good shot with his bow. He was brought to
task [by a] promise of every coin he could hit at a distance
of thirty feet. He did better than we expected and we discontinued the coin shooting as a bad investment on our side. He
was promised a square meal if he could hit a cap in the air.
A new cap was furnished willingly by a recruit who had been
led to believe by us that the Indians were bad marksmen with
bows and arrows. The cap was thrown up and we all thought
he had lost, but a hole was found through the middle, to the
great sorrow of the owner.

Our stay at the picket camp was soon to end as a courier
arrived from the fort ordering the men from our company
immediately back. After our return we found the company
busily engaged in packing boxes. The company had been
ordered to Fort Gibson, Indian Territory, about 300 miles
northeast. We [were] to start the next morning to walk to a
railroad station in Texas, from whence we were to take the
train. Transportation was furnished for the necessary military
materials only. There was no corner to pack my carefully
collected pressed plants, or money enough in my possession
to express them to a safe place. They had to be left behind
and abandoned to the wind and the cows.

7

. . . .

Fort Gibson, 1880

The wind was blowing strongly from the north as we left the place with almost three years of pleasant recollection behind, directing our steps to the south. [We took] one more glance back at the place we entered three years ago with the firm conviction of finding wild men in this country on the same level with beasts, but instead were welcomed by a race who in every respect were equally intelligent to the Caucasian.[1]

The sun was getting warmer as the road led us across the dry rolling prairie with nothing to ·break the light brown glare and the vibrating heat of the surface, while we in our march suffered from severe thirst. At last we saw the dark line of timber [to be] the campground. Our throats became dryer and dryer and the distance seemed to increase as we walked with more vigor to cover the uniform level between us and the creek.

A few hours later, after a refreshing rest in camp at Beaver Creek, I mounted a horse to cross the prairie to pay a neighboring village a visit, but the horse meant different. With bit firmly between his teeth he raced over the country, regardless of trees, ditches, and all my attempts to hold him. At last, after a wild chase of a mile or two, he agreed to go where I wanted.

My appearance at the village seemed to spread consternation amongst the quiet villagers, people were excitedly running to and fro, keeping their eyes on me as if the evil one had appeared in their midst. Well they might be frightened by the presence of U.S. troops so long as they were setting on forbidden ground in the Territory, consequently living under the apprehension of being expelled and driven from their present homes by the government.[2]

We left the creek the next morning with our canteens filled with clear cool water in forbearance of another day of suffering. The heavy fog which had been hanging over the earth all morning turned into steady rain, soaking our clothes thoroughly, filling our shoes to the brim. We tried to take the situation philosophically and look sheepful. Under this favorable condition for a drunk we crossed the Red River into Texas and entered a small village. The few saloons and grog shops were soon crowded with soldiers who invested what little money they had in whiskey to keep the chill from their bones and prevent further rheumatism.

After a reasonable satisfaction most of them followed the wagons into camp, while others remained and misused the confidence given them by their commander. It was a miserable afternoon and evening for the sober ones in camp. After pitching a tent and changing clothes I scrambled out to obtain the names of the men who were going to be on guard with

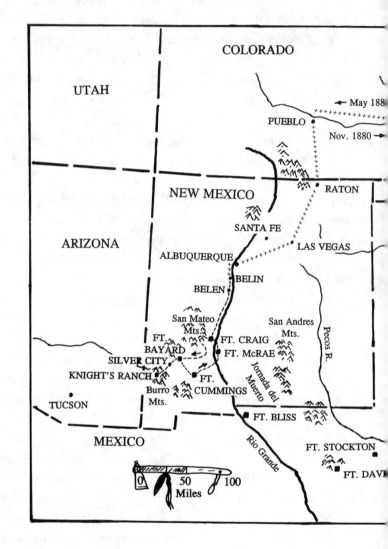

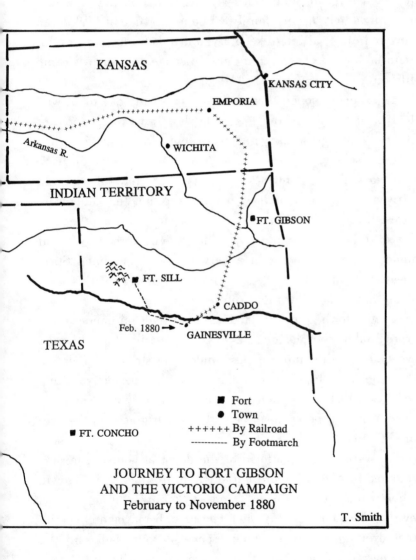

KANSAS

KANSAS CITY

EMPORIA

Arkansas R.

WICHITA

INDIAN TERRITORY

FT. GIBSON

FT. SILL

CADDO

Feb. 1880 → GAINESVILLE

TEXAS

■ Fort
● Town
++++++ By Railroad
---------- By Footmarch

■ FT. CONCHO

JOURNEY TO FORT GIBSON
AND THE VICTORIO CAMPAIGN
February to November 1880

T. Smith

me that night. The sights I met were anything but desirable. [The] camp under a couple of inches of water; a newly created muddy stream passed close by; cooks trying to build a fire; [a] drunken sergeant and men swearing and fighting; a soldier pitching a tent [for his] family, while four or five little children cowered under a tree to keep dry; a drunken man striking his wife because he has nothing else to strike at — such is camp life on a rainy day.

The morning opened as pleasant as a spring day to all who had been temperate the foregoing day. It was discovered at roll call that a great many men were absent. Some had returned to the last town for a drink, or had walked ahead and were waiting at the next town for us to pass. [A] few [of the] first arrived in time to march with the camp, but the latter were arrested as the camp arrived in town. Here was another disgraceful display of soldiery, over half the camp had to be put under guard, behaving in a very disorderly manner. Strict measures had to be abided to control some violent prisoners, while others lay down and refused to move.

Thanks to the cool collected action of the commander there were no more serious breaches of the men after this. Although we had to suffer more or less under the strict order drawn over the camp by a few drunkards, we were perfectly willing to have a little restriction put upon our liberty and complete our journey in peace, as to be still more disgraced in the eyes of civilians.

We were on the platform of the depot at Gainesville, surrounded by a guard to prevent any man from going into town, when a dish full of fat pork and crackers was brought to us by the cooks for supper. Only a few men displayed an appetite that evening, owing to the presence of some ladies in the windows above, and the civilians around us, who stared as if we were a set of wild beasts caged up behind iron bars and exhibited for two bits.[3]

What a relief to us as we were ordered to the car, away

from the eyes of the civilian idlers. One night's comfortable sleep in the cars and we entered once more the Indian Territory. Here the orange vendor entered the car and offered fruit for sale – twenty-five cents an orange, and for one [dollar] the orange was filled with whiskey. This was only one of the numerous devices to smuggle whiskey in small lots into the Territory.

We left the cars at Gibson Station and pursued our way past Indian farmhouses and forests, after having [been] thoroughly soaked by a thunderstorm crossing the ferry at Gibson. What a miserable place we thought as we entered and took possession of the fort. A two-story wooden barracks with a cistern in front and rear [stood] on one side of the parade ground. On the other side the officer quarters [were] situated. Visa via of these was a small miserable looking shanty destined [as] the guardhouse. Back of this place, adjoining the post garden, a space where banks of cart wood were stacked.[4]

Fort Gibson was situated in the Cherokee Nation, on the left bank of the Grand River, two and one-half miles above the confluence with the Arkansas River. There was very little prairie in this vicinity. The fort stood on a little elevated ground on the banks of a lovely stream which passed at the foot of the hill where, in former years, boats were anchored. Hills and high bluffs lined the river to the north, while to the south the country became more level and marshy. Heavy fogs and mists hovered over the water after sunset and in the mornings.

Innumerable wild ducks bred in the high grass and reeds along the river and creeks. The waters were well stocked with fish and soft-shell turtles. Deer, panthers, and turkeys gave life to the forest which covered the hills and valleys where, day and night, birds sent forth their melodious songs. Different varieties of squirrels hid in wild plum and apricot trees, while poisonous reptiles coiled under blackberry and dewberry vines.

The town of Gibson lay on the foot of the little hill on which Fort Gibson was located. [It] had a population of four to five hundred with two churches and schools. The principal buildings were a brick store, a frame store, a steam mill, one drug store, and the private residence of Bushyhead, the principal chief of the Cherokees. Isolated farmhouses, surrounded by peach orchards, [were] here and there, and a mile beyond we saw the flag of a national cemetery playing in the breeze. Standing on the rocks at the creek [we] watched a herd of cattle swimming across the river. In the place at the ferry where we saw the cows crossing soldiers had lost their lives from diving off the boat and striking the sharp pointed rocks below.[5]

It was here that we witnessed the baptism of negro women. I don't think there is a religion better suited for that race than Baptist and Methodism. The congregation slowly walked down the narrow road to the edge of the water, singing hymns. The minister selected a secure place in the river and, aided by an assistant, baptized an old woman, who went through the ceremony quietly. The next one was a young mulatto woman with [a] prepossessing appearance, dressed in a long gown or night shirt. Slowly she walked to where the minister stood, singing her hallelujah, but stifled by the dunking she wildly threw up her arms and burst forth in, "Ah Lord, I is baptized!" Carried back to the bank by the assistant, she changed her gown, while friends held up shawls as a protecting shield against "mean" eyes on the banks above.

After our arrival at the fort we did not see the sun for three or four weeks. Our outside enjoyments were naturally very limited so in order to repay us for our loss we made arrangements for a grand ball, inviting all the "aristocracy" of the Cherokee nation, that is a select few of the Indians, besides the farmers in the vicinity. Naturally disappointed to swing to the reputation of soldiers in general these "select few" remained at home. Nevertheless we had a splendid time and found the girls pretty, intelligent, and well-educated, besides extremely modest.

The seat of the government and the high schools were at Tahlequah, twenty-eight miles east of Fort Gibson, where their only paper was published. The *Cherokee Advocate* was printed partly in the Cherokee language, the types of which are a mixture of English and assumed letters. The principal difference from a civilized nation were the laws, yet very incomplete. Only the school laws were strict, but the execution of the law for murder was loose, when comparing it with the laws of the New England states.

In summer they had their old Indian dances, altered a little. The right of settlement could be gained through marriage in the nation, or by paying a heavy fee to the nation fund, which was payable yearly. The slaves of the Indians, when set free, assumed the rights of the nation. Remarkable was the beauty of the Cherokee and Chickasaw women.[6]

I was on guard when a man was brought to the guardhouse for disorderly conduct and placed under my charge. He had my utmost confidence. Taking advantage of this he made his escape, going direct to the saloon, where he was unfortunately seen by my captain before I could recapture him. My goose was cooked, I thought, as I saw the prisoner brought back to the guardhouse, but after a satisfactory explanation I was permitted to go free of the punishment which invariably would have been the consequence of permitting a prisoner to escape.

The same afternoon I arrested three negroes for malicious conduct and placed them in the strongest cell, with the intention of giving each a twenty-five pound log to carry for an hour or so. One of them complained about a dislocated shoulder which at first seemed to be so, but proved a willful action after a careful examination.

The following morning a man was ordered to the parade ground to hoist the flag. Through his stupidity the flag went

. . . .

to the top of the pole without any means of lowering it. A man at last volunteered to climb the swinging pole and brought the flag down after a desperate struggle. A sigh of relief went from everyone's heart as the man returned the flag to our midst without having come to grief. Nobody imagined what a narrow escape the man really had from being dashed to pieces on the ground below until we saw the pole laying on the ground the next morning, blown over by a heavy storm during the night.

We went to the river to rebait a fishing line with about fifty hooks we had stretched across the water where a catfish of sixty-five pounds had been caught that morning. Finding nothing on the line, we hoisted a small sail on our boat and went flying up the stream, until we came to a place where the combined force of the sail and oars were insufficient to overcome the swift descent of the water. We were compelled to draw the boat by a rope past this rapid. During our stay at [Fort] Gibson I frequently extended my fishing trips further up the river and adjoining bluffs. One day I saw a red and black snake with black diamonds lazing in the road, sunning herself. Thinking that I had a harmless water snake I walked close to kill her with a stick. How great was my consternation as I heard the rattles of rattlesnake under those harmless coils, which she gradually unrolled, and soon disappeared unharmed into a crevice under the rocks.

I responded to an invitation one pleasant evening in May [and] a friend and I took a stroll after the sun had disappeared behind the western horizon. The vampire bats were enjoying themselves by whizzing past our faces and around our heads. The mocking bird sounded the last notes of the day when a pair of steers harnessed to a carriage passed us at a lively gait. In astonishment of that singular turn-out we returned to the fort.

A few days after the above occurrence we saw an Indian crossing the river. He was attired in a civilian suit, a pistol fastened around his waist, the hair long, falling in curls over his shoulders, [with] a large hat completing his dress. He was drunk and returning from a dance in town where his friends, [at] the risk of their own lives, prevented him from killing a negro whom he was going to shoot, "for the fun of it." This man was the quickest shooter in the country and nobody would believe that that pleasant face and laughing eyes could do more harm than kissing a girl.

Some whiskey was smuggled from Arkansas and Texas, while most was distilled by moonshiners in the Territory and was called "White Mule," because it kicked a man higher than the sky.

After skirmish drill and blank cartridge musketry one day I was setting on the porch reading when my attention was called to a cat whose eyes were steadily fixed on a swallow. We saw the bird let go its hold on the rafter and drop to the ground as if under the influence of liquor, too stupid to fly. The cat made a quick move to get hold of the bird, but [was] intercepted by us. She retired while the swallow rose and joined the rest.

A negro, who had stopped to look at the cat in her bird-charming act, [had] two wives, a white and a black one. He was married to a colored woman and living in Arkansas when he made the acquaintance of a white woman. Deserting his lawful wife he eloped with the latter and settled at Gibson. Traced there by his first wife he accepted her, a reconciliation followed, and they all lived happy and contented under one roof.

[One day] I took up my gun to seek a little variety in hunting. While penetrating the dense forest below the fort my eyes met a fat little porker industriously rooting the ground. The temptation was too great and the opportunity too good to pass this game and look for uncertainties. With a quick bullet and a quick plunge of the knife the work was soon over. I returned to the fort with a "deer" in a gunny sack. A half hour afterwards saw us going to the theater in town as if nothing had happened.

Unfortunately for us we received orders to repair for a campaign in New Mexico and were compelled to abandon our already far advanced garden, and our new acquaintances in the neighborhood.[7]

8

The Victorio Campaign, 1880

Twenty-four hours after the notice was received we were speeding again over the country on the iron horse, passing villages and farms on the boundless prairie of Kansas. We passed a "city" of new wooden houses facing the railroad, flying through a cut on the prairie where fences were erected as a protection against the snow in winter. [In places] we saw houses of which nothing but the stone weighted roofs were visible above the ground, level country with [no] change of scenery except the low treeless banks of the Arkansas River.[1]

[Once] our iron horse moved slower and slower, blowing

the whistle [at] a young heifer lazing in the ditch along the road while a herd of cattle accompanied by a couple of tame buffalo ran for their lives.

At last we entered Colorado and stopped at a place to change cars. The weather was warm and we went to the river for a bath to obtain a little relief of the heat and the hot sand which seemed to float in the air. On our return some went after [haircuts. The barber] placed a seat cushion across the aisle. My barber was standing in front with his scissors over me when a shift engine bumped against our cars, sending me heel over head in the middle of the aisle, after giving the barber a terrible kick in the ribs.

We were at last fairly started for the south. After amusing ourselves by firing from the cars at antelope, and passing some square mud houses, we got to the foot of a branch of the Rocky Mountains. Slowly we entered a valley and gradually ascended the high hills before us, an extra engine pushing the rear of our three cars. The sides of the mountains were steep, almost perpendicular, and here and there we could see them dotted with the black entrances of coal mines.

We seemed to float in midair as we crossed a gulch on a high bridge. Hundreds of feet below a flowing brook edging its way from rock to rock between inaccessible mountains. Gradually ascending into the higher region we found the trees small and the summits crowned by a cape of snow. At last we penetrated the backbone of the range, over 9,000 feet above sea level. Soon [we] emerged from the tunnel, a broad plateau of New Mexico spread before our view. Our descent was easily accomplished and our train thundered across the plain while the Rocky Mountains, like a row of gray headed patriarchs, kept guard on our right.[2]

We passed Las Vegas [New Mexico] and entered the mountains again, the cars rocking like a steamer on the ocean [as] we held on to the seats to prevent us from being dashed through the windows. [We] descended into darkness after a short stop where the road branches off to Santa Fe.

We awoke the next morning at Albuquerque, a Mexican village on the Rio Grande, [of] about 3,000 inhabitants. The building material was adobe, a sun dried brick. Irrigation ditches of over twenty miles furnished the necessary supply of water for the fertilization of the valley. The principal produce was red pepper, onions, corn, wheat, and grape vines. The wine was brought into the market pure. Mescal, a frequently used spirit of the Mexicans, was made of cactus commonly called the Spanish Dagger.

The houses of adobe [had] rooms of ten by fifteen feet, placed as to enclose a court of forty to fifty feet. Nothing [could] be seen from the outside, except an arched entrance, which terminated in the court. The flooring was made of mud, the interior and courts of the houses were according to the owner's wealth and taste, sometimes magnificently furnished. By the rich the court was nicely laid out in flower beds, with fountains to cool the air. Cloth-covered stone vessels filled with cactus coal [to] purify the water furnished a cooling drink in hot weather. The poorer classes kept their "carras," an entirely wooden wagon, garden tools, and sometimes their stock in the court. Conical ovens of different sizes were at every dwelling. They were in average four feet in diameter. The wash tub was a large clay vessel made of burned clay with a diameter of two feet and a depth of one foot and a half.

The habits of the Mexicans were very different [from] the Americans, especially in old towns. The Spanish and the Indian seemed to be amalgamated in the Mexican. Their only good habit was the cleanliness of their clothing. The dress of the women was similar to "civilized" dress, except in some lonely place or Old Mexico, where they dressed only in a skirt. The men dressed civilized, shirt and white pantaloons. Their religion was Catholic.

Very entertaining it was to attend a Mexican fandango, besides to study the character and music of those people. Their hospitality was their only virtue, they were fond of drinking and gambling like the Indian.

The ass was the universal riding animal all over the country. The ox was yoked by the horns with leather strings to the cross. The shepherd dog was an indispensable animal of the herder, his value exceeding three hundred dollars. Herds of sheep by the thousands were herded only by dogs, nothing attended to by man, except to take meals to the dogs. The sheep, goat, burro, and ox was the wealth of the native. Sheep were frequently used for thrashing wheat and other grain.[3]

New houses were erected at the station as the new town, about one half-mile from the old town. Suspicious looking individuals, followers of the new railroads, were lounging in the vicinity of the provision and mess cars. We were placed for further transport on flat-car freighters with railroad ties. From there we had an excellent opportunity to admire the beautiful Rio Grande valley.

We traveled over a sand constructed road, the speed of the train enveloping us in a cloud of this fine material. We discovered a conspicuous bank ahead which developed into a Mexican village. We crossed the river where the Mexicans, men and women, were bathing together in blissful innocence. Belin was the end of our rail journey and we camped a few days in order to join [together] the wagons which had been taken apart for easier transportation at the beginning of our trip.[4]

Enough leisure time left us for a tour of inspection through a town of ancient looking buildings with a population three hundred years behind present civilization. The materials with which all the buildings were constructed were adobes. We saw what must have been two or three store buildings, [a] town hall, a nicely constructed Catholic church with ancient fittings and carved rafters and doors, [which] relieved the eye of its weary surroundings. A man [was] driving his steers through town with nothing but a white shirt and a large hat to cover his body. It [was] already a puzzle to me how they could get their clothes white in such a dirty [river] which was so yellow and muddy [that our] camp kettle was covered with two inches of sand after boiling the coffee.

In the evening the population gathered for a little musical entertainment or dance, attired in calico loose dresses. Even these were found a little warm [by] the women for dancing, who generally unrobed on the veranda during intermission.

[At] a well with salty water only two feet below the surface, in front of a store, a man with a strangely Hebrew nose and decidedly German accent addressed us as we entered the store. He was the proprietor of the institution, and moreover, with his sect, had the sale trade of the valley under his control. [He] kept the prices stimulated by the formally difficult and long transportation of freight.

Our next move was [to] a saloon and gambling house where fantastically dressed Mexicans seemed to have more money and looks than sense. We went to [a] hall where a fandango was in full blast. The heavy walls and roof had protected this hall comparatively well against the hot rays of the sun during the day. Merry pairs of dancers were moving by the strain of the string band Mexican music. Heavy clouds of dust created by the fast and beautifully shaped feet of graceful señoritas were floating in the air. We returned to camp with pleasant vistas of coquettish women before us.

Early the next morning we started over the country on foot in credit of our nickname do-rays [doughboys?], infantry, to do active duty against a hostile tribe of Indians who terrorized the southern section of the territory and committed depredations in large towns as well as the settlements. Only a few days before our arrival they had set a whole mountain range afire, which was yet burning, descended into a village, killed the population, and drove off the stock. Their number was variable, estimated from 750 to 800. Assuming the smaller

number as the one nearer to the truth we still found them of
sufficient strength to withstand successfully a large force for
some time which may be deemed necessary to put against
them, especially as they were commanded by a very intelligent
chieftain who had lawless whites in his command to sell the
stolen stock and purchase rifles.[5]

The Indians were well acquainted with the country, knowing all the out of the way watering places in the almost
inaccessible mountains. The Apaches were mountain Indians
and could, if necessary, travel on foot faster than any body of
whites in the country. They [wore] buckskin leggings and
moccasins with heavy soles. It was said they could run down
a young deer in a long run. The Apache, when on the warpath,
either laid in ambush or sneaked up on his victim. When in
an attack or fight no war whoop was heard. Comanche generally frightened a timid person half to death with their yells,
while the Apache prefered to take their enemy unawares.

It was a great mistake of emigrants, when going through
a defile or dangerous place, to keep together. An Apache would
not attack a party if he could not kill most of them with the
first volley, even if the Indians should be ten to one. Their
object was to kill, and not get killed. A single man or party
could travel with greater safety at night. An Indian was in
average a poor marksman with the rifle, especially firing from
an elevated position.

A Comanche would shake hands with you before he commenced a blow. [A] Kiowa would seek your confidence through
attention, and stab you in a suitable moment in the back. The
Mescalero [Apache] never took scalps or mutilated the dead,
they even kept their prisoners alive. Only the roaming plun-
dering bands of different tribes mutilated the dead and tortured
the living.[6]

They had been on the warpath over one year and, in spite
of the endeavors by the negro cavalry regiment and an infantry

regiment, were still making noses to the authorities. Unfortunately the troops had to be scattered as small detachments over the territory to guard towns and stations against raids. What was left of the command, including over one hundred Indian troops or scouts, were poorly maneuvered by the commander of the district at Santa Fe who, instead of being at that place, should have been with the troops in the field to act instantly and not leave a splendid opportunity to pass. Receiving information and giving high-sounding orders from headquarters may be well enough in a civilized war, but never against a band of Indians.[7]

We started fresh with good spirit to our destination, but after a walk of ten or twelve miles in the sand we experienced a soreness of feet and a pain in the upper legs. Halt was given and we dropped exhausted under the shade of a tall cottonwood tree. [The] lieutenant, too proud for anything [and who] used to ride in an ambulance, emerged from between coffee kettles and greasy pans on the cook wagon.

After a rest of ten or fifteen minutes we proceeded, soon comfortably lodged in camp, feeling as fresh as ever after a foot bath and a couple of days rest. [This] feeling seemed to improve instead of diminish through the rest of the trip.

[Because] the road was hardly traceable on the sea of sand and hills we had to guess the way. The surface was covered with small waves [like] water, we frequently saw a pipe-shaped whirlwind carrying sand 800 or 1000 feet in the air. The houses and mud fences [were] half buried in drift sand, difficult to distinguish from the surrounding country. Here and [there] we saw Mexicans with bull teams [and] ancient looking vehicles with wooden axles and two heavy wooden wheels. The steers were bound with rawhide to their horns to a crosstree of the "carra" while the drivers walked along with a pole in hand.

We saw a magnificent forest of deerhorn cactus ten or twelve feet high, covered with innumerable red flowers, which gave the appearance of a tall rose garden. This cactus was frequently used by the Mexicans for the construction of hedges around exposed fields.

We moved along the ground with our eyes on the tracks of the man ahead of us while a hot air, constant from the south, dried our throats, filling our lungs with sand. At last we were in a place waiting for the wagons to come up [to camp], but owing to the contrariness of the commander, who was in one of the wagons under strong stimulation, he sent a messenger ordering us back three miles to a place where the wagon had gone into camp. There laborers were engaged in cutting trees and clearing track for the construction of the railroad. Not far [away] a large colony of beaver had built a dam, gathering the scanty waters of a small spring.

The tents were soon pitched and blankets spread in the sun for an airing to clear the rattlesnakes and tarantulas who might have secreted there during the previous night. After a foot-wash and a meal of "Cincinnati chicken" and hardtack we went out for a hunt or retired for a game of cards. At sundown we retired with nothing to unrobe but the shoes and blouse, the gun and cartridge belt placed conveniently on the blanket.

Early in the morning, long before daybreak, the bugle awoke us for reveille. The tents were struck, the blankets rolled, bacon and crackers consumed, and we left camp twenty minutes after the first sound of the bugle. We never washed our faces in the morning while on the road for fear of softening the skin or catching cold in the eyes, but we always made it a rule to bathe if possible in the evening.

We stopped at Fort Craig, awaiting further orders from district headquarters, giving ourselves a general hauling-over in the Rio Grande. Our clothes needed a wash and we started for the river armed with a bar of soap, the river high, muddy yellow water passing through the channel at a great fall. Into this water we took frequent plunges from the bank while we were waiting for our washed clothes to dry in the sun.

The fort was situated on a little hill on the right bank of the Rio Grande. [The] quarters, built of adobe, were in a decaying condition. The post was the only one on the frontier with proper earthworks, all other forts were merely quarters built in a square.[8]

West of Fort Craig the dark mass of the San Mateo Mountains could be traced on the horizon for a considerable distance. South of the plateau ran a plain on which in former years hundreds of Spanish troops perished for the want of water and has since borne the name "Journey of Death" [Jornada del Muerto]. East of the fort [was] a dark mass of mountains with abrupt deep cuts, [Sierra del Oso].

Stopping at the fort and also awaiting orders was a scout by the name of Jack Crawford. "Captain Jack," as he was generally called, had a beautiful entirely white Newfoundland dog who shortly after our departure saved his master's life from a watery grave while the former was bathing in the river and got overpowered in the quicksand and stray current.[9]

Orders were received by our captain to scout the [San Mateo] Mountains [to] the west for Indians. We found ourselves on our way the next day. The heat was intense and the air dry as we walked over the hills or through the sand in the valley. It was in one of the latter places where I passed the remark that some people had their brains in their heels, for which I was placed under arrest by a sergeant who thought my remarks referred to him. For this he received a reprimand from our captain while I was released after our arrival in camp. I and two other men were selected for advance guard as the troop entered the foothills of the San Mateo Mountains, to prevent any contemplated surprise by the Indians while the men were engaged in lowering the wagons down steep hills.[10]

The camp was selected at the head of a deep canyon which in former years, judging by the work on the eighty-foot wall, must have been the outlet for water from the San Mateo, whereas then only a little water appeared at the surface which was honored with the name Nogal Spring. The flow [was] greatly improved by clearing the water hole of its slimy substance, lining the sides and bottom with gravel, and placing charcoal on the bottom to purify the water. Shelter tents were erected by some men in the middle of the ravine, while others less particular selected caves, the retreats of innumerable rattlesnakes, for their abode.

The range still seemed to be in the hands of its original owners, the Indians. Very few ranchmen let the cattle or sheep enter the meadow in the foothills. Very little use was made of the forest in the mountains, [and] the prospectors in search [of] precious metals seldom penetrated this region. During the time of occupation we experienced a feeling of separation from the rest of the world. We were prevented from obtaining a fresh supply of tobacco, smoking dried walnut leaves as a substitute.

Small forts or redoubts [were] erected as breastworks and every precaution taken to guard against a surprise by the Indians. Pickets were thrown out every night in the ravines and different approaches to the camp, in addition to a permanent guard on top of one of the hills.

Up this hill we went one evening to relieve the guard and take their place for the next twenty-four hours. After a few rests and many puff-outs we succeeded in reaching the summit. We were six to seven hundred feet above the camp in a place hardly large enough for four men to lay down, only accessible by one narrow path. From this little natural fortress protected by perpendicular walls we kept guard day and night over the safety of the camp below. From there we saw at night the fire telegraphing of the Indians in the mountains, and watched their signaling with smoke in the day. But we were safe and well provided with ammunition in case of attack, in fact didn't need to fret about Indians or their signaling so long as our scalp locks were in place, nor holes through our bodies.

We gathered some of the thick flower stems which grew

on the sides of the hill on rosette-like cactus [to] support a
blanket for shade over our little fort. Our attention was drawn
to a piece of paper which ascended from the camp and carried
six hundred feet over our heads, descending somewhere on
the plain. We [later] learned that a whirlwind passed over the
camp and took a paper from the hands of the company clerk
who had just emerged from the Captain's tent with the payroll
[list] in his hands.

The sun disappeared behind a black cloud from which a
heavy rain soon poured down. Our blanket roof was useless
and I found shelter in a small cave. After the rain [I] was
climbing back when I heard a rattlesnake above me. My
position [on] the precipice was [too] dangerous on wet stones
to stand much agitation so I returned to the cave and called
to my friends for assistance. The snake [was] killed, a beautiful
dark green reptile with black velvet stripes, nine rattles and
a button on her tail.

A few days afterwards I was on picket guard in one of the
ravines, rolled up in a blanket and laying between the rocks
with my blouse for a pillow. The [other] sentry was cautiously
moving about watching the different objects in the neighborhood. Indians frequently when advancing for a night attack
carried a bush in front of them to prevent detection. Everything
was quiet except the call of an owl in the canyon. Without
previous introduction some coyotes came up and started a
concert at almost arms-length from where I was concealed. I
enjoyed the entertainment as well as I might in that lonely
place, besides [being] the evidence that no other grisly beast
or Indian was near. A puma or Mexican leopard appeared on
the scene with a roar. The coyotes broke up their concert very
unceremoniously and beat a hasty retreat while I, with gun
in hand, looked for the beast. But it did not [show itself] and
everything was quiet for the rest of the night.

The following day a friend and I went on an exploring tour
down the canyon and were richly rewarded with a string of

small trout caught by hand under rocks in the pools of fresh water. We [found] the remains of a small sheep which only a few days ago had been stolen from a herd on the plains by a large grisly bear. We turned out for a bear hunt but there were too many green hunters and too much notice for the bear to wait for us to shoot him, so we returned without having seen a thing.

At our arrival in the mountains we noticed a young hog which were known in Texas and the Indian Territory as the razorback, having a sharp pointed back with a long snout, and were considered the poorest breed. This little porker [was] quite tame, becoming the pet of the place. He was permitted to live on account of his leanness, picking up the wasted grain to fatten himself for future usefulness.

Besides this porker there were daily visits of cattle and other animals at our spring. There was only one narrow gate in the rock [to the spring] large enough to permit one animal at a time to pass through. This place was selected as the best for appropriation. [The] suitable animal was hit with an ax [and] the carcass easily strayed where the wolves would clear any evidence of the slaughter while the meat was taken to a cave and secreted for our daily use. We were compelled to keep this secret or pay for the cattle we ate owing to the occasional visits of a ranchman who had been engaged by the government as a guide for us, and who, by the way, was always fed [only] bacon whenever he put in his appearance at the camp. The object of our staying at the spring in the first place [was] to protect the stock ranches.

One pleasant morning we left camp provided with a canteen full of water and a couple of pack mules, starting for a scout through the mountains. I and two more were again selected as advance guard to prevent surprise by the Indians. We advanced steadily, directed by the guide, keeping a sharp lookout. After a five or six mile walk we were relieved by another advance guard. We arrived at the foot of the range and entered a pine forest. We climbed steep hills and passed under high bluffs on our way to a spring way up in the mountains said to be guarded by Indians. Now we were coming down to business, frequently using our hands to climb over rock. Even our captain, who at first attempted to scale the mountain [on] a mule, had to come down and use his legs a little.

In spite of that exhaustive work and empty canteens the men kept cheerful all the way, jokes passing by those whose tongues were not too dry. Even the mules, packed with our rations and one blanket for every man, needed very little urging as they followed us in a zig-zag up the mountain. Everything went well until one of the mules lost his foothold and fell, mule and cracker boxes chasing each other as they rolled down the hill. Fortunately his life and the crackers were saved by some small trees in the path.

After hours of hard crawling we gained the summit, taking an extended rest while a man and our guide volunteered to go to the spring to bring water on their ponies. [This] was the place where the Indians had herded their stolen sheep and cattle for which the signs on the ground gave sufficient proof. We waited patiently for an hour for the return of the scout, during which time we experienced the effect of an elevated position, shaking with cold. The party at last returned but without water, the scout confessing his inability to find the spring.

There was only one thing for us to do, to return to a spring which we passed in the morning three miles from our permanent camp. The command was accordingly given to retrace our steps. On our way back no precautions were observed when there was the most danger of being surprised by Indians and massacred. The commander and everybody else went their own way, only thinking of themselves and their individual wants. How easy it would have been for a small number of good marksmen to do effective work in our ranks, killing a great many before we could have realized and avoided the danger. We learned afterwards in one of the Mexican towns that the Indians had been within one hundred feet of us as we scaled the mountain that morning.[11]

We were fortunate reaching the water without a more serious mishap beyond that of a little fright, which happened when we were within a half-mile of the spring. It was getting dark as we heard a sharp quick report of rifles in front. Our first thought was that the Indians had taken possession of the water and were now defending it. Our thirst was temporarily gone and we prepared for a little fun with the redskins, everybody being in anguish for an engagement, preferring rather a good fight to walking for days and nights through sand and hills. But less dangerous "game" than expected, deer, came into the evening to the spring and were surprised by our men who blasted without killing anything.

All of our men arrived but two, one was considered the meanest man in camp and disliked by all, receiving now very little sympathy. He was always without water, being too lazy to carry it, in the habit of depending on others for drinking on all our marches. He was generally accommodated by kind souls but [that] day left high and dry. It was a pitiful sight to look at, going from one to another begging for only one drop but there was no pity, everyone recalled all the water they had for themselves. Late that evening he arrived in camp with the other man, more dead than alive, finding all the men asleep peacefully, with the exception of a few timid ones [who] selected an isolated bush for their bed with the hope of being overlooked by the Indians in the event of a massacre.

In the morning we returned to our permanent camp without having anything at all accomplished. Another party sent out afterwards returned with five or six Indian ponies and a mule which they had found in the mountains.

It was July and the middle of the rainy season. A storm or

two was the order of the day, making camp life miserable for those who were living under their shelter tent and had not been fortunate enough to capture a cave. But relief was near and one rainy morning we left the mountains and entered the sunshine on the plains to go to a stage ranch in the extreme southwestern portion of the territory.

We went back to the river again a little better provided with transportation since the capture of the Indian ponies. The little mule proved himself a very intelligent and useful beast through the rest of the campaign. He would follow us all day with our dinner and a keg of water securely strapped on his back.

After following the course of the Rio Grande for some time the Captain took a cut-off across the plain between the mountains and the river. We found the road smooth and hard as a boulevard or park drive, but equally hard on feet and legs. After an hour's rest it required at least one mile to ease the stiff limbs. Deep drains of considerable depth ran over this plain, their existence not perceptible until we were within a short distance.

We were camping in one of these drains, not far from a Mexican village with a name as long as the town, when our second lieutenant caught up with us. This poor fellow was a complete wreck from marching. After our arrival at Fort Craig, after riding on the camp kettle in the cook wagon, he had an opportunity to go on sick report and get excused from further duty, which kept him at that place while we were in the mountains running after shadows.

Vegetables were slim, bacon and hardtack plentiful on our march. One or two of the ponies we had captured in the mountains could hardly be used for anything and some of us were sent to the village with orders to sell them. With a reasonable amount of money, ten dollars, and a sack full of onions we returned to camp perfectly satisfied we had not got the worst of the bargain. Here the nemesis of heaven over-hauled us and a thunderstorm crashed over our heads, blew down the tents, water swamping the place.

Good spirit prevailed and as much fun as possible was drawn from the situation. While we were putting up our tents again we could see the men and women in the town climbing up on the houses and repairing the roofs with mud. It seemed as if we were going to get the full benefit of the rainy season, although we had been informed on the Rio Grande that there had not been a strong enough shower for three years to wet clothes. We were inclined to brand all the Mexicans as a set of liars. But this was easily explained, in fact [there] had been very little rain in the valley of the river, while only a few miles away heavy showers were daily falling in the mountains.

The next day found us walking two by two with our guns over shoulders to see more of that strange country. Our path led us past another town where we saw a man standing on top of a wheat stack with a long pole in his hands while dozens of sheep were running, thrashing the wheat spread around the stack. The wheat was spread on cloth exposed to the sun while a man industriously cleaned it. We passed a sage bush, breaking off some of the needle-like leaves for a tea in the evening. We camped on a river again a mile or so from a large Mexican town where the Indians only nine months [before] reduced the population one-third.

Newly created rivers from the mountains made a swamp of the usual meadows, the wagons sinking up to their axles in mud. We had to unload the wagons and carry the cartridge boxes at the worst places. [The] men crossed a rivulet on two unhitched and most gentle mules, while one, proud of his superior horsemanship and under considerable "blowing," mounted a kicker. No sooner had his legs encircled the body of the animal [than] the spirit of the mule was aroused with one short jump followed by a high kick. [The] man went flying through the air with his gun across his shoulder, going head foremost into the mud, leaving nothing but heels above water to indicate where our rider disappeared. With assistance he was extricated and prevented from eating more mud than was good for his constitution.

At last we were past this morass and westward to the mining region, entering the foothills of the Mimbres Mountains where the town of Hillsboro was situated. The town was a very important and flourishing mining town before the Apache went on the warpath. The stamp mills and other machines to work the ore were not working and the few miners who lingered were idle. The prices of articles and vegetables were enormous.[12]

From there we passed through the richest, most fertile section of the territory. [Around] a lake some [sixteen miles] distance south of the town was a beautiful valley about a mile in circumference [McEvers Ranch]. Small hills surrounded the valley from where the Indians laid siege to a house in the center, succeeding in compelling the occupants to abandon the house and leave their fields to the mercy of the hostiles. Two Irishmen were captured by the Indians and compelled to herd their stock all day without being offered any food or water, or permitted to wear their clothes, but were graciously excused in the evening and directed to leave for their homes.

To the Black Range we directed our steps and soon camped on the divide at [Mule Spring] many feet above the level of the sea. Twenty-one miles from Mule Spring was Hot Springs, sprouting out of the ground on the top of a little hill, twenty feet high, caused by the deposits of the water rich in iron and other minerals. The temperature of the water was 160 degrees Fahrenheit. Bath houses and a hotel were erected on the foot of the hill for the accommodation of the sick. A garden, irrigated by the surplus water of the spring, furnished necessary vegetables. The only drawback was the scarcity of shade trees. An alley of trees [a] few years old was yet too small to afford such.[13]

Fort Bayard, twenty-one miles from Hot Springs, was established in 1866 in the center of the southwestern mining district of New Mexico. The houses were built of rocks and adobe. After stopping for a few days we continued to march to the principal city of the district, Silver City.[14]

[Silver City] was situated in a beautiful valley where here and there we saw the entrances of the mines on the slopes. The city was a composition of Mexican shanties and frame houses. The frame houses, with the exception of a few private dwellings, were hotels and saloons fitted up in grand style. One of the latter even went so far as to bring a piano to these wild regions and place [it] in the barroom. Of the Mexican houses, some were the usual mud while others were constructed in the shape of the letter "A" with the reed-like leaves of cactus used for the roof.

We camped on a small creek at the outskirts of town and some of the men went in, got drunk, and were put in the lockup, while others entered dining halls and were bounced for not paying. A friend and I visited two stamping mills operated by the last syndicate running, our pockets loaded with specimens of fine silver ore. [The mills] pulverized the ore, washed it, [and] separated the silver with quicksilver, after which the silver was melted into bars.[15]

Leaving the camp the next morning we were marched through town, stopping at a place to take one more drink for fear of never returning alive to take another. Some got more than their share and the consequence was a demoralized mob leaving the town. Even the commanding officer found the beverage too strong for his legs and took an extended rest along the road which kept him in the rear of his command until the next morning when the men were already prepared to leave camp.

The commander was not the only one. Our Frenchman again got lost, took another road and stumbled over human bones under a destroyed house in the mountains. Frightened by this he regained the main road, returning a few days after.

We started on our last days march, crossing the Continental Divide on the southern side of the Burro Mountains, soon settling in a camp to rest after passing over 370 miles of ground, averaging about twenty miles per day, at Knight's Ranch, thirty-four miles southwest of Silver City. We were one-half mile from the stage ranch, living under oak and fir trees, with a roof of tent and flour sack to shelter us against the weather, passing the days as best we could.

Some played cards in front of the tents under a big oak tree, others hunted or ran over the mountains in search of minerals, while some secretly worked with pick and shovel in lonely places, expecting to strike it rich and become millionaires in a short time. At times the men lounged under trees, being taught the signals of the bugles, or drilling by the sound of the bugle. [Others] enjoyed themselves with two orphaned donkeys, going through the feats of a circus performer, much to the amusement of the audience.

Beside us were about one hundred negro cavalry with a large pack train and a camp of about twenty Indian scouts to guard the four or five different Indian trails which the hostiles generally took on their way to the north. Nightly our Indian scouts danced at camp, rending the air with yells, after which they would sleep in a circle with their feet toward the campfire. In the mornings some scouted the country while others amused themselves trying to roll a small wheel past a ridge with a long pole.

[That] these [Indian scouts could be depended upon] for the cause they were enlisted . . . is exampled [by] the man who could not get a shot at the enemy, [and in] anger shot himself, trying to commit suicide. The constitution of these people and the amount of hardship they were capable of enduring was extraordinary. They could travel on foot for forty or fifty miles in a day without taking nourishment, rest, or indulging in a drink of water. This made them, as soldiers, superior to the white who had to carry water and food, which the former gathered along the road as needed. In fact eighty Indians well trained and maneuvered were strong enough to fight a hostile force four or five times their number.

The negro troops in the forts were a success, but in the field lacked in endurance and did not fight as well as the whites. [In] the words of some, "I isn't going to stay there and let them shoot at me 'fo' thirteen dollars a month. No sir! I isn't goin to do it!"

In our own camp the officers were engaged with a small cannon, firing at a high cliff. As if the elements were in with them a heavy thunderstorm drew up, struck the cliffs, and paralyzed our captain and the operator in the telegraph [tent].[16]

[In the] evening preparations were made to place a guard over camp. After relieving a man of duty who claimed to be blind and could not see after dark we went on guard and I placed a sentry with the necessary instructions over the stock. My watch was given to the first one with the order for the last man to wake me one hour before daybreak, the time for reveille in hostile country. The night passed without being awakened and I awoke at last with the sun shining brightly in my face, two horses and my own watch gone. A pursuing party was at once sent after the fugitive, but they returned soon, leaving the man to follow his own way, and time the distance by my watch.

After a month's rest all the troops and my company were ordered into Old Mexico to join the U.S. troops already there to assist the Mexican troops in capturing marauders. I was left at [the camp] in charge of ten men to guard the ranch. Our position was not a very secure one. If the troops failed to capture the Indians they would [have] surely passed and probably given us a call.[17]

That did not worry us, [henceforth] being relieved of all restrictions from the presence of officers and superiors. Our old camp was abandoned and a nice site at a small spring below the ranch selected as the most suitable and strong place for such a small band. Here the site was cleared of rubbish and a strong house erected at the entrance to a small valley, while loopholes in the sides of the house gave it the appearance of a fort. Our victuals were cooked on a nicely constructed oven and the "washwomen" — everyone being his own laundress — found a large rock below the spring a very commodious washboard.

We lived like lilies of the valley, nothing else to do but cook and eat. We were stepmotherly dealt with by the company [first] sergeant, who left us with less than our allowance of rations, compelling us to live on acorns for a while, until our rations were sent from the fort. Then we lived high, that is considering the frontier. We lived like the flowers around us, surplus bacon, flour, and yeast powder were sold to prospectors and freighters, while we bought or traded vegetables and live sheep for our kitchen. The latter supplying us also with bedding, of which we were in need, especially in cold nights of the latter part of our stay.

We were never in want of excitement [to] pass the time. Playing cards was our usual amusement. American and Mexican freighters would stop to fill their water barrels, the first generally drove six mules while the latter had ten mules, four abreast, on the wagons. Bull freighters driving ten or more yokes of oxen also [stopped] when on their way from mining towns in Arizona and Mexico to Silver City. Besides these transients there were horse thieves in the vicinity who stole the cattle and stock of emigrants, or attacked and robbed the stage that passed. Tramps passed daily in quest of a handout. We were overrun by these bums since the construction of the railroad had progressed [within] twenty miles, and could not afford to feed every hungry soul who passed.

[One day came] the appearance of a civilian scout. He claimed to be a government scout on his way to headquarters, but finding us he concluded to be flush with money. With two of my soldiers [he] went on a spree, which I would not have objected, if they had remained away from camp. They returned to our camp and made it very disagreeable for our peace loving community. That evening two men from the ranch, who probably were also in good spirits, came galloping down the road, yelling like Indians, which seemed to arouse the spirits of our scout who commenced to fire his pistol in rapid succession, causing something like a stampede from the fire where we had been sitting.

The scout, being informed that any such nonsense had to be discontinued, settled down at the fire and began telling stories. In this art he was undoubtedly a master. I can not recall any of his hair-breadth escapades and daring deeds for the simple reason that I put them down at the start as lies and consequently passed from my mind as soon as they were told. Only one thing I recollect — he had killed so and so many "greasers" this year already and there were so and so many more to make a hundred. He was undoubtedly a tough case judging by the pistols in his belt, the lameness of one shoulder, and his general action. I was glad when his back was turned upon our camp the next morning.

A scout of our party returned with unpleasant news, having seen an Indian trail, which sent the whole camp into excitement. More scouts were sent out to discover the whereabouts of the hostiles who might have been hundreds of miles from us. One of these scouts returned with the news that a cave, about four miles [away] was inhabited by a puma.

A panther hunt was exactly what I wanted for a change, having chased skunks and wolves long enough from our camp. The next morning bright and early [I] started out, provided with matches and candles. [At] the cave with a burning candle in one hand and gun in the other I made my way into the darkness, while my friend waited outside, ready to assist me at my call.

I was [proceeding] through [the] edifice when two glittering eyes checked my advance. I called to my pal to be ready and

come in, waited but [heard] no noise in [the] rear of me,
[while] the eyes in front were preparing for an attack. Not
caring to take up the combat single-handed I beat my retreat
to see what kept my partner. He was gone – nowhere to be
seen. Thinking it prudent to hunt him first, instead of the
panther, I started up the ravine where I soon caught up with
the man. [He] positively refused to go into the cave or remain
to smoke the animal out. I abandoned the hope of having that
puma's hide for my bed sheet and we proceeded up the canyon
for a scout.

Walking a little in advance of my friend I saw an animal
hastily leave its course and ascend a hill. My always ready
rifle stopped its flight, a well directed bullet sending it rolling
into the bush. My first impression was that I had killed a
wolf, but it proved to be a female panther [of] six foot, my
wish gratified, and a puma skin was to decorate our shanty.

There were also numerous bears, but I never had the luck
to meet one of the bruin family, except once. I was one day
preparing to leave camp when I saw to my astonishment a
big black bear trotting leisurely along the road, turning a
corner at our camp. Calling the attention of the others I quickly
loaded my gun, [but] saw a man behind the bear – with a
rope in his hand with which he was leading the animal.

At all times during my enlistment I had a mania to climb
mountains, stroll over the country, gather rocks and flowers,
[or] try to bring home everything eatable. I would in stocking
feet venture up steep and dangerous places to pluck a flower,
[and] in fact commit frolics and risk my life where there was
no reward gained. [On] one of these dangerous tours I ascended
a steep mountain from where I obtained truly a magnificent
view of the country. [Upon] descending [I] decided upon a
shorter route to camp. The place was steep and dangerous so
I removed my shoes to get a firmer handle on the rocks.
Smelling a rattlesnake I made a quick move. In my eagerness
to get away from that poisonous reptile I lost my hold, feet

went from under me and I went sliding where I intended
to walk. Only for my gun, which I pressed against a rock to
check my descent, I would have made a well beaten steak
for a puma. My descent was slow enough to keep the bones
together but too fast to prevent myself from falling into a
cactus where I got my body full of needles which took some
time to shave off.

We remained [at Knight's Ranch] until November when
orders were received from headquarters to rejoin our company
at Fort Gibson and further to proceed to Fort Davis, Texas.

Here we had a clear case [of] how foolishly the money of
the people, appropriated by Congress for the protection of the
settlers on its frontier, was expended by its servants to the
gratification of their own individual whim. Our company, or
at least the main portion of it under the command of the
Captain, was somewhere on the Rio Grande and about two
hundred miles from Fort Davis, the point of destination.

Through the mere whim of the Captain [to return to Fort
Gibson] we had to walk about six hundred extra miles, besides
being transported over 3,000 extra miles by rail, making an
expenditure of about 10,000 dollars to the government, for
which nothing was gained by the people.

At last we [were] to return to civilization and enjoy the
gifts of that institution of which we had so long been deprived.
To read once more a newspaper, to listen once more to the
sweet notes of music, and to look upon the fools of the refined
society. We gave a parting glace and retraced our steps with
light heart to join our friends at Fort Gibson, from where we
started with the firm belief that some of our comrades would
never return, paying the earth with their blood for the benefit
of the country and its citizens. But we were safe and hearty
without having received a wound from the arms of the enemy,
every man answered to his name, except the one who took
my watch and lit out while on guard.

Although we were in the heart of a dangerous country we

had the satisfaction to know that our presence was sufficient guarantee for the safety of the inhabitants and sojourners, of which even our own President was one who knew that he was tolerable safe to travel in this country with a strong guard.

We managed to retreat from these dangerous mountains without having lost any of our hair by one of those numerous devils. The morning was cold as our wagons passed between the walls of the Burro Mountains and ascended from where water sought the two great oceans of our continent, passing a couple of freight wagons which had, previous to our arrival, been attacked and burned by Indians.[18]

In Silver City we received a disagreeable addition to our party in the shape of a deserter who, while his company passed here, got drunk and left behind. On our way to the fort we crossed a valley where some time previously I narrowly escaped from having my head blown off. During my last trip to Fort [Bayard] on detached service [I] saw a wolf on the roadside. I took my gun, which had been laying on some corn sacks, loaded it and dismounted to fire. Before I could execute my intention the wolf disappeared behind the trees. On my return to the wagon I took the cartridge from the chamber, noticing a few grains of corn rolling out. Examining the barrel I saw it was stocked with corn up to the muzzle. What a narrow escape! Had I fired the barrel would have exploded and blown my head off, and made a cornfield of a wolf's hide.

The wind blew forty miles an hour as we camped on the bald hill on which Fort Bayard was situated. We had prepared for a nice open air rest after [temporarily] turning the prisoner over to the commanding officer of the fort, but our little shelter tents were blown into all shapes. The sand and pebbles flew around our head as if from a blowpipe, the temperature low enough to be disagreeable.

Morning awoke us with a pleasant smile and we started on our way to Fort Cummings afoot, there being only enough room on the wagon to pack our blankets. Over rolling barren country we moved, having again charge of the deserter to be taken to headquarters at Fort Cummings.

The road entered Cook's Canyon [where] mesquite brush was the principal growth. Five miles from the entrance to the canyon the road bent to the north, ascending the pass through Cook's Range. In this pass the depredations of Indians took frequent place. There were breastworks of the Indians on the roadside hills where an encounter took place between Indians and U.S. troops. Scattered bones of man and beast indicated the place, [including] the unburied bones of Victorio's son, laying in one of the ravines west of the divide.[19]

Fort Cummings, an old abandoned fort established in 1863, had a wall twelve feet high enclosing a square of 6400 yards, [with] one arched entrance on the south side. [It] had been made the headquarters for the troops in the field. We saw long rows of cavalry and infantry tents in the rear of the dilapidated fort. Under the shadows of a ledge of rock a company of Indian scouts [was] roasting a hindquarter of deer on the coals of a small fire. From there scouts were dispatched in different directions to scour the country while the troops were always ready to take up the Indian trail at a moments notice.[20]

In spite of this vigilance the hostiles, within twelve miles of there, attacked a stagecoach and killed the occupants. The cavalry were at once ordered to the scene to punish the marauders, but were badly punished themselves by the latter who permitted the troop to enter a ravine, attacking from both sides, compelling them to retreat with heavy loss.

[In] the evening we ascended the hill to the fort to listen to the music as the regimental band played a lively march for the troop to mount guard. It was a poor band, not better than a curbstone band, nevertheless it was music and sounded sweet, filling our hearts with delight and greater joy than the voice of a Paddy. The details of the different companies for the night guard were drawn in line to be inspected by the adjutant and placed in command of the officer of the day.

We had different branches of the service forming one company to guard against surprise and destruction by the enemy. On the right side of the line stood a negro sergeant in charge of the company. Next to him stood a couple of infantrymen abreast [of] white and black cavalrymen.

[At] a row of infantry tents the habitually lazy infantrymen either played cards or lounged around. Not far [away] were the cavalry tents where saddles [were] suspended from a rope in front, while the men had blown [up] a beef bladder, kicking it about for a football. Further on [I heard] the merry laugh of the colored troops, playing ball and going through all sorts of antics which they endeavored to amuse themselves. Vis-a-vis of the row of tents, on the other side of the street, was a line of wall tents where the officers of the command were quartered, and where the difference between the cavalry and infantry was as distinct as with the men.

The cavalry officers, as a rule, were more cordial and intelligent [than] infantry officers, and did not consider their West Point teachings supreme in a frontier campaign. They would listen to the suggestions of experienced enlisted men and would shape actions accordingly, or would follow the advice of one who had gone through the mill before.

Our way from this fort took us back [to] the mining town of Hillsboro again where we met a company of soldiers with Indian scouts returning from a scout through the Black Range. We entered the valley of the Rio Grande to take a more difficult but shorter route to Fort Craig. Our wagon sank up to the axles in sand hills on an imaginary road, but at last we crossed the Rio Grande and followed a rocky foundation to a spring called the Mexican name of Ojo del Muerto, appropriately "Spring of Death" from the fact that it was death to every single man or small party who camped there overnight.

Houses were erected there and Fort MacRae established in 1863 to protect the emigrants and freighters against an ambuscade by the Indians. A graveyard close by with the names

of California Volunteers on the headstones showed plainly
how well the Indians succeeded in those days in carrying on
their murderous work, giving free passes to the happy hunting
ground to a careless civilian or reckless trooper. The fort was
abandoned and the dwellings fallen to pieces, but the mountains were still there and the Indians, although in less numbers,
still hovered and paid an occasionally unexpected visit to the
unsuspecting Mexican freighter.[21]

The next morning we passed through mountains and descended to a dry plain, the Jornada del Muerto, [and] a well-
beaten road hollowed out to a depth of three or [more] feet
by wagons passing for three hundred years from Old Mexico
to Santa Fe. After one cold night on this plain we regained
the river valley and crossed the river to Fort Craig.

We selected a former kitchen as the best room in the abandoned barracks for our temporary shelter. The woodwork of the
doors and windows was torn off and the fresh autumn wind
had free access to our den, but [we] fastened blankets in the
openings and [had] a roaring big fire kindled in the room,
soon forgetting that there were some people who have a better
time than soldiers. A terrific snowstorm sprang up during the
night, opening our door and windows with ease, covering us
with a soft white sheet of a foot of snow before morning.

We remained only a few days, sold coffee [beans] to buy
liquid coffee on the road, baked bread in one of the old ovens,
and mounted a train one night which took us back again from
where we started over four months [before]. We reached our
destination without further mishap except a laughable incident
east of Colorado where a new conductor took charge of the
train. He entered our car to collect tickets from the passengers
when he spied one of our men comfortably behind the stove,
selecting this place as the warmest in the car. Mistaking him
for a tramp the conductor collared him with intention. My
recognition of the man satisfied the conductor that the man

was alright, the man's clothes [being campaign] worn, dusty, and sun faded.

We reached Emporia, Kansas where we had to change cars for a south-bound train about four o'clock in the morning. Instructing our cook to retrieve our rations and luggage from the baggage car I attended to the men and we were soon lodged comfortably, through the generosity of the station keeper, in a nice warm room at the station.

That evening we stood around a fire at the station a few miles from Fort Gibson, anxiously waiting for a couple of venison hams to fry which had that morning been thrown into our possession by mistake by the baggage [man] at Emporia with the impression that they belonged to us. In answer to my telegram to the commanding officer at the fort a wagon appeared the next morning to convey our luggage to the fort. Here we found everything in the old same track as we had left it the last spring.

9

. . . .

The Texas Frontier,
1881–1882

The Indian girls were as pretty as ever and [at] the first opportunity I went down to see the "girl I left behind me." I found her in the milk house, but there was a man admirer in the shape of a young Indian who seemed to have the inside track and had taken my place in her heart. [After] one glance from her pretty black eyes, a few words of warm greeting, and I was escorted to the house and ushered into the parlor.

We remained at the fort only one week when all our property was taken to the railroad and we started on our way to Fort Davis, Texas. At Eastland, Texas, at that time the end station of the unfinished Texas railroad, we transferred our property to government teams and from there to Fort Davis had another series of camp life.[1]

Before leaving that station we had anything except a pleasant time. The money was flush [after] the soldiers received four months pay at [Fort] Gibson. The place suited them to perfection to blow it in, having what they called a good old time for their few dollars after their exposures in New Mexico. All the scum of humanity were represented at that place; gambling houses, dance halls, whiskey dens, and women joining hands to extract the hard-earned money from the railroad constructors and our worthy comrades and fellow soldiers. Drunks and fights were the order of the day while camping there and I was glad when it was time to leave.

Our first days were not a pleasant one for the guard, of which I unfortunately was again a member. We had charge of a dozen quarrelsome drunken men, in the meantime trying to keep up with the rest of the command and wagons. Frequent rests delayed us on the road, darkness overtaking us [when] yet there were miles between us and the camp. During one of our rests one of our prisoners sufficiently sobered up to know what he was about, taking French leave, as he told us afterwards, walking back to a farmhouse to have a good rest. I, as corporal of this guard, was held responsible by the officer of the day for the man's action and was subsequently tried but acquitted by a general court-martial after our arrival at Fort Davis, contrary to general rule without having been placed under arrest.[2]

After our first night's rest everything went smoothly, most of the prisoners liberated and returned to their respective companies for duty. The marching regulated into one hour marching and ten minutes rest, the leading companies of the column changing daily, there being four companies [of the regiment]. The dull time of the march passed with the men singing and joking. The appearance of a jack rabbit was followed by a

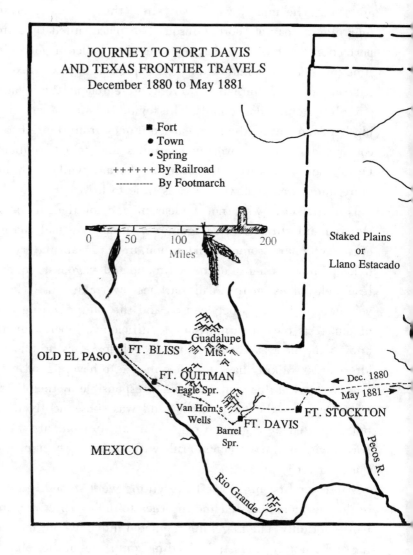

JOURNEY TO FORT DAVIS
AND TEXAS FRONTIER TRAVELS
December 1880 to May 1881

■ Fort
● Town
• Spring
++++++ By Railroad
---------- By Footmarch

0   50   100   200
Miles

Staked Plains
or
Llano Estacado

Guadalupe
FT. BLISS   Mts.
OLD EL PASO

FT. QUITMAN
Eagle Spr.   Dec. 1880
                              May 1881
Van Horn's
Wells   FT. DAVIS   FT. STOCKTON
    Barrel
    Spr.

MEXICO

Rio Grande   Pecos R.

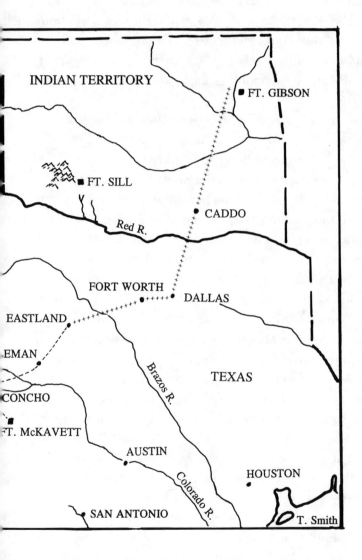

lively chase by our hounds, furnishing excitement for the occasion, making us forget the distance to camp and tired legs.

Near Fort Concho we saw the colored cavalry band mounted on splendid white horses advancing to escort us into that place. We were delayed at the fo t a few days, joined in the meantime by a few more companies and recruits. The weather was cold, the ground covered by a soft layer of snow as we slept under our small shelter tents, doubling up to keep each other from freezing.[3]

One morning I felt something crawling over my body, which proved to be a louse. My partner, a wreck, had been out the night before and brought home a few of these for free. We dissolved partnership at once and I went to the icy river to change clothes. With a little imagination of a hot summer day [I] took a fire-ash bath, changing clothes with the catfish.

The snow and ice had disappeared and the sun was shining softly as we left Fort Concho to resume our march west. We soon came to a remarkable valley where only five years [before] we could have seen thousands of buffalo, but where only their bleaching skulls and skeletons gave evidence for their former existence, while cattle, almost as wild as the buffalo, took their places keeping abreast of the times and wants of mankind.

We crossed a waterless plateau, a corner of the Staked Plains, where the grass dried in summer under the burning rays of an equator sun, and the blizzard had an unhemmed sweep in winter, which no animal life could face. It was Christmas as we crossed a plain of cactus and sage, and occasionally a mesquite tree, while here and there a pretty prairie flower would repay us with its beautiful color.

A guarded spring at the head of one of the numerous valleys made our home for one night. We lay that evening under the bright rays of luna, thinking of the happy days of boyhood when standing around a decorated Christmas tree admiring our presents. We [thought] of a poor wretch from the ranks of the colored troops stationed to guard the spring who had been killed by one of his comrades and buried that afternoon a short distance from camp with all the military honors due a soldier, but over whose grave the wolves were howling. This was surely a loss to the government but there was [also] a small party of emigrants who had met with a great calamity by having their stock stolen, and only for the assistance of the military who brought them [to the spring] they would have perished on this God-forsaken plain.[4]

[We left] on the day of joy of all Christian nations, following a valley which gradually deepened, terminating at the river Pecos. The sun overhead burned and our water supply dwindled to the last drops as we passed [a] natural cistern constructed by wise mother nature in the rocks where the rain water, as fresh as spring water, kept for months. The valley of the Pecos ran for miles to our right and left, bordered by table mountains. We made our descent by a road running diagonally across the face [of a steep hill]. [We had] another race in marching by the companies, of which the officers of the command had a little delight to test the endurance of the different commands. [The others] increased the cadence of the steps to five miles per hour. [There was] at least one sensible captain of the command who did not indulge in unnecessary haste, bringing his men, if not as soon, in better condition to the [river] than the rest, this one our captain.

Tents were pitched on the bank of the river and after a supper of government straight we took a plunge into the water. There was nothing which equalled a good bath to refresh and ease the limbs after a long hot day's marching, that is if it can be done without wishing a furnace under the river to heat the water.

Nothing of note occurred on our march from that point to Fort Stockton, except that we stole wood from a woodpile at a ranch near a spring over which we had been placed as guard to keep anyone from stealing [wood]. We went into camp for a few days at Fort [Stockton] in order to give our teams a rest.

A clear stream of lukewarm water passed our camp. The ground was white from the alkaline of the soil where our tents were pitched in a triangle, flaps fastened [together], forming a large room [of] three chambers with a low fire burning in the center with the pleasant odor of mesquite root.[5]

The weather was intensely cold and we couldn't think of taking a bath in the creek whose waters were invitingly warm, so we either remained in the tents, or crossed the little barrel bridge to pay visits to our friends in warm quarters at the fort, or at the warm stoves of the traders in the town nearby.

The weather was moderate [when] we left on New Year's day to complete our march to Fort Davis. We came to a marshy valley [and] Leon Spring, thirty feet in diameter, [it] was said to be over 1500 feet deep. A long plank had to be used to go near the water on the account of the insecurity of the edge surrounding the hole. On solid ground [we] went into a dry camp, awaking the next morning to find a heavy layer of snow and a cold wind blowing from the north.[6]

Little time was lost in breaking camp and starting on the road. A walk of eight miles in the snow was more fatiguing than walking thirty miles over a good road [so] we were compelled to go into camp again to wait for colder or warmer weather. In the morning the sun brought a milder air which melted the snow and made the day one of the most disagreeable of the march. It was impossible to step in a dry place so we waded through snow-water and mud. At our last camp of this march, in a canyon at the foot of a line of cliffs [on] Limpia Creek, we found that some officer had brought his intellect to bear by having cart wood sent to the command from Fort [Davis], while better wood for camp purposes was growing within easy reach. The creek ran through one of the most dangerous canyons in Texas, [Limpia Canyon], especially a stretch of seven miles where the walls were vertical, two hundred yards apart and three hundred feet high. The canyon opened four miles from Fort Davis in a fertile valley where Mexicans had made their homesteads.[7]

[After] our four hundred mile walk from the railroad the fort was soon in sight and we were once more lodged under a warm comfortable roof of the military barracks. We were almost strangers [to] a civilized habitation and felt a little out of place after [almost] seven months of continual camp life. Nevertheless it appeared our health had improved since we sat before the camera of a traveling frontier artist at Fort Gibson last spring. One thousand miles of walking and exposure to direct change of weather, not to mention the three thousand miles of railroad ride, seemed to have knocked all the diseases of the men and brought health to their bodies, but sickness to their clothes.[8]

We fairly returned to the civilized way of living and usefulness of society people, playing pool and billiards, drinking whiskey, besides other accomplishments. We felt that our lives were not thrown away with the idle amusement of a useless occupation of chasing Indians from one section of the country to another.

Some [men] went to the hospital for treatment of real or imaginary diseases, frost bite, and the effect of cold spells on the road. Men went to the Mexican village for a dance or to seek excitement with the señoritas, while others barged off to take in the gambling and dance hall of a German Jew whose pretty daughters were not too proud to accept the love of a negro.

Others took their guns to the mountains for black bear and other game, there being a great many of the former in the hills. It was not unusual for the sentries in the fort to see a bear passing their post in the dark to examine the swill-barrel of the kitchen, and we had a couple of bears chained up at the hospital.

Small Mexican farms dotted the bottom of the valley where

the land was low enough to be cultivated by irrigation. [On] the steep hills we noticed small rooms hidden beneath huge rocks and caves in the cliff where some human hand had been once at work to construct a shelter. Flint arrowheads gave evidence of former battles with Indians. Natural wells, almost inaccessible to human beings, [were] only known to one well-acquainted with the country.

[As to] the people of the country we discovered [a] deviation from those in the eastern sections of Texas. [The] frontier dude – a flannel shirt with colored designs, a wide pair of breeches, a pair of boots with fancy stitching, a rimmed white hat with heavy silver band covered his top-knot, a pair of pistols in a belt around his waist, this was a Texas dude.

[The] colored soldiers at the fort were very fond of this showy display – although I had frequently seen white commissioned officers make the same display in order to gain easier access to the fortified hearts of the Mexican señoritas – the outer seam of the pants was ripped at the bottom as far as the knee and a red piece of triangular cloth inserted which enlarged the bottom of the pants enough to completely hide the shoe. When returning from a ball or visit to town this red piece disappeared for plain military regulation suit [by] drawing the seams together and fastening with hooks and eyes.

One morning when sleeping soundly in my bunk I heard heavenly music, a small Mexican band – two violins, guitar, and clarinet I think – on their return from a ball, who took it in their heads to serenade the post trader. The piece they were playing, a wild Mexican air, was played with the mellowness of a southern nature. The notes, soft and sweet, seemed to float in the air as I lay in a trance, unable to move a limb or perceive anything beyond the music. The trance gradually wore off after the strong sound of the morning bugle called us for reveille, arousing us to the full realization of life.

I always considered detached service a pleasure and a nice

pastime. [An] order with instructions to repair a telegraph line was given to me one morning and I immediately repaired with an escort wagon to the telegraph office to get the necessary instruments. We were soon on our way and, after adjusting a few insulators near the fort, entered a canyon through which the line was running. Following the line on its angular way [as] it zig-zagged through the canyon it was necessary for me to climb one of the [leaning] poles. I securely adjusted a pair of iron [climbing] spurs to my boot and managed to reach the top but while I was trying to repair the damage I lost my spur hold, swung around to the inclining side of the pole, and came down with a velocity that slowed on top of a large pile of rocks.

My fall was soon forgotten as we moved on, shortly passing a suspicious looking individual who, although dressed like a Mexican, had a certain Indian air about him, which forced us to keep a watchful eye and guns convenient when at work. At camp coffee was quickly prepared while a section of a hawk was roasting on a pole. The supper was an unusually tough one, but even a tiresome walk through that evening did not elevate our bill of fare above the standard bacon.

We returned to the fort [the next] morning to take a few days rest before going on another trip as an escort to El Paso. It was a cold Sunday morning [when] an ambulance and escort left the fort with an inspecting officer to inspect the various forts on the frontier.[9]

We traveled fast and little spoke by the men who sat on their wagons with a blanket wrapped around à-la-Indian, while rifles rested conveniently between their knees. The scenery was magnificent, the road winding through mountain defiles [and] over hills to Barrel Springs [where] the Indians frequently visited in dry season for water. The rock was mostly white-red marble [and] game such as antelope plentiful. [At] Elmurto [El Muerto] Springs, eighteen miles west of Barrel Springs, I saw one camp not over two days old. Elmurto was the last watering place for sixty miles [to] Eagle Springs. The road [to] Van Horn's Well led mostly over rolling prairie. [At] Van Horn's Well water was only found in the wet season. From there the road gained Bass Canyon [where] projecting rocks and ledges afforded good hiding places for hostile Indians to ambush emigrants and the stage. Their depredations were numerous in 1880, but mostly induced through the carelessness and ignorance of the travelers by keeping cowed around their wagons. Eagle Springs was enclosed by mountains, and the most dangerous place on the road. Indians were compelled to go there for water when on their route to or from the Guadalupe Mountains.[10]

We entered some canyons [Quitman Canyon] where the Indians had attacked a stagecoach, leaving behind nothing but scattered letters, charred trunks, and dead mules. They also left the dead bodies of the passengers besides the mutilated and outraged body of one of the women victims.

We shall pass over the details of this horrible crime and [mention] the acquaintance of the Texas State Militia Rangers whom we met at a spring in the mountains. They were all fantastically dressed and painted in Indian dresses and wigs, [as if] to go on a variety stage in a city. They came to our camp on a visit before returning .to the trail of the hostile Indians. The life of these men can not be compared with a regular soldier.[11]

The state paid them only thirty dollars a month including rations, while each furnished his own horses and ammunition, besides what they could make raiding the Indians. As frontier soldiers they were far superior to the [Army] regulars, in fact twenty-five of [them] were more efficient in an Indian outbreak than one hundred U.S. troops commanded by high sounding West Pointers. But this superiority was gained through their uncivilized treatment of the unfortunate beings of the Plains. Their orders were to kill every Indian on sight without pardon, treating them like beasts. While the

U.S. troops endeavored to kill as few as possible and to capture alive if possible in order to take them back to the reservation to be kept there by their "game-keepers," depriving them of what was natural through birth [and] citizenship of America, placing them in this respect below the negro, whose superior [they] were in every respect.

On our way to El Paso we were soon in sight of the Rio Grande Valley. The road was very sandy and our progress slower, but for this we were sufficiently repaid by the smiles of señoritas as we passed houses and homes. [A] Mexican, with one corner of his plaid thrown over the shoulder and a large brimmed sombrero on his head, leaned leisurely against the pillars of a mud arcade, matching the blue [smoke] rings from a cigarette. Close by his side we saw vessels suspended by a rope from the ceiling, in which water was lowered to an icy temperature by circulation. From the house stood a scaffold where yellow river water was kept in a bull's hide to be purified with cactus charcoal.

We greeted a Mexican whose hand lay on the head of a ferocious looking dog. [He] escorted us through the arched entrance into the courtyard of his house, showing us the inside of the building, a suit of rooms placed in a square with doors and windows open to the court and a strong door protecting them against the outside world. The block of [adobe] mud was only one story high, as most of the buildings were, covered with a twenty-inch thick roof. After enjoying the hospitality and admiring his ancient farm machines we took our departure to seek further adventure.

Our steps to that place had been observed by some of the female inhabitants of the village who were on top of a roof and by all appearance had made us the subject of their talk. Seeing themselves discovered they hastily withdrew beneath the protecting roof of the "old man." We had just directed our steps in that direction to make, if possible, their acquaintance, when our attention was drawn to another object of interest, a young girl in her best calico dress passing us on her way to church. Besides her there were other well-dressed beauties going to the same place of worship to repent their sins and pray.

By this time we experienced a strong longing for salvation, a feeling that our sins needed a thorough overhaul and cleaning, and that it was best to have this done at once while it was within easy reach, not waiting until it was too late. So we entered the structure and went through the ceremony at the holy water basin but there came to the end of our wits. Being Protestant in our beliefs we did not know what to do next.

The congregation, all ladies kneeling before the altar, did not aid our comfort by frequently turning their heads and drawing a bee-line of us, seeming to find more interest in our presence than [that] of their own salvation. We stood this for a while but the heavy cross-fire of black eyes was getting too hot for us and we beat a hasty retreat without having received forgiveness for our sins, or even a chance to repent them.

The following day we [visited] the home of our Mexican friend. The old man, [who] by the way had in the meantime his pistol stolen from him by one of our men while indulging in the evening in too much Mexican agenda, was feeling a little hostile towards us.

We continued our journey toward El Paso where a few days later we pitched our tents on the banks of the Rio Grande, a short distance above that old Spanish settlement. Fort Bliss lay about one mile above El Paso at a place where the river, after cutting through the Franklin Mountains, resumed a winding and sandy path. Above [a] falls the river [had] been dammed and used on the American side for working a flour mill, on the Mexican side for supplying a large irrigation ditch which furnished the old town of El Paso with water. Franklin, or El Paso, Texas, was one-half mile from the river and was the seat of the custom house of the district. On the opposite bank of the Rio Grande the Mexican town of El Paso [had] a population of six thousand.[12]

We forded by ferry for the nominal sum of five cents and entered the [old] city. The town was laid out in irregular narrow streets and sidewalks paved with limestone and sandstone. Only a few streets were entirely bordered by houses, the rest intermixed with wine gardens surrounded by adobe walls. In the center of the city was the plaza, two hundred feet square, with two rows of adobe seats surrounding it. In the center of the plaza had been a fountain but it was broken. [The plaza] was shaded by high cottonwood trees, on the east side were stores, on the north and south dwellings. On the west [stood] a celebrated three hundred-year old Catholic church built of adobe, the rafters and other wood works carved in a style different from the altar, pulpit, and Holy Mary shrine. Beyond this structure we observed an arcade, probably used as a market or stables, and extensive vineyards irrigated by a network of ditches.[13]

[We] returned to camp as the sun neared the horizon, [as] night would endanger the life of an unarmed roamer. It was not very safe for a man to travel after dark, a boy had been killed only a day or two [before] by some knights of the road and our men held up and relieved of their valuables while returning from an entertainment in town. We lay in the tent that evening listening to the exceptionally melodious notes of a fife and drum band as they sounded tattoo in the garrison, while the rattle of a flour mill near the river lulled us to sleep for our last night of stay.

The morning sun found us traveling over the sandy road down the Rio Grande valley on our return to Fort Davis. Our second or third day from El Paso we met the Texas Rangers again. They had followed and overtaken the Indians, killed and captured their stores since we met them at the spring in the mountains, and were loaded with plunder and scalps, going to El Paso to do police duty there.

Back in Fort Davis I tried to get my witnesses together for my approaching trial by general court-martial, which might have meant in this case [being] reduced to the ranks and confined in the guardhouse for six months. I found there were some men in my company already aspiring for my [corporal's] place, the first step to [a] general's position. But they were to be disappointed in this respect, as the court found me not guilty of the charges preferred against me.[14]

There was no rest for the soldier, especially if he, individually, did not like too much of it. This time it was the telegraph line between [Fort Davis] and old Fort Quitman on the Rio Grande which needed repairing. Our party consisted of four men: myself, a colored driver, and two recruits from my company. Two of my party were pleasant company for such a trip, but one of the recruits was the "gorilla" in the company, deserving the name so far as his intellect and physical appearance was concerned.

We left on a pleasant day in May 1881 provided with fifteen days rations and all necessary repairing tools. How pleasant it was to travel across the country with a brisk morning breeze fresh from the green mountains. We saw big volumes of smoke rising from the plain ahead, carried before the wind [as] a messenger of death and destruction. Turning a mountain and entering the valley, smoldering black surface at our feet, the [fire] ascended the hills to our right until checked by rocks.

The fire had done its work. Telegraph poles, rotten and dry from long standing, were still burning while some of the stumps dangled on the wire. We replaced them with iron poles which had previously been distributed in different places along the road. [We traveled] a few miles further [to] a stage ranch to camp and share the scanty water of a small spring with the station keeper.

Stagecoaches plied regularly between towns and forts to carry the mail [and] make connections to railroad stations. [Stage stations] were established along the road at intervals of twenty to forty-five miles where the stock was exchanged. Broncos or Mexican mules, owing to great endurance, were principally used on the line. These animals were the toughest and keenest little creatures on the frontier. When started at a station they would travel the whole distance without needing much urging from the driver but neither would they mind the reins when scenting wolves or Indians on the road, in which case they would turn as fast as convenience would permit and return to the starting point.

A stage driver was always a very interesting individual. He had been driving stages on every line in the country since he was a boy. He had many adventures with road agent and Indian, fought Indians in Missouri and Dakota, and had hair-breadth escapes in Texas and New Mexico. He was never too tired to enlighten you on the subject [and] could tell more frontier stories than any man alive, and was never in want of having seen an Indian on the last trip only a few days ago.[15]

The following day, after discovering an Indian trail during our day's work, we went into camp at another stage ranch near a small spring at the mouth of a canyon. We met a party of emigrants already camped for the night. They hailed from Tennessee and were on their way to Silver City, New Mexico. We went down to their camp to see if there were any girls with the party. We found the leader of the pack in a very downhearted mood about the safety of his family. He had received information from the stage drivers that the country was swarming with Indians and that there was eminent danger if he should venture further. Even my assurance of the absurdity of such an assertion did not elevate his spirits, not until I promised my escort past the most dangerous places for the whole length of my trip. They felt themselves safe to continue their voyage.

Our way led us across very dry country, to Devil's Backbone, in fact the devil's country – no water for sixty miles except in some of the valleys where water from the last rain was retained in pockets in the rocks. Men had tried to obtain water by digging [at] Van Horn's Well but as of then there was no sign of any water and consequently the work had to be discontinued. Water had to be transported in barrels for a distance of twenty-two miles.[16]

Our next stopping place was Eagle Springs, where we met the Rangers on our last trip to El Paso, perpendicular rocks and cliffs where the eagle felt at home, where bear and mountain lions lurked under the shadows of the cedar, and where marauding Indians [would] lay in ambush for their prey. A very interesting place, that, and the only spring and watering place for a distance of 105 miles on the road. A very sweet consolation for a thirsty wayfarer, to travel there knowing he might be compelled to exchange his own blood for each drop of water to drink. No wonder the emigrants displayed signs of fear to cross there on their own merits and the good looks of the females under their protection. A strong stone house had been erected by the station keeper as protection against Indians, [and] a detachment of soldiers was stationed there as a guard to afford temporary protection to sojourners.

We resumed our work on the telegraph line, continuing alone as our friends the emigrants remained under the protection of the soldiers for a few days in order to give their exhausted teams a rest. We saw a valley of roses, a whole forest of beautiful red flowers in the midst of the "Devil's country," deerhorn cactus in full bloom. We entered [Quitman] Canyon where only a month [before] the old [devil], in the form of Indians, got away with one of his followers — a gambler — and burned him on a stake for the amusement and delight of the family.

With the fate of that man still fresh on my mind I left the wagon to follow the telegraph line on foot when — bang! I heard a shot and a bullet whistled close to my ear. Indians! I thought, my body dropping behind the thick stump of a cactus. After a quick glance in front I discovered that the shot had been fired accidentally from our wagon in the rear. Past the habitual Indian trail we entered the canyon. Strange feelings take possession of a man when he is about to pass a place where death may meet him at every step. We kept our eyes suspiciously on every stone, expecting to see a gun or hear the report of a rifle, but nothing of that sort happened and we passed the last natural breastworks of rocks, [which] by the way were painted with hieroglyphics.

After passing the carcasses of the mules who had been killed at the time when the gambler met his redeemer we went through that back door of hell without losing our hair and came into full view of the Rio Grande. At last we were comfortably encamped near an old fort on the banks of the river, taking a much needed rest after one hundred forty-five miles of labor.

We took a stroll up to old Fort Quitman [to] pay a visit to some friends temporarily stationed there and to see if the telegraph was in working order. The fort, first established in 1852, lay at a point where the valley of the Rio Grande narrowed between steep mountains, eighty-five miles from El Paso. The fort had been abandoned at different times and the buildings left without care, and with the exception of one or two houses, was consequently in very bad condition. Owing to the insecurity of the country by hostile Indians and lawless whites the place was again occupied by a detachment of soldiers, while small detachments were distributed at different stage ranches along the line to act as escort.[17]

We found everything satisfactory but an hour or two later I returned to the camp loaded with the unpleasant news that Indians, or whites clad like Indians, had crossed the river on the regular Indian trail only twelve miles above us and fired at a surveying engineer of the proposed railroad. This intelligence was inconvenient to us but more so for the man [who] was our "gorilla" of little use who I learned through the other men, intended to cross the river into Mexico and desert. [That would have been] of little loss to us, that is if he would leave without taking a mule from our team. He changed his mind, concluding to stay with the crowd, by which I was thrown out of heaven as I was in hopes that he would desert and deliver us of his disagreeable presence.

We resumed our return trip [to] to Fort Davis, passing a bull team slowly drawing a section of heavy iron boiler over the dreary country for the distant mines while the poor beasts were having to be content with salted cactus as their supper. I had a little experience in that myself. Having heard once that the new sprout of a Spanish dagger, while in the shape of a cabbage, was good to eat when boiled and afterwards fried. I tried it and found it a good substitute for anything better. We camped at one of the stage ranches, dining on the cactus with the station keeper as our guest for the royal dish. This old worthy pronounced our preparation a decided success, intimating that the secret be divulged to him and his own table [be] supplied with this valuable dish of the plains.

We left the station the [next] morning, not waiting to see how he succeeded with his cabbage. We heard a few days later that the "greens" had played havoc with his bowels and acted [as] bitter [as] a dose of oil. He was yet very weak but sent his best wishes and prayers to us, with a hope to meet us again sometime.

When returning to Fort Davis [we] learned that our company had in the meantime been ordered away and were now stationed at the regimental headquarters at Fort McKavett, Texas, about three hundred miles east. We were assigned temporarily to another company of our regiment. After their arrival from the different stage ranches where most of them had been stationed we started east to Fort McKavett.[18]

We left Fort Davis on the same road which led us there and retraced our steps to Fort Concho. From there we had fifty odd miles to our destination. A few days later we were camping near a ranch on the Concho River [and] found cowboys out in full force engaged in rounding up cattle to subject them to the cruel treatment of branding. The whole side of a steer was sometimes covered with brands. [We] passed quickly over the road and got into permanent quarters at Fort McKavett, joining our company again.

Fort McKavett was established in 1852 in what was then the haunts of the Comanche Indians. These original inhabitants have since greatly diminished in number and were on a reservation in the Indian Territory, the shadow of their former strength. The fort lay at the dividing line in Texas where the well-watered and timbered valleys of the eastern portion are bordered by the dry timberless plateau of the northwestern section. The country was generally rocky and the rocks principally limestone composed of millions of petrified shells. The valleys were fertile but [required] irrigation as it very seldom rained in the summer. The winters were mild while summer nights were cold. With the healthy climate and beautiful country life was worth living – even for a disappointed lover.[19]

[As] to the military life at the fort, the joys and sorrows of soldiers at a regimental headquarters, the guard duty was light. One hour's drill two or three times a week kept our limbs from growing stiff. [This] besides a couple of spectacular displays of dress parades for the amusement of the women constituted our post duty. The privates, if they were not policing around the garrison or scrubbing the company kitchens, were marched to the river to work from morning to night with pick and shovel building dams for the post gardens, or else some other kind of slaving about the fort.

The noncommissioned officers, on the other hand, had less work to perform, [being] only required to superintend. But their money was well-earned by drilling recruits, putting them through their first military instruction. The most disagreeable job was surely to have a dozen green shavetails (a new army mule) and instruct them in the different maneuvers. No one

[can] imagine that there is such ignorant class of men alive on this earth until he puts a dozen or so through the different maneuvers and manual of arms.

EDITOR'S NOTE:

Emil A. Bode's memoirs end rather abruptly at this point. He was promoted to sergeant in February 1882, taking his discharge the same month at the expiration of his term of service. From several letters and notes included in his manuscript it is apparent that he worked for a while for the government, perhaps as a surveyor. From the letters it seems that he was a businessman by the end of the 1880s, traveling frequently in the area of Chicago and Dayton, Ohio. Nothing further has surfaced about his later life. I close his story with a simple statement, one he might regard as rather high praise. Corporal Emil A. Bode saw his duty and did it; he was a good soldier.[20]

INTRODUCTION

1. There are very few monograph-length memoirs by soldiers in the enlisted infantry on the frontier in the post–Civil War era; among these is James D. Lockwood's *Life and Adventures of a Drummer Boy* (Albany, N.Y.: John Skinner, 1893). Lockwood, a regular in the Eighteenth Infantry, served in Montana and Wyoming from 1866 to 1868. An account from the First Infantry is Rev. John E. Cox, *Five Years in the United States Army* (Owensville, Indiana: 1892; reprint, with Introduction by Don Russell, New York: Sol Lewis, 1973). Article-length memoirs of the post-Civil War regular infantry are almost as scarce but include Sergeant John E. Cox, First Infantry, "Soldiering in Dakota Territory in the Seventies: A Communication," *North Dakota History* 6 (Oct. 1931): 62–82; Michael D. Hill and Ben Innis, eds., "The Fort Buford Diary of Private Sanford, 1876–1877," *North Dakota History* 52 (Summer 1985): 2–40. Sanford served in the Sixth Infantry; Jon G. James, ed., "Montana Episodes: Sergeant Molchert's Perils: Soldiering in Montana, 1870–1880," *Montana: The Magazine of Western History* 34 (Spring 1984): 60–65. Molchert soldiered with the Seventh Infantry at Fort Shaw in the 1870s.

Enlisted cavalry memoirs of the post–Civil War frontier are more numerous and include, by regiment, the First Cavalry: George F. Brimlow, "Two Cavalrymen's Diaries of the Bannock War, 1878," *Oregon Historical Quarterly* 68 (Sept. 1967): 221–58, (Dec. 1967): 293–316, which combines an officer's and private's diaries; the Third Cavalry: Thomas R. Buecker, ed., "The Journals of James S. McClellan, 1st Sgt., Company H, 3rd Cavalry," *Annals of Wyoming* 57 (Spring 1985), 21–34; the Fourth Cavalry: John B. Charlton, *The Old Sergeant's Story: Fighting Indians and Bad Men in Texas in 1870 to 1876,* Robert G. Carter ed., (New York: Hitchcock, 1926; reprint, Mattituck, N.Y.: J. M. Carroll, 1982); James B. Kincaid, "Diary of Sgt. James B. Kincaid, Co. B, 4th Cav., August 1876 to 1881," *Winners of the West* 16 (July 1939); James Larson, "Manuscript," James Larson Papers, Arthur Arndt Collection, Barker Texas History Center, University of Texas at Austin, published as *Sergeant Larson, 4th Cavalry* (San Antonio: Southern Literary Institute, 1925); Sherry L. Smith, ed., *Sagebrush Soldier: Private William Earl Smith's View of the Sioux War of 1876* (Norman: University of Oklahoma Press, 1989); Henry P. Walker, ed., "The Reluctant Corporal: The Autobiography of William Bladen Jett," *Journal of Arizona History* 12 (Spring 1971): 1–50, (Summer 1971): 112–44; The Fifth Cavalry: Paul

H. Hedren, ed., "Campaigning with the 5th Cavalry: Private James B. Frew's Diary and Letters from the Great Sioux War of 1876," *Nebraska History* 65 (Winter 1984): 443–66; the Sixth Cavalry: H. H. McConnell, *Five Years a Cavalryman: or, Sketches of Regular Army Life of the Texas Frontier* (Jacksboro, Tex.: J. N. Rogers and Co., 1889; reprint, Jacksboro, Tex.: Jack County Historical Society, 1963); the Seventh Cavalry: Ami Frank Mulford, *Fighting Indians in the 7th United States Cavalry* (Corning, N.Y.: Lee & Mulford, 1878), and a Seventh Cavalry enlisted biography of one of Custer's orderlies, John Burkham, by Glendolin D. Wagner, *Old Neutriment* (Boston: Ruth Hill, 1934).

The rarest of all enlisted accounts are by black soldiers of the Ninth and Tenth Cavalries or of the black infantry regiments. Three outstanding works on black enlisted soldiers on the frontier are William H. Leckie, *The Buffalo Soldiers: A Narrative History of the Negro Cavalry in the West* (Norman: University of Oklahoma Press, 1967); Arlen L. Fowler, *The Black Infantry in the West, 1869–1891* (Westport, Conn.: Greenwood Press, 1971); and John M. Carroll, ed., *The Black Military Experience in The American West* (New York: Liveright Publishing Corp., 1971).

2. For a discussion of the soldiers' sympathetic attitude toward the Plains Indians see Sherry L. Smith, *The View from Officers' Row: Army Perceptions of Western Indians* (Tucson: University of Arizona Press, 1990), and Richard N. Ellis, "The Humanitarian Generals," *Western Historical Quarterly* 3 (April 1972): 169–78.

3. For a historical synthesis of the enlisted soldier in the frontier army see Edward M. Coffman, *The Old Army: A Portrait of the American Army in Peacetime, 1784–1898* (New York: Oxford University Press, 1986); Oliver Knight, *Life and Manners in the Frontier Army* (Norman: University of Oklahoma Press, 1978); John J. Lenny, *Rankers: The Odyssey of the Enlisted Regular Soldier of America and Britain* (New York: Greenburg, 1950); Don Rickey, Jr., *Forty Miles a Day on Beans and Hay: The Enlisted Soldier Fighting the Indian Wars* (Norman: University of Oklahoma Press, 1963); idem, "The Enlisted Men of the Indian Wars," *Military Affairs* 23 (1959–1960), 91–96; Robert M. Utley, *Frontier Regulars: The United States Army and the Indian, 1866–1891* (New York: Macmillan, 1973); Henry P. Walker, "The Enlisted Soldier on the Frontier," in *The American Military on the Frontier: The Proceedings of the 7th Military History Symposium, U.S. Air Force Academy, 30 Sept.–1 Oct. 1976,* ed. James P. Tate (Washington, D.C.: GPO, 1978), 118–33.

4. Letter to author from Rolf Nowak, 15 January 1992, Archivpfleger des Kirchenkreises Uslar, Uslar, Germany. Register of Enlistments, vol. 72, 1871–1877, 198 entry 118, Records of the United States Army Adjutant General's Office, 1870–1917, Record Group (RG) 94, National Archives and Records Service (NARS) (hereinafter cited as Adjutant General's Records); Muster Roll for 28 February to 30 April 1882, box 474, Regular Army

Muster Rolls, Sixteenth Infantry, Company D, 31 Oct. 1872–31 Dec. 1902, ibid.

5. "Report of the Recruiting Service from October 1, 1875–October 1, 1876," *House Exec. Doc.*, 44th Cong., 2d sess., no. 1, pt. 2, Serial 1742, 73.

6. The army as "handyman" quote is from Samuel P. Huntington, *The Soldier and the State: The Theory and Politics of Civil-Military Relations* (New York: Vintage Books, 1957), 261; "Report of the Secretary of War, 10 Nov. 1876," *House Exec. Doc.*, 44th Cong. 2d sess., no. 1, pt. 2, Serial 1742, 5–9, 12–13.

7. "Report of the Secretary of War, 10 Nov. 1876," 12–13.

8. Ibid., 5; "Report of the General of the Army, 10 Nov. 1876," *House Exec. Doc.*, 44th Cong., 2d sess., no. 1, pt. 2, Serial 1742, 46–50.

9. "Report of the Secretary of War, 10 Nov. 1876," 6.

10. For an overview of the army struggling toward professionalism see William B. Skelton, "Professionalism in the U.S. Army Officer Corps during the Age of Jackson," *Armed Forces and Society* 1 (Summer 1975): 443–71; Russell F. Weigley, *History of the United States Army* (New York: Macmillan, 1967), 265–92; Clyde R. Simmons, "The Indian Wars and U.S. Military Thought, 1865–1890," *Parameters: Journal of the U.S. Army War College* 22 (Spring 1992): 60–72; Jerry M. Cooper, "The Army's Search for a Mission, 1865–1890," in *Against All Enemies: Interpretations of American Military History from Colonial Times to the Present*, ed. Kenneth J. Hagan and William R. Roberts (Westport, Conn.: Greenwood Press, 1986), 173–95; Allan R. Millett and Peter Maslowski, *For the Common Defense: A Military History of the United States of America* (New York: Free Press, 1984), 233–66.

11. For views on the U.S. Army's frontier strategy and tactical doctrine see Francis Paul Prucha, *The Sword of the Republic: The United States Army on the Frontier, 1783–1846* (New York: Macmillan, 1969; reprint, Bloomington: University of Indiana Press, 1977), 249–68, 352–64; Russell F. Weigley, *The American Way of War: A History of United States Military Strategy and Policy* (New York: Macmillan, 1973; reprint, Bloomington: Indiana University Press, 1977), 153–63; Robert M. Utley, *Frontiersmen in Blue: The United States Army and the Indian, 1848–1865* (New York: Macmillan, 1967; reprint, Lincoln: University of Nebraska Press, 1981), 18–90; Robert M. Utley, "The Frontier and the American Military Tradition," in *Soldiers West: Biographies from the Military Frontier*, ed. Paul Andrew Hutton (Lincoln: University of Nebraska Press, 1987), 1–10; Robert M. Utley, "A Chained Dog," *American West* 10 (July 1973): 18–24, 61; John M. Gates, "Indians and Insurrectos: The U.S. Army's Experience with Insurgency," *Parameters: Journal of the U.S. Army War College* 13 (March 1983): 59–68; Utley, *Frontier Regulars*, 45–59, 147–67; Coffman, *The Old Army*, 42–103, 215–87. For discussions on national policy and broad military policy toward the nineteenth-century American Indian see Robert Wooster,

The Military and United States Indian Policy, 1865–1903 (New Haven: Yale University Press, 1988), 1–12; Smith, *The View from Officers' Row*, 7–14, 182–85; Robert G. Athearn, *William Tecumseh Sherman and the Settlement of the West* (Norman: University of Oklahoma Press, 1956), 25, 31; Dan L. Thrapp, *The Conquest of Apacheria* (Norman: University of Oklahoma Press, 1967), 87–107; William B. Skelton, "Army Officers' Attitudes toward Indians, 1830–1860," *Pacific Northwest Quarterly* 67 (July 1976): 113–24.

12. Chief of Military History, *Infantry*, vol. 2 of *The Army Lineage Book*, 7 vols. (Washington, D.C.: GPO, 1953), 108–9; "Report of the Secretary of War, 10 Nov. 1876," 24–25; Regimental Returns, Sixteenth Infantry, January 1880–December 1889, microfilm no. 665, roll 176, Returns from Regular Army Infantry Regiments, June 1821–December 1916, Adjutant General's Records, NARS. (hereinafter cited as Regimental Returns, Sixteenth Infantry).

13. In comparing the troopers of 1876 to the soldiers Custer led in the Civil War Gregory J. W. Urwin writes "A large portion of the 7th Cavalry, on the other hand, were composed of poor white trash and semiliterate immigrants. They were on no great mission. They merely looked to the Army to provide them with a secure livelihood." From *Custer Victorious: The Civil War Battles of General George Armstrong Custer,* (reprint, Lincoln: University of Nebraska Press, 1990), 288. A profile of the typical soldier of the army of the mid-1870s is found in Coffman, *The Old Army*, 330–32 and Rickey, *Forty Miles a Day on Beans and Hay*, 17–32. The generalization about the army of the mid-1970s is from the author's personal observation in the ranks.

CHAPTER ONE: *Enlisting in the Infantry*

1. Bode joined the Sixteenth Infantry Regiment, which had 368 present for duty of its authorized enlisted total of 375. He was assigned to Company D, which was nearly at full strength, with 36 of its authorized 37 enlisted men. During Reconstruction duties through 1876 the Sixteenth Infantry had been scattered in company garrisons in Alabama, Arkansas, and Louisiana. In November 1876, three months before Bode joined, the regiment, minus one company, assembled in New Orleans with the Third Infantry to prevent political violence during the contested vote count in the presidential contest between Samuel J. Tilden and Rutherford B. Hayes. The Sixteenth took up station at Jackson Barracks, three miles south of New Orleans. "Report of the Secretary of War, 19 Nov. 1877," and "Report of Brigadier General C. C. Augur, Headquarters Department of the Gulf, 12 Oct. 1877," *House Exec. Doc.*, 45th Cong., 2d sess., no. 1, pt. 2, Serial 1794, 24, 40, 47, 99–100; Joseph G. Dawson III, *Army Generals and*

Reconstruction: Louisiana, 1862–1877 (Baton Rouge: Louisiana State University Press, 1982), 224–34.

2. In 1877 Congress required a five-year enlistment for soldiers, compared with twelve years in the British Army. The minimum height for an infantry recruit was five feet, four inches. Minors of sixteen years could enlist, with parental consent, as musicians. One-half of the recruits of this period were foreign born, with Irish and Germans predominating. The majority of recruits joined, as did Bode, because they were unemployed. Most were from the unskilled labor class or the lower economic strata. A medical officer performed a required physical examination to look for grounds for rejection, such as disease or alcoholism. As a part of a reform movement to improve the quality of the ranks, beginning in 1874 the recruit's application and medical results were forwarded to the Adjutant General's Office for a data search to determine if he had been previously discharged for bad character or was a deserter. The waiting period for the return of final confirmation gave the company leadership a chance to observe the behavior of the new soldier and look for further grounds for rejection. Bode joined just before all recruiting for general and mounted service halted on 9 May 1877 because of the lack of appropriated funds, leaving the army short 2,692 of its authorized 27,442. "Adjutant General's Report of the Recruiting Service for the Year Ending October 1, 1877," *House Exec. Doc.*, 45th Cong., 2d sess., no. 1, pt. 2, Serial 1794, 44–46; Coffman, *The Old Army*, 330–32; Rickey, *Forty Miles a Day on Beans and Hay*, 17–32.

3. In 1877 a ration by regulation was worth about twenty cents per day and consisted of 20 oz. salt beef, fresh beef, or mutton; 12 oz. pork or bacon; 18 oz. flour or soft bread, or 16 oz. hard bread, or 20 oz. cornmeal. Additions per man for each one hundred rations included 2.4 oz. peas or beans, 1.6 oz. rice or hominy, 2.4 oz. sugar, .6 oz. salt, 1.2 oz. roasted coffee or .2 oz tea. The flour was exchanged for an equal weight of bread at the company or post bakery. Each one hundred rations also included 1 gallon of vinegar, 1.1 lbs. of candles, 4 lbs. of Babbitt's soap, and 4 oz. of pepper. In 1879 the salt beef ration increased to 22 oz. and the per–one hundred issue of tea to 2 lbs, and of salt to 4 lbs. The ration was barely adequate to maintain health under difficult labor. The soldiers supplemented their diet with vegetables and fruits when available through the company garden or a personal purchase. Wild game gained through hunting was also important; it was a skill at which Bode excelled. "Report of the Commissary-General of Subsistence, 10 Oct. 1881," *House Exec. Doc.*, 47th Cong., 1st sess., no. 1, pt. 2, Serial 2010, 484–85, 515; Coffman, *The Old Army*, 340; Rickey, *Forty Miles a Day on Beans and Hay*, 39. Utley, *Frontier Regulars*, 88–89.

4. A private of this period earned thirteen dollars per month, with longevity pay of one dollar per month for each year of service after the

third year. A private in his fifth year of service earned sixteen dollars per month, less the three dollars' time in service pay that was held to discourage desertion until his honorable discharge. A corporal earned fifteen dollars per month base pay, a sergeant seventeen dollars. Rickey, *Forty Miles a Day on Beans and Hay*, 21; Coffman, *The Old Army*, 346–47; Utley, *Frontier Regulars*, 23.

5. In the summer of 1877 the majority of troops in Louisiana were ordered to Northern and Midwestern cities to put down labor strikes or, like Bode's regiment, sent to the frontier. The Sixteenth Infantry was ordered to take up stations in Kansas and the Indian Territory. This movement effectively ended Reconstruction occupation in the South. The notion that the Compromise of 1877 was a direct trade – that the Democrats would ratify the disputed electoral vote count to Republican candidate Rutherford B. Hayes in exchange for withdrawal of troops in Reconstruction duties in the South and other concessions – is a historical generalization. But as historian Clarence E. Clendenen has pointed out, only 12 percent of the army was in the South; the majority had long since departed for the practical necessities of dealing with labor strikes and Indian uprisings. Clendenen, "President Hayes' 'Withdrawal' of the Troops: An Enduring Myth," *South Carolina Historical Magazine* 70 (Oct. 1969): 240–50; Dawson, *Army Generals and Reconstruction*, 261–62.

CHAPTER TWO: *En Route to Fort Sill*

1. Jefferson Barracks, Missouri, on the west bank of the Mississippi a few miles below St. Louis. Founded in 1826 it served as an ordnance depot from 1871 to 1878. Bode was there in 1877. In the period 1878–94 Jefferson Barracks became a cavalry training post. It was last used by the regular army in 1946 and was afterward turned over to the Missouri National Guard. National Park Service, *Soldier and Brave: Historic Places Associated with Indian Affairs and the Indian Wars in the Trans-Mississippi West*, The National Survey of Historic Sites and Buildings, vol. 12, Robert G. Ferris, ed. (Washington, D.C.: United States Department of the Interior, National Park Service, 1971), 177–80.

2. "Cincinnati chicken" was soldier slang for a piece of salt-preserved pork ration. Rickey, *Forty Miles a Day on Beans and Hay*, 266.

3. Fort Gibson, Oklahoma. Bode's company transfered there in 1880.

4. Caddo, Bryan County, Oklahoma, then a small town on the Choctaw reservation, was a stop for the Missouri, Kansas, and Texas Railroad, 120 miles southeast of Fort Sill, 153 miles by way of the old military road of this period. The Missouri, Kansas, and Texas Railroad was, like most of the western lines, a land-grant railroad, required to transport government troops and equipment free of charge. "Report of the Quartermaster General,

1 Nov. 1881," *House Exec. Doc.,* 47th Cong., 1st sess., no. 1., pt. 2, Serial 2010, 359.

5. The Union Agency managing the Cherokee, Creek, Choctaw, Chickasaw, and Seminole statistics reported these tribes had about 168,000 head of cattle in 1877. In addition to the Indians' herds grazing these lands, white cattlemen routinely allowed their herds to graze freely on Indian lands, especially when northbound across the Territory on one of the large cattle trails. In 1877 the commissioner of Indian Affairs set a penalty of one dollar per head for those cattle grazing away from the main trails. In the late 1880s a lease, or "grass-money" system, was eventually established to allow the legal grazing as a source of cash for the tribes. "Report of the Commissioner of Indian Affairs, 1 Nov. 1877," *House Exec. Doc.,* 45th Cong., 2d sess., no. 1, pt. 5, Serial 1800, 704–7; Ernest Wallace, "The Comanches on the White Man's Road," *West Texas Historical Association Yearbook* 29 (Oct 1953): 3–32.

6. Crossing the Big Blue River, about twenty-two miles northwest of Caddo. Bode's Journal, page 64, Western box 2, W2, Special Collections of the Sterling C. Evans Library, Texas A&M University, College Station, Texas (hereinafter cited as Bode's Journal).

7. Harris' camp, recorded in Bode's Journal, page 65, as being twenty-seven miles west of the Big Blue River. Cyrus Harris was the Chickasaw governor in the periods 1856–58, 1860–62, 1866–70, 1872–74. B. F. Overton served as tribal governor from 1874 to 1878 at the time of Bode's assignment to Fort Sill. Arrell M. Gibson, *The Chickasaws* (Norman: University of Oklahoma Press, 1971), 265–66.

8. The Texas-Kansas Cattle Trail or the Chisholm Trail of 1867, near Rush Springs, Grady County.

9. Signal Mountain, on the present Fort Sill Reserve. The army built the blockhouse in 1871 to serve as a signal and heliograph station, as well as a weather observation point. Gillett Griswold, "Old Fort Sill: The First Seven Years," *Chronicles of Oklahoma* 36 (Spring 1958): 2–14.

10. The highest peak of the Wichita Mountains is 2,479 feet above sea level.

11. Founded by Major General William B. Hazen, the Kiowa-Comanche Indian Agency originally began near Medicine Bluff at Fort Sill, established in conjunction with the post in 1869. The first agent was Lawrie Tatum, a Quaker who resigned in March 1873 after President Grant's Quaker Peace Policy failed. The agent in 1877, at the time of Bode's arrival, was another Quaker, J. M. Haworth. The reservation encompassed 2,968,893 acres and contained 1,090 Kiowas, 1,545 Comanches (Komantsus), 343 Kiowa-Apaches, and a few Delawares. In 1877 the Indians had 4,194 horses and 1,343 head of cattle. In 1878 the Agency was consolidated with the Wichita Agency, thirty-five miles north of Fort Sill at Anadarko, but the Indians were reluctant to move and remained at Fort Sill more than seven

years after the consolidation. The army officers at Fort Sill were equally
reluctant to force them, believing the local stock-raising conditions and
grass were better than in the valley of the Wichita, and also being concerned
that the Indians would be cheated by white contractors if transactions were
not monitored by the soldiers. "Report of the Commissioner of Indian
Affairs, 1 Nov. 1877," 664, 689, 705; William T. Hagan, *United States–
Comanche Relations: The Reservation Years,* (New Haven: Yale University
Press, 1976), 135–40; National Park Service, *Soldier and Brave,* 251, 268.

12. Bode arrived at Fort Sill 29 June 1877. Bode's revised manuscript,
15, typescript, 348, Western box 2, W2, Special Collections of the Sterling
C. Evans Library, Texas A&M University, College Station, Texas (hereinafter
cited as Bode's revised manuscript and typescript); Post Returns, Fort Sill,
Oklahoma, June 1877, microfilm no. 617, roll 1174, Adjutant General's
Records, NARS (hereinafter cited as Post Returns, Fort Sill, Adjutant
General's Records); Post Returns, Fort Sill, Oklahoma, March 1869–January
1917, Fort Sill Archives microfilm number NAS-E88-Roll 1.

CHAPTER THREE: *Fort Sill*

1. Fort Sill, Comanche County, Oklahoma. On a site selected by Colonel
Benjamin H. Grierson, Tenth Cavalry, Major General Phil Sheridan established Camp Wichita, which was briefly known as Camp Sheridan but
later came to be called Fort Sill, in January 1869 to supervise the newly
created Kiowa-Comanche Reservation, to protect the exposed northern flank
of the Texas frontier, and to serve as a base of operations for future
campaigns by Custer's Seventh Cavalry and Grierson's Tenth. Sheridan
named the post for Brigadier General Joshua Sill, one of his brigade
commanders killed at Stones River in the Civil War. One of the most
important forts of the post–Civil War frontier, Fort Sill was home to the
Fourth Cavalry when Company B, and Bode's Company D of the Sixteenth
Infantry arrived 29 June 1877. The post garrison, commanded during that
period by Colonel Ranald S. Mackenzie, consisted of the headquarters and
Companies A, C, D, K, L, and M of the Fourth Cavalry, and Companies B
and D of the Sixteenth Infantry, a total of 22 officers and 536 enlisted
men present for duty. Except for the wooden infantry barracks mentioned
by Bode most of the post buildings were of cut limestone, quarried and
constructed by the soldiers of the Tenth Cavalry and Sixth Infantry in
1871. In 1905 the army expanded Fort Sill into an artillery command and
training center, a mission it retains at the present. Post Returns, June 1877,
Fort Sill, Adjutant General's Records "Report of the Secretary of War, 19
Nov. 1877," 17–18, 31; National Park Service, *Soldier and Brave,* 268–72;
Captain Wilber S. Nye, *Carbine and Lance: The Story of Old Fort Sill*
(Norman: University of Oklahoma Press, 1937); Griswold, "Old Fort Sill:

The First Seven Years," 2–14; Paul Andrew Hutton, *Phil Sheridan and His Army* (Lincoln: University of Nebraska Press, 1985), 91, 100–101.

2. The image of contractor fraud and corruption in the quartermaster department has become almost a historical generalization for the frontier era. Historian Darlis A. Miller, in her study of the military economics of the Department of New Mexico in the post–Civil War years, found that a detailed examination does not support this negative generalization. "Fraud was not rampant," she writes. "A dishonest contractor was the exception rather than the rule." During this same period actual cases of corruption by quartermaster officers did occur but were relatively few in number. Most of the inefficiency in the post quartermaster departments was the result of the high turnover and inexperience of the young officers detailed to the temporary duty. Miller, *Soldiers and Settlers: Military Supply in the Southwest, 1861–1885* (Albuquerque: University of New Mexico Press, 1989), 331–55.

3. Bode lined through Theaker's name, Bode's revised manuscript, 40, typescript, 383. Hugh Albert Theaker, from Ohio, was commissioned as a regular first lieutenant in the Sixteenth Infantry, 14 May 1861, and received a brevet at the battle of Missionary Ridge. Theaker spent most of his career in the Sixteenth Infantry, serving as colonel of the regiment from 1896 to 1898. Francis B. Heitman, *Historical Register and Dictionary of the United States Army*, 2 vols. (Washington, D.C.: GPO, 1903), 1:952.

4. Lieutenant Henry O. Flipper, born in Georgia in 1856, was the first black graduate of the United States Military Academy (June 1877). He was assigned to Company A, Tenth Cavalry, which transferred to Fort Sill while Flipper was en route. He joined his company at Fort Sill on 1 January 1878. Flipper boarded with his company commander, Captain Nicholas Nolan, an Irishman and former Second Dragoon ranker commissioned in the Civil War. Flipper became friends with Mrs. Nolan and with her unmarried Irish sister, Mollie Dwyer. In November 1880 Flipper and his company were transferred to Fort Davis, Texas, where he participated in the Victorio Campaign. Bode's Company D, Sixteenth Infantry, arrived there in January 1881, so Bode would have witnessed or had direct knowledge of the controversy that followed.

At Fort Davis Lieutenant Flipper, as is usually the lot of very junior officers, was appointed acting assistant quartermaster and acting commissary officer, both assignments requiring the handling of considerable funds. Colonel William R. Shafter, former commander of the black Twenty-fourth Infantry, took over as post commander in March 1881. In the process of a self-audit Flipper discovered a shortage of $1,440 in commissary funds. Although he and his friends subsequently made good the missing money he had lied to Colonel Shafter about the status of his accounts and had written a personal check to cover the deficit, a check that had no bank account to make it good. In August 1881 Shafter arrested Flipper for embezzlement and for conduct unbecoming of an officer and gentleman. Against all custom and tradition Shafter had the officer placed in the guardhouse. In December 1881 the court-martial ruled that Flipper did not intentionally defraud the government, but did lie to his commanding officer and was therefore guilty of conduct unbecoming. Flipper's regimental commander, Colonel Benjamin H. Grierson, stood by the young officer with letters of character testimony, but President Chester A. Arthur confirmed the verdict and sentence. Flipper was dismissed from the service 30 June 1882. He went on to become a talented civil and mining engineer, dying in 1940 at the age of eighty-four. Three decades after his death Flipper received a posthumous honorable discharge after a 1976 review of his case. Henry O. Flipper, *Negro Frontiersman: The Frontier Memoirs of Henry O. Flipper, First Negro Graduate of West Point,* Theodore Harris, ed. (El Paso: Texas Western College Press, 1963); Bruce J. Dinges, "The Court-Martial of Lieutenant Henry O. Flipper: An Example of Black-White Relations in the Army, 1881," *American West* 9 (Jan. 1972): 12–15; Donald R. McClung, "Second Lieutenant Henry O. Flipper: A Negro Officer on the West Texas Frontier," *West Texas Historical Association Year Book* 48 (1971): 20–31.

5. Bode's statement on Shafter was lined through, probably because Shafter was still alive when Bode wrote his memoirs. This statement was inserted from its original position on page 39 of the revised manuscript, or page 381–82 of the typescript. Bode was at Fort Davis while Shafter was in command in 1881. Born in Michigan in 1835, Shafter began his army career during the Civil War as a volunteer first lieutenant in the Seventh Michigan Infantry. He was wounded at Seven Pines in 1862, for which he was later awarded the Medal of Honor, and by 1864 had advanced to full colonel of the Seventeenth U.S. Colored Infantry, and was breveted volunteer brigadier general in 1865. In the post–Civil War years Shafter served as a regular with black regiments, leading the Forty-first and Twenty-fourth Infantries on the Texas frontier and was eventually promoted full colonel of the First Infantry. Shafter obtained the rank of volunteer major general in the Spanish-American War and was highly criticized for his command of the campaign to capture Santiago, Cuba. He died in Bakersfield, California, 13 November, 1906. Paul H. Carlson, *"Pecos Bill": A Military Biography of William R. Shafter* (College Station: Texas A&M University Press, 1989). Roger J. Spiller and Joseph G. Dawson III, eds., *American Military Leaders* (New York: Praeger, 1989), 278–80.

6. On page 39 of Bode's revised manuscript this paragraph was written as an insertion and began with "Lut. Col. Davidson (Bvt. Brgd. Genneral) of the 10th Cavly. a gentleman under the strict leadership of his wife . . ." Davidson's name was lined through and a sentence beginning "Commanding Officers were at times . . . " put below in its place. Lieutenant Colonel John W. Davidson, Tenth Cavalry, replaced Colonel R. S. Mackenzie

as post commander in early 1878 while Bode was present. Davidson, a Virginian born in 1823, graduated from West Point in the class of 1845 and was commissioned in the First Dragoons. He served in the Mexican War and was wounded in the Indian Wars in 1854. At the start of the Civil War he was a major of the Second Cavalry and advanced by brevets for valor to volunteer major general at the end of the war, earning the regular lieutenant colonelcy of the Tenth Cavalry in 1866. He was promoted to colonel of the Second Cavalry in 1879 and died 26 June 1881 in Minnesota, only a few years after he left Fort Sill.

Bode's comments about opium are not surprising. Opium pills were a ubiquitous cure-all for wounds, diarrhea, and dysentery, and were often issued in conjunction with quinine for malaria, a disease common at Fort Sill. Many soldiers, especially older veterans with wounds or chronic disorders, became opium addicts, victims of "the army disease." During the Civil War the Union Army issued nearly ten million opium pills and over two million ounces of various opium preparations. David T. Courtwright, "Opiate Addiction as a Consequence of the Civil War," *Civil War History* 24 (June 1978): 101–11. On Davidson's biography see Homer K. Davidson, *Black Jack Davidson: A Cavalry Commander on the Western Frontier* (Glendale, Calif.: Clark, 1974); Heitman, *Historical Register*, 1:355–56; *Register of Graduates and Former Cadets, 1802–1964, of the United States Military Academy* (West Point, N.Y.: West Point Alumni Foundation, 1964), 232.

7. Colonel Ranald S. Mackenzie, nicknamed "Bad Hand" by Southern Plains Indians, commanded Fort Sill on and off in the period 1875–77. He not only was a fiercely tenacious campaigner but proved also to be stubbornly committed to fair treatment for the Indians and soldiers placed in his charge. He appears to have been universally popular with his soldiers and with most of his officers. Born in New York City, 27 July 1840, Mackenzie graduated first in his West Point class and was commissioned as an engineer in 1862. He distinguished himself in important Civil War battles such as Second Manassas, Fredericksburg, Chancellorsville, Gettysburg, Cedar Creek, and Petersburg. Mackenzie emerged from the Civil War as one of the boy generals, a twenty-five-year-old volunteer major general. Earning a regular colonelcy of the Fourth Cavalry Mackenzie served for two decades as one of the master tacticians on the frontier, leading his soldiers in the few decisive battles of the era such as the one at Palo Duro Canyon, Texas, in 1874. Mackenzie received a promotion to brigadier general in 1882. While in command of the Department of Texas he suddenly developed a problem with alcohol and was, in 1884, committed to Bloomingdale Asylum in New York City. He died, insane, in 1889. Jean L. Zimmerman, "Colonel Ranald S. Mackenzie at Fort Sill," *Chronicles of Oklahoma* 44 (Spring 1966): 12–21; Ernest Wallace, *Ranald S. MacKenzie on the Texas Frontier* (Lubbock: West Texas Museum Association, 1965).

8. In 1880 Bode served in New Mexico in Colonel Hatch's district. In

the original manuscript Bode drew an "X" across this entire passage, revised manuscript, 38, typescript, 381. Colonel Edward Hatch, Ninth Cavalry, was born in Maryland and commissioned a volunteer captain in the Second Iowa Cavalry in August 1861. Hatch rose to volunteer major general by the end of the Civil War, serving most of the conflict in the Western Theater. Hatch received brevets at the battles of Franklin, Tennessee, and Nashville. In 1866 he took a regular commission as colonel of the newly formed black Ninth Cavalry, performing long and creditable service on the frontier. In spite of Bode's statement that the colonel was tied to his headquarters, Hatch took to the field and personally lead one of his columns during the Victorio Campaign of 1880. He died 11 April 1889. Heitman, *Historical Register*, 1:510.

9. Bode left Buell's name in the revision, perhaps because he knew Buell had died in 1883. Bode served in one of Buell's New Mexico base camps for the Victorio Campaign in 1880. At the beginning of the Civil War George P. Buell was commissioned as a lieutenant colonel from his native Indiana in the Fifty-eighth Indiana Infantry, being promoted by the end of the war to brevet volunteer brigadier for gallantry at Missionary Ridge. He received the regular lieutenant colonelcy of the Twenty-ninth Infantry in 1866, transferred to the Eleventh Infantry in 1869, and became regimental commander of the Fifteenth Infantry in March 1879. He died 31 May 1883. Colonel Martin L. Crimmins, "Colonel Buell's Expedition into Mexico in 1880," *New Mexico Historical Review* 10 (April 1935): 133–42; Heitman, *Historical Register*, 1:260.

10. Colonel Galusha Pennypacker, Sixteenth Infantry, was Bode's own regimental commander. Born in Pennsylvania, Pennypacker began the Civil War as a volunteer quartermaster sergeant in the Ninth Pennsylvania Infantry, became a major of that regiment in August 1861, and finished the war a volunteer major general. Pennypacker received a brevet volunteer brigadier rank and, in 1891, was awarded the Medal of Honor for his leadership in the capture of Fort Fisher, North Carolina, a battle in which he was badly wounded. In 1866 Pennypacker earned the colonelcy of the Thirty-fourth Infantry, transfering to the Sixteenth Infantry in 1869. He retired in July 1883. Heitman, *Historical Register*, 1:783.

11. Colonel Benjamin H. Grierson, Tenth Cavalry, 1826–1911. Bode lined out this comment, revised manuscript, 39, typescript, 382. Bode served with Grierson at Fort Davis, Texas, in 1881. In 1863, Grierson led the famed "Grierson's Raid" of Union cavalry through Mississippi, emerging from the war a brevet regular major general. He was a clever and resourceful frontier commander who served for many years in the Southwest and successfully used a web of small patrols rather than large-scale columns in the Apache campaigns of the 1880s in the trans-Pecos of Texas. William H. Leckie and Shirley A. Leckie, *Unlikely Warriors: General Benjamin H. Grierson and His Family* (Norman: University of Oklahoma Press, 1984).

12. Lieutenant Colonel James Van Voast, Sixteenth Infantry, Bode calls by the name of "Van Horn Vost." The passage is lined out on page 39 of the revised manuscript (typescript, 382). From New York, Van Voast graduated from West Point in 1848, served in the Third Artillery, Ninth Infantry, and during the Civil War in California with a slot as major of the Eighteenth Infantry. For a short period in 1882 he was colonel of the Ninth Infantry. He retired in 1883 and died in Ohio, 16 July 1915. *Register of Graduates,* 240.

13. Major George W. Schofield, Tenth Cavalry, committed suicide 17 December 1882, before Bode wrote his memoirs; therefore Bode leaves the name in the passage. From New York, Schofield received a volunteer commission as a lieutenant in the First Missouri Artillery in October of 1861 and was a volunteer brevet brigadier by 1865. Schofield's promotions and brevets came from the Western Theater in the Battle of Champion's Hill, the siege of Vicksburg, and the Georgia Campaign. He took a regular major commission in the black Forty-first Infantry in 1866 and moved to the Tenth Cavalry in 1870, earning the lieutenant colonelcy of the Sixth Cavalry in 1881. He died 17 December 1882. Schofield perfected the automatic ejector on the .45-caliber Smith and Wesson pistol used on the frontier. Heitman, *Historical Register,* 1:865; Utley, *Frontier Regulars,* 73.

14. By regulations established in 1835 the profit from the sale of surplus flour, plus a tax on the post trader, went into the "post fund" to pay for the bakery, garden seeds, utensils, schools, library, gym, printing press, and other benefits. After 1841 cash profits from the sale of surplus rations except flour, i.e. primarily bacon, coffee, and sugar, went into the "company fund" for the exclusive benefit of the enlisted men. Although most of the company funds were spent on additional types of food, a portion went toward the purchase of a wide variety of group items to serve the majority of the company. These included utensils for the mess, sports equipment, books, clocks, coffee mills, dominoes, fishing gear, stationery, and on occasion, beer and cigars. Because the rations were cut to turn a profit many frontier officers complained that this practice left their men underfed. Ironically one commander in 1880 complained that the soldiers of the Plains expeditions had depended on buffalo to supplement the ration and were going hungry in the field because of the extermination of the herds. "Report of the Commissary-General of Subsistence, 10 Oct. 1881," 484–515.

15. Bode was detailed as a hospital attendant on 7 September 1877 and relieved of that duty because of illness on 9 October. Special Orders No. 170, 7 Sept. 1877, and Special Orders No. 200, 9 Oct. 1877, from Special Orders, Headquarters, Fort Sill, vol. 1, no. XD6213763, Fort Sill Archives (hereinafter cited as Special Orders, Fort Sill Archives).

Cooks were normally detailed for ten days at a time. Extra pay was given if a soldier had to perform an extra duty for more than ten days of the month. Laborers, assistant cooks, teamsters, and clerks received twenty cents per day, raised to thirty-five cents in 1884. Skilled laborers, mechanics, and schoolteachers received thirty-five cents, increased to fifty cents per day in 1884. Coffman, *The Old Army*, 347; Utley, *Frontier Regulars*, 88.

16. In 1877 the post surgeon reported that malaria and chronic diarrhea were the major health problems at Fort Sill. In 1878 Dr. J. W. Smith, the agency doctor, reported the prevalence of malaria among the Comanche and Kiowa tribes camped at Fort Sill. The soldiers of Fort Sill ate quinine pills every morning for breakfast. Record of Medical History of Fort Sill, I.T., Feb. 1873–May 1880, no. D62.137.140, Fort Sill Archives (hereinafter cited as Medical History of Fort Sill); Bernice Norman Crockett, "Health Conditions in the Indian Territory, from the Civil War to 1890," *Chronicles of Oklahoma* 36 (Spring 1958): 21–39; Robert G. Carter, *On the Border with Mackenzie; or, Winning West Texas from the Comanches* (Washington, D.C.: Eynon, 1935; reprint, New York, Antiquarian Press, 1961), 258.

17. In August 1876 Congress directed the secretary of interior to issue rations for only one week at a time to the Southern Plains Indians on the reservations, and only to those who were actually present. This was to prevent them from acquiring enough surplus to mount raiding expeditions using, as the army often claimed, the reservation as a sanctuary and base of supplies for their forays. "Report of the Commissioner of Indian Affairs, 1 Nov. 1877," 622–23.

18. For purposes of sanitation the army authorized one laundress per seventeen soldiers, or four per company, a practice begun as early as 1786 and written into the regulations of 1802. Many of these laundresses were the wives of soldiers but others were single and sometimes the source of trouble at a post. The laundress received an army ration per day, quarters, bedding straw, and a set price per soldier as payment for her cleaning. An army general order of 1876 and congressional legislation of 1878 prohibited the enrollment and further use of laundresses but allowed those in current positions to continue. The regulations of 1883 removed the authority to issue rations to the laundresses. See the third chapter of Patricia Y. Stallard, *Glittering Misery: Dependents of the Indian Fighting Army* (Fort Collins, Colo.: Old Army Press, 1978), 53–73; Miller J. Stewart, "Army Laundresses: Ladies of 'Soap Suds Row,'" *Nebraska History* 61 (Winter 1980): 421–36; Robert Wooster, *Soldiers, Sutlers, and Settlers: Garrison Life on the Texas Frontier* (College Station: Texas A&M University Press, 1987), 64–68; Coffman, *The Old Army*, 24–25, 112–15, 308.

CHAPTER FOUR: *Indians and Indian Territory*

1. Bode went to cook for the camp guard.

2. In 1876 forty-eight Quahada Comanches broke away from the reservation. They were captured and imprisoned until 1 August 1877, when they

were turned over to the Kiowa and Comanche agent, J. M. Haworth. With the help of the military he opened for them a farm four miles from Fort Sill, building on it two houses. Haworth optimistically reported, "The decision of the Department to build them houses has been very gratifying to the Indians," but he does not confirm Bode's observation that they used the houses for their horses. "Report of the Commissioner of Indian Affairs, 1 Nov. 1877," 485; "Report of the Commissioner of Indian Affairs, 1 Nov. 1878," *House Exec. Doc.*, 45th Cong., 3rd sess., no. 1, pt. 5, Serial 1850, 555.

3. Indian agent P. B. Hunt reports a slightly different version of this story. He had relieved the Agent Haworth in April 1878 and therefore relates some of the details second-hand. After returning from three years' confinement at Fort Marion, Florida, for participating in the breakout of 1874, one of the Comanche warriors, in early 1878, entered the tent of the farm guard and attempted to assassinate one of the soldiers. Agent Hunt gives no apparent reason, although Bode states that the soldier had been sleeping with one or more of the Indian's wives. Hunt reported that the man escaped. On 26 July 1878 a deputy United States marshal arrived with an arrest warrant from the closest federal court at Fort Smith, Arkansas. The warrant was for the Comanche and two "accessories," not for a witness, as Bode writes. The principal Indian defendant was at that time already in the guardhouse, having been arrested and brought in by Quanah Parker.

The post adjutant, interpreter, and marshal rode out to the Indian farm to arrest the two "accessories." The small infantry guard at the farm went under arms to help. The two Indians at first appeared ready to submit but were encouraged to resist by an unnamed medicine man. An army officer ordered a large negro teamster to seize and hold the medicine man. When he attempted to do so the three Indians attacked the soldiers with knives. The marshal and soldiers immediately opened fire, killing two Indians and wounding the medicine man. The feared outbreak of violence over this incident did not materialize, according to Agent Hunt, because the Comanches "to a certain extent, recognize[d] the supremacy of the law." "Report of the Commissioner of Indian Affairs, 1 Nov. 1878," 555.

4. Bode spells the name "Tassitovey" in the revised version (typescript, 427).

5. In her study of army perceptions of Indians, Sherry L. Smith finds that soldiers' descriptions of Indian women of the nineteenth century generally fall into two stereotypes, the "Indian princess" view and the "dirty squaw" perception, both of which are displayed by Bode in this and other passages. Bode's observations are also interesting in light of new studies that suggest that historical generalities about the status of Plains Indian women is an image based more on projections of Anglo-Western values than on their actual and relative situation. Some current studies have suggested that the woman's role in Plains Indian society should be reconstructed to present these women as occupying a more powerful and

vital role than in past stereotypes. Sherry L. Smith, *The View from Officer's Row*, 55–91; Patricia Albers and Beatrice Medicine, *The Hidden Half: Studies of Plains Indian Women* (Washington, D.C.: University Press of America, 1983).

Some of the details on Comanche dress and of the role of women are included from Bode's Journal, 89–97, and typescript, 45–49.

6. Eveline Alexander, the wife of a Third Cavalry officer, also reported the use of canvas tepees by the Ute Indians in New Mexico in 1866. See Sandra L. Myres, ed., *Cavalry Wife: The Diary of Eveline M. Alexander, 1866–1867* (College Station: Texas A&M University Press, 1977), 98.

7. Woman's Heart was a Kiowa leader, not a Comanche as Bode indicates. "Report of the Commissioner of Indian Affairs, 1 Nov. 1875," *House Exec. Doc.*, 44th Cong., 1st sess., no. 1, pt. 5, Serial 1680, 775; Martin F. Schmitt and Dee Brown, *Fighting Indians of the West* (New York: Bonanza Books, 1968), 67.

8. Indian Agent Haworth complained in 1875 that the federal court was too far away to serve justice. "One of our greatest difficulties . . . is the great distance and expense in going to Fort Smith; it is a financial sacrifice to almost anyone to go, hence parties who might give valuable evidence conceal their knowledge." "Report of the Commissioner of Indian Affairs, 1 Nov. 1875," 776.

In May 1878 Congress passed the provision authorizing the organization of a total force of fifty officers and 430 privates as Indian police at the various agencies. The Indian police at the Kiowa and Comanche Reservation were organized in November 1878, with two officers and twenty-six men, primarily to deal with horse thieves and whiskey sellers. "Report of the Commissioner of Indian Affairs, 1 Nov. 1878," 471–72; Hagan, *United States–Comanche Relations*, 148–50.

9. Bode mentions part of this story about Major Schofield earlier in Chapter Three.

10. The "mill" was soldier slang for the guardhouse. See, for example, Hill and Innis, "Diary of Private Sanford," 2–40.

The "Bull Ring" was the generic place of punishment for soldiers. Carefully supervised by a sergeant, defaulters were put through grueling drills at the double-time. Rickey, *Forty Miles a Day on Beans and Hay*, 44.

11. Fort Leavenworth, Kansas, founded in 1827 on the Missouri River, was the headquarters for the Department of the Missouri. The military prison, called the U.S. Disciplinary Barracks, was established in 1874. National Park Service, *Soldier and Brave*, 145–48.

Typical of guardhouse prisoners while Bode was on guard were the nine present on 22 August 1879. Two were citizens confined "until further notice," the remainder were two Tenth Cavalry troopers and two Sixteenth Infantry soldiers serving sentences of one year, twenty days, or ten days. In addition three Tenth Cavalry troopers were awaiting courts-martial for theft. Guard Reports, Fort Sill, I.T., 3 July 1879–29 Nov. 1879, no. D62.137.20., Fort Sill Archives (hereafter cited as Guard Reports, Fort Sill).

12. General Winfield Scott established post libraries in the Army Regulations of 1821. The funds to support libraries were derived from a tax on the post sutler and augmented by donations from religious and education societies. Companies and regiments also maintained libraries, as did individual officers. These libraries held a wide range of material, from fiction, history, and even philosophy, to newspapers and religious tracts.

In 1838 Congress passed legislation creating the position of Army chaplain, stipulating that they perform extra duties as schoolmasters for extra pay and rations. Often chaplains were the mainstay of post education for soldiers, teaching in schools financed by the surplus of the post bakery and flour fund. In 1866 Congress approved legislation for soldier education, especially for new regiments of black troops. These schools were likewise often run by the regimental chaplains. Miller J. Stewart, "A Touch of Civilization: Culture and Education in the Frontier Army," *Nebraska History* 65 (Summer 1984): 257–82.

13. The authorized strength for an infantry company of 1877 was 37 enlisted men. Seven regiments of cavalry were authorized 100 men per company and three regiments had 70 per company, more than twice the manpower of the infantry units. "Report of the Secretary of War, 19 Nov. 1877," 47.

14. In 1877 the post surgeon recorded that the soldier's rations were sufficient when supplemented by vegetables from the company gardens, indicating the garden program was successful at Fort Sill. Entry for 25 July 1877, Medical History of Fort Sill.

15. The guardhouse reports of 1877–79 are incomplete, but in the available records there is no indication of which Indian Bode could be describing. Guard Reports, Fort Sill.

16. The "Rattlesnake pilot" was probably some member of the Colubridae family of common snakes, such as the bull snake, and was unlikely to have been poisonous, as Bode states.

17. The shortage of frontier artillerymen required infantry to be detailed to artillery drill to learn the fundamentals of firing cannon. See for example the diary entry for 29 October 1876 in Hill and Innis, "Diary of Private Sanford," 27.

CHAPTER FIVE: *Frontier Duties in the Territory*

1. Colonel W. S. Nye, in his history of Fort Sill, states that the telegraph between Fort Sill and Fort Richardson, Texas, was established in June 1877, and the telegraph from Fort Sill to Fort Reno about 1877. Nye, *Carbine and Lance,* 366; Bode's original manuscript states that the construction of the

Fort Sill to Fort Reno telegraph was in June 1878. However, in June 1878, Bode, a sergeant, and another Sixteenth Infantry private were ordered to draw six days' rations and repair the Fort Sill to Fort Richardson telegraph as far as the Red River. Special Orders No. 129, 16 June 1878, Special Orders, Fort Sill Archives.

The Fort Sill to Fort Richardson telegraph was approved in 1874 and constructed in the summer of 1875 by a party under Captain W. C. Beach, Eleventh Infantry. One group worked from Fort Sill south, the other started north from Fort Richardson at Jacksboro, Texas. The parties met on the Red River, completing the line on 22 June 1875. Tuffly Ellis, ed., "Lieutenant A. W. Greely's Report on the Installation of Military Telegraph Lines in Texas, 1875–1876," *Southwestern Historical Quarterly* 69 (July 1965): 67–87.

On 5 August 1879 Lieutenant Lassiter, two noncommissioned officers and eight privates of Company K, and one noncommissioned officer and nine privates of Company D, Sixteenth Infantry, were ordered to draw fifteen days' rations and leave Fort Sill the following day to construct the Fort Sill to Fort Reno telegraph to the midway point between the two posts. However the Fort Sill Post Returns for August 1879 show that Lieutenant Evarts S. Ewing with ten men of Company K, ten of Company D, and five of Company B, Sixteenth Infantry, left the post on 10 August 1879 to build the telegraph line to Fort Reno. The construction party returned in September of 1879. Special Orders No. 163, 5 August 1879, Special Orders, Fort Sill Archives; Post Returns, Fort Sill Archives, August 1879.

A final piece of evidence that indicates Bode was mistaken and the Fort Sill to Fort Reno telegraph was constructed in 1879 is the report of the secretary of war for 1881. The chief signal officer reports that this telegraph line was established 31 August 1879. "Report of the Chief Signal Officer of the Army, 15 Nov. 1880," *House Exec. Doc.*, 46th Cong., 3rd sess., no. 1, pt. 2, Serial 1957, 106.

2. This is Cache Creek, north of Fort Sill, which runs south and intersects Medicine Creek near the post.

3. The William Penn Treaty with the Delawares was in 1642. Black Beaver, a Delaware chief, had a farm of three hundred acres and a considerable stock of hogs, cattle, and horses. He had been a trapper on the upper Missouri River for the American Fur Company, led an Indian company in a Texas volunteer regiment on the Texas frontier during the Mexican War, and served the Union during the Civil War. In 1849 he was a guide to Captain Randolph B. Marcy during his explorations of Texas. Marcy considered him a dependable friend and wrote of Black Beaver, "His life had been that of a veritable cosmopolite, filled with scenes of intense and startling interest, bold and reckless adventure." Marcy, *The Prairie Traveler* (New York: Harper & Brothers, 1859), 188–96; Thomas H. Kreneck, "The North Texas Regiment in the Mexican War," *Military*

History of Texas and the Southwest 12, no. 1 (1975): 109–17; "Report of the Commissioner of Indian Affairs, 1 Nov 1879," *House Exec. Doc.,* 46th Cong., 2d Sess., no. 1, pt. 5, Serial 1910, 169; Schmitt and Brown, *Fighting Indians of the West,* 75.

4. The Wichita (Anadarko) Agency was located in present Caddo County, Oklahoma. It was established in 1871 on the north bank of the Wichita River as an attachment to the Kiowa-Comanche Agency at Fort Sill and the two agencies were consolidated in 1878 and relocated on the south bank. Moved slightly west in 1895 the reservation became the center of the last great Oklahoma land rush when opened to settlement in 1901. National Park Service, *Soldier and Brave,* 251–52.

5. The Quaker agent Lawrie Tatum opened the Kiowa-Comanche Agency school in 1872 with a few students. Although Quaker missionaries continued to teach, by 1875 the boarding school ran on contract management and had twenty-seven students, both boys and girls, from the various tribes. Agent J. M. Haworth reported at that time that he had room for sixty scholars, optimistically adding, "We could have had more if we had the room for them." In 1879, of a school-aged Indian population of five hundred, only sixty-five, or 13 percent, of the Indian children were enrolled. The lack of sufficient funds and parental discouragement greatly inhibited the boarding school system but it did produce a few students who became articulate Indian spokesmen to the white community by the 1890s. "Report of the Commissioner of Indian Affairs, 1 Nov 1875," 775; Hagan, *United States–Comanche Relations,* 134–35.

6. Agent P. B. Hunt took over duties in April 1878, ending the era of Quaker control. Hunt, a former lieutenant colonel, had been badly wounded and crippled in the Civil War. He served as the Indian agent until 1885. Bode mentions meeting Hunt while going on the beef inspection trips. Company commanders at Fort Sill were routinely assigned the special duty of conducting a weekly beef inspection of the cattle that were bought on contract and given to the Indians as ration on the hoof. Bode accompanied his commander, Captain H. A. Theaker, to the Wichita Agency on several of these inspections. Theaker was seldom satisfied with the cattle. In March of 1878, for example, he reported the beef to be "in very poor condition and very much under weight." The contract specified the weight would be not less than 850 pounds per animal and he found them at 650 pounds. Captain H. A. Theaker, Sixteenth Infantry, "Report of Cattle Inspection," Wichita Agency, 24 March 1878, microcopy no. 234, roll 930, Letters Received by the Office of Indian Affairs, 1824–1880, RG75, NARS; Hagan, *United States–Comanche Relations,* 139, 164–65.

7. In 1878 a few Indians of the Indian Territory reservations were on the payroll as freighters and were paid the same rate as whites. At the Fort Sill Agency the Indians produced 140,000 board feet of lumber and 3,200 rods of fencing. In 1879 at Fort Sill and at the Wichita Agency

Indians received fifty wagons and transported much of their own supplies, in convoy, from the Caddo railhead. They used the opportunity to haul to Caddo their own goods and crops to barter and trade. In 1879 at the Cheyenne-Arapaho Agency the Indians hauled 451,000 pounds of freight at the rate of $1.50 per one hundred lbs. per 165 miles, and earned about $7,121 dollars making bricks, chopping wood, cutting hay, hauling wood, and splitting rails. "Report of the Commissioner of Indian Affairs, 1 Nov. 1879," 167, 172; "Report of the Commissioner of Indian Affairs, 1 Nov. 1878," 553, 796–97; Hagan, *United States–Comanche Relations,* 148.

8. The Wichita Agency school burned in 1877. "Report of the Commissioner of Indian Affairs, 1 Nov. 1879," 174.

9. Fort Reno activated in 1874 as a post south of the North Canadian River from the Cheyenne and Arapaho or Darlington Agency and remained an installation until 1949. In 1878 the garrison consisted of six companies of the Sixteenth Infantry and the Fourth and Tenth Cavalries under the command of Lieutenant Colonel J. W. Davidson. "Report of the Secretary of War, 19 Nov. 1878, *House Exec. Doc.,* 45th Cong., 3rd sess., no. 1, pt. 2, Serial 1843, 12; National Park Service, *Soldier and Brave,* 265–68.

10. The Cheyenne-Arapaho Reservation, on the north bank of the North Canadian River, began in 1869 under the Quaker agent Brinton Darlington. After the Cheyenne uprising of 1874, nearby Fort Reno was established. Dull Knife and more than nine hundred Cheyennes were brought to the reserve in 1877 after Custer's defeat at the Little Bighorn. Dull Knife and others broke out on 9 September 1878 but were captured and returned. In 1878 the four-million-acre reservation, under the agency of John D. Miles, held a population of 3,298 Cheyennes and 2,676 Arapahos. It opened to white settlement in 1889. "Report of the Commissioner of Indian Affairs, 1 Nov. 1878," 780; "Report of the Commissioner of Indian Affairs, 1 Nov. 1879," 164; National Park Service, *Soldier and Brave,* 266–68.

11. There is no mention of the incident of Big Bow's arrest in the Fort Sill post returns, the guard reports, or in the commissioner of Indian Affairs reports.

12. By "blue-beans" Bode means bullets. Grass fires on the prairie and in camp were a very real danger in this era, creating considerable anxiety among soldiers and travelers. In her classic memoir army wife Lydia Spencer Lane tells how all of her and her children's winter clothing and possessions were destroyed in a similar incident involving grass set ablaze by a cooking fire. Lane, *I Married a Soldier; or, Old Days in the Army* (Philadelphia: J. P. Lippincott Co., 1893; reprint, Albuquerque: University of New Mexico Press, 1987), 86, 120–22.

13. Bode was promoted to corporal in November 1879. Report for November 1879, Guard Reports, Fort Sill.

14. This new second lieutenant of D Company, Sixteenth Infantry, was

Walter A. Thurston. Born in Alabama, he graduated from the United States Military Academy and was commissioned in the regiment in June of 1879. Thurston remained a lieutenant for nearly twenty years and was finally promoted to captain in 1898. His career reflected the slow advancement of the "Old Army" after the Civil War. Thurston accepted a commission as a lieutenant colonel of volunteers in the Second Alabama Infantry during the Spanish-American War, serving in the Philippine Insurrection. He retired as a regular major in 1905 and died in 1911. *Register of Graduates,* 270; Heitman, *Historical Register,* 1:960.

15. The paymaster was Major William H. Johnston, stationed out of St. Louis, Missouri. From Ohio, Johnston served as a paymaster in the Civil War, was breveted a volunteer lieutenant colonel of the paymaster department, and obtained a regular commission as a major in 1866. Promoted to lieutenant colonel as a paymaster in 1884, he finally retired in 1888. Johnston died 6 May 1896. Post Returns, Fort Sill Archives, September 1879; "Report of the Secretary of War, 19 Nov. 1878," 59; Heitman, *Historical Register,* 1:579.

CHAPTER SIX: *Prairie Adventures*

1. By 1878 the heretofore reliable sources of game on the reservation had become scarce. The commissioner of Indian Affairs authorized Indian parties to leave the reservation to hunt for buffalo in the summer of 1878. In January 1879 Army cavalry escorts went with Indian hunting parties to the Texas Panhandle but met with little success, because the buffalo were nearly extinct in that area. The agency at Fort Sill had to send supplies for the relief of the hunting party. This was probably the supply train for which Bode was on escort duty, which would have occurred before, not after the paymaster escort duty of September 1879. Hagan, *United States–Comanche Relations,* 141.

2. Bode is mistaken in his generalization concerning Quanah Parker being the chief of the Comanche Indians. Quanah was one of the more famous because of his ability as a warrior and his unusual background in having a white mother, but in 1878 the young man had ninety-three Quahada Comanches in his ration band, making it only the third largest on the reservation. About twenty years old in 1875, Quanah was too young to assume a leadership role in the natural Comanche hierarchy, but became the chief of this reservation ration band through the orders of Colonel Ranald S. Mackenzie. Historian William T. Hagan writes that Quanah became influential among the Quahada because of his ability to deal with the white establishment, an eminence possibly resented by the older Comanche leaders. Hagan, *United States–Comanche Relations,* 154–57.

3. Established as a cavalry camp on Otter Creek for the Wichita expe-

dition in 1858, Camp Radziminski was active for only a year, occupying three different locations up and down the creek. The site was often used by passing patrols and expeditions after the Civil War. Robert W. Frazer, *Forts of the West* (Norman: University of Oklahoma Press, 1965), 122–23; Herbert M. Hart, *Tour Guide to Old Western Forts* (Fort Collins, Colo.: Old Army Press, 1980), 125.

4. Although Bode was often on telegraph repair detail, the only record of one in which he was the noncommissioned officer in charge was in January 1880, when he and three privates were ordered to repair the line between Fort Sill and the Red River. Special Orders No. 1, 2 Jan. 1880, Special Orders, Fort Sill Archives.

5. Bode is referring to the fact that these cowboys, probably Texans, since they were close to the border of that state, were illegally grazing their cattle on grass within the Indian Territory. Legally this grass belonged to the Comanches. This type of trespassing was common and a constant source of complaint by the Indians and agents. Bode, as a noncommissioned officer, should have chased away or arrested these trespassers. For a discussion of this issue see Hagan, *United States–Comanche Relations*, 150–51; Wallace, "The Comanches on the White Man's Road," 6–7.

6. Mount Sheridan, on the current Fort Sill military reservation, is about 2,450 feet high.

CHAPTER SEVEN: *Fort Gibson*

1. With families in tow, D Company, Sixteenth Infantry, departed Fort Sill for Fort Gibson on 28 February 1880 under telegraphic change of station orders from Headquarters, Department of the Missouri, dated 26 February 1880. Post Returns, Fort Sill Archives, February 1880.

2. In 1879 and 1880 the military departmental commander officially complained to the secretary of war about white encroachment and illegal settlement on Indian lands. Although he had made numerous arrests he did not have enough troops to completely stop the invasion of early "sooners," who were encouraged by the pending legislation that would open part of the Indian Territory to settlement a decade later. "Report of Brigadier General John Pope, Headquarters Department of the Missouri, 3 Oct. 1879," *House Exec. Doc.*, 46th Cong., 2d sess., no. 1, pt. 2, Serial 1903, 80–81; "Report of Brigadier General John Pope, Headquarters, Department of the Missouri, 22 September 1880," *House Exec. Doc.*, 46th Cong., 3rd sess., no. 1, pt. 2, Serial 1952, 89–91.

3. The spur at Gainesville, Texas, would link D Company with the Missouri, Kansas, and Texas Railroad to carry them to Fort Gibson.

4. Portions of this section describing Fort Gibson and the Cherokee

Indians are from Bode's Journal, pages 60–62. D Company, Sixteenth Infantry, arrived 6 March 1880 to become the garrison of Fort Gibson, replacing four companies of the Twenty-second Infantry. It remained a one-company post, with Bode's company commander, Captain Hugh A. Theaker, commanding the post until October 1880, when K Company, Nineteenth Infantry, and H Company, Twenty-third Infantry, arrived. The army established Fort Gibson in April 1824 during a time of conflict between the Osage and Cherokee Indians. It was constructed above a convenient rock ledge, used as a boat landing, on the Grand River, three miles up from the three forks of the Grand, Verdigris, and Arkansas rivers. As the the upper terminal of river navigation it became an important depot and staging area for antebellum military and survey expeditions to the Southern Plains. Later moved to a nearby hill site and abandoned by the Army in 1857, the stockaded post served the Confederacy before being reoccupied as a Union stronghold in the Civil War, remaining on active service until 1890. Post Returns, Fort Gibson, March 1880, in Post Returns, Fort Gibson, Oklahoma, July 1872–October 1897, microfilm no. 617, roll 406, Returns from United States Military Posts, 1800-1916, Adjutant General's Records, NARS (hereinafter cited as Post Returns, Fort Gibson); Brad Agnew, *Fort Gibson: Terminal on the Trail of Tears* (Norman: University of Oklahoma Press, 1980), 25–62; National Park Service, *Soldier and Brave*, 264–66.

5. The controversial Dennis Wolfe Bushyhead led the National party, and was elected principal Cherokee chief in 1879 and 1883. The great grandson of a British officer and briefly a student at Princeton University, Bushyhead was a forty-niner, a merchant, and later the tribal treasurer. H. Craig Miner, "Dennis Bushyhead," in *American Indian Leaders: Studies in Diversity*, ed. R. David Edmunds (Lincoln: University of Nebraska Press, 1980), 192–205.

6. One of the Five Civilized Tribes, the Cherokee originated in the southeastern United States, living primarily in western South and North Carolina, southern Tennessee, and northern Alabama. Expelled in 1838– 39 the tribe made the infamous Trail of Tears journey to the Indian Territory, where they had an immediate conflict with the Osage tribal groups in residence. The slave-owning Cherokees supported the Confederacy in the American Civil War, and their tribal lands were open to white settlement in 1906. Grace Steele Woodward, *The Cherokees* (Norman: University of Oklahoma Press, 1963); Charles H. Fairbanks, *Cherokee and Creek Indians* (New York: Garland Publishing, 1974).

7. D Company, Sixteenth Infantry, departed Fort Gibson for the Victorio Campaign in New Mexico on 28 May 1880, in compliance with telegraphic orders from the headquarters of the Department of the Missouri. Post Returns, Fort Gibson, May 1880.

CHAPTER EIGHT: *The Victorio Campaign*

1. D Company, Sixteenth Infantry, was being transferred to New Mexico
to participate in the Victorio Campaign, departing Fort Gibson on 28 May
1880. In September of 1877 Victorio, a highly skilled small-unit leader and
principal chief of the Mimbres Apaches, led 310 Chiricahuas and Mimbres
in a break from the San Carlos Reservation in Arizona to return to their
New Mexico homelands. After being rounded up and held at Ojo Caliente
the group was being returned to Arizona in 1879 when Victorio, leading
eighty warriors, made a second break and settled in with the Mescalero
Apaches at the Tularosa Agency. Believing he was to be arrested and tried
Victorio went to war in September 1879, killing eight soldiers of the Ninth
Cavalry and stealing several dozen horses. Establishing a base of operations
in the mountains of northern Mexico, Victorio raided back and forth across
the border, gaining strength from various Apache bands until he had nearly
150 warriors. After numerous skirmishes with army columns, Victorio went
on a spree between March and May of 1880, attacking sheep ranches,
miner camps, and travelers in Arizona and New Mexico.

New Mexico District Commander Colonel Edward Hatch requested and
received additional units to strengthen the campaign against Victorio, of
which Bode's Company D, Sixteenth Infantry, was one. In late May 1880,
after being wounded by Indian scouts attached to the army, Victorio and
most of his warriors returned to Mexico. This is about the time Bode and
his unit were en route from Fort Gibson. Although raiding south of the
border and in west Texas, Victorio did not again return to New Mexico.
In late July and early August he attempted to cross into Texas but was
turned back after two bruising encounters with Colonel Benjamin Grierson
and detachments of his Tenth Cavalry. Victorio then retreated into the
Candelaria Range in Chihuahua, raiding and roaming over much of that
northern Mexican state. In September 1880 Don Joaquin Terrazas, a Mexican volunteer colonel, organized a force to campaign against Victorio. In
September Sixth Cavalry companies from Arizona and a force from New
Mexico under Colonel George Buell, which included part of Bode's Sixteenth Infantry Regiment, crossed the border into Mexico to try and find
Victorio.

On 15 October 1880 Colonel Terrazas's column caught Victorio's small
band at Tres Castillos, where Victorio was killed in the battle with Mexican
soldiers. Post Returns, Fort Gibson, May 1880; "Report of Brigadier General
John Pope, Headquarters, Department of the Missouri, 22 September 1880,"
86–89; "Report of Colonel Edward Hatch, Headquarters, District of New
Mexico, 5 August 1880," *House Exec. Doc.*, 46th Cong., 3rd sess., no. 1, pt.
2, Serial 1952, 93–100; Crimmins, "Colonel Buell's Expedition," 133–42;
Utley, *Frontier Regulars*, 368–74; Dan L. Thrapp, *Victorio and the Mimbres
Apaches* (Norman: University of Oklahoma Press, 1974); Joseph A. Stout,

Jr., *Apache Lightning: The Last Great Battles of the Ojo Calientes* (New York: Oxford University Press, 1974).

2. Bode apparently changed cars in Pueblo, Colorado, and went south through Raton Pass to Las Vegas, New Mexico.

3. Much of the description of Albuquerque is from Bode's Journal, pages 31–35.

4. After a rail journey of 1,081 miles, D Company arrived in Belin, New Mexico, on 1 June 1880. Regimental Returns, Sixteenth Infantry, June 1880.

5. It was typical of soldiers' rumors that Victorio's force was greatly exaggerated. He had at this time, including stragglers still in New Mexico, no more than 150 fighters, including a few Comanche warriors. At this point he was already in Chihuahua, Mexico, but his son, Washington, was killed in Cook's Canyon on 5 June in a skirmish with Major Albert P. Morrow and a patrol of the Ninth and Sixth Cavalries. Thrapp, *Victorio*, 270, 277, 281–82; Stout, *Apache Lightning*, 144–46.

6. These observations on Indians are from Bode's Journal, pages 101–2.

7. Although much of Bode's criticism is valid, the district commander, Colonel Edward Hatch, did take to the field to direct operations in 1880.

8. Part of this description of Fort Craig is from Bode's Journal, page 41. Located in Socorro County, New Mexico, Fort Craig was constructed by the Third Infantry to replace Fort Conrad, a post slightly further north, in April of 1854 to guard the Santa Fe–El Paso Road. The Union troops at Fort Craig fought the Battle of Valverde, the first major Civil War battle in the Southwest. The post remained active until 1885, serving in the Apache campaigns of the period. National Park Service, *Soldier and Brave*, 224–25; Frazer, *Forts of the West*, 98.

9. Jack Crawford, the "poet scout," was waiting for orders to scout the Sacramentos. Crawford later found Victorio's camp in Mexico, volunteering to try and convince the Indian leader to surrender. The plan was abandoned after a long, hazardous journey because Crawford's interpreter refused to enter Victorio's camp. Thrapp, *Victorio*, 291–92.

10. On 29 June 1880 Bode's Company D entered the San Mateo foothills near Nogal Spring, apparently traveling up Nogal Canyon toward what is now called Vicks Peak in the present Cibola National Forest. Bode's Journal, page 42.

11. Although there were a few small hostile groups still in New Mexico, most of Victorio and his band were in Mexico by this time.

12. The twenty-seventh of July, 1880, according to Bode's Journal, page 47, from which most of this passage was taken.

13. Bode's Journal, pages 50–51.

14. Bode's Journal, page 51. Established in August 1866 by the 125th Infantry, California Volunteers, Fort Bayard was an important post in the Apache Wars. Abandoned in 1900 it became a veterans hospital. Frazer, *Forts of the West* 96–97; National Park Service, *Soldier and Brave*, 223, 224.

15. The description of the silver extract process is from Bode's Journal, 2 August 1880, page 52.

16. The small cannon was probably one of the two Hotchkiss 1.65-inch, 2-pounder rifled "mountain guns" to be used in the Buell Expedition into Mexico. Crimmins, "Colonel Buell's Expedition," 141.

17. On 9 August 1880 D Company arrived in this temporary base camp probably at the base of what is now Knight Peak in the Gila National Forest. On 30 July Victorio had crossed the Rio Grande from Mexico into Texas, engaging in several serious skirmishes with Colonel Grierson's Tenth Cavalry patrols, which were screening the network of water holes Victorio used along the Texas border. About the tenth of August, Victorio was forced back into Mexico by a battle at Rattlesnake Springs, Texas. However, at the time of Bode's arrival at Knight's Ranch, Indians attacked and killed three persons in a stagecoach thirty-five miles east of Bode's position, an indication that small raiding bands were still active in his vicinity.

The soldiers departing Bode's camp at Knight's Ranch were taking part in the Buell Expedition into Mexico. The Department of the Missouri commander, Brevet Major General John Pope, ordered a concentration of units in southern New Mexico at Fort Cummings and Knight's Ranch for operations against Victorio. Commanded by Colonel Buell, Fifteenth Infantry, the three-hundred-man task force of Ninth and Fourth Cavalry companies, several Fifteenth and Sixteenth Infantry companies, and two Apache scout companies acted as the large pursuit force, while a number of Ninth Cavalry companies served as a screen, as did Bode's little group, splitting into small detachments to guard nearly every water hole and ranch in southern New Mexico. The purpose of the screen was to give notice if Victorio's band slipped back north while Buell's force was headed south into Mexico to campaign in concert with the Mexican forces under Colonel Terrazas. Bode's D Company of infantrymen were part of the escort for Buell's large supply train as the command moved into Mexico the last week in September 1880. The supply train included a unique four-hundred-gallon water wagon. After three weeks the Mexican military authorities ordered Buell's expedition to return to the United States just as Colonel Terrazas's troops found and killed Victorio. Bode's Journal, pages 52–53; "Report of General John Pope, Headquarters, Department of the Missouri, 22 September 1880," 86–89; Crimmins, "Colonel Buell's Expedition," 133–42; Thrapp, *Victorio*, 287–90; Stout, *Apache Lightning*, 153–59.

18. Bode records he left Knight's Ranch on 6 November 1880 and the Sixteenth Infantry returns state that D Company left Fort Craig for Fort Gibson on 1 November. Bode's Journal, page 60; Regimental Returns, Sixteenth Infantry.

19. Bode's Journal, pages 55–56. Bode is referring to the skirmish of 5 June between Major Marrow's detachment and Victorio's son Washington. See note 5, above.

20. Part of this description is from Bode's Journal, page 57. Twenty-one miles northeast of Deming, New Mexico, Fort Cummings was established in 1863 as a Civil War frontier post by the First California Volunteer Infantry to guard Cooke's Spring. The site had been a Butterfield Mail Station until 1861, when it was attacked by Apaches. Used by expeditions until 1873 the post was again occupied from 1880 to 1886, the troops living in tents. National Park Service, *Soldier and Brave,* 225–26; Frazer, *Forts of the West,* 98.

21. After the 1863 massacre of a wagon train party at Ojo del Muerto the New Mexico Volunteers established Fort McRae three miles east of the Rio Grande, at the northern end of the Jornada del Muerto. It remained in active use until 1876. National Park Service, *Soldier and Brave,* 226–27; Frazer, *Forts of the West,* 100.

CHAPTER NINE: *The Texas Frontier*

1. In 1881 the Sixteenth Infantry Regiment was transferred to the Texas frontier. In compliance with Department of the Missouri Special Orders No. 260, 26 November 1880, D Company, Sixteenth Infantry, was ordered to Fort Davis, Texas, leaving Fort Gibson on 3 December 1880. Post Returns, Fort Gibson, December 1880; Regimental Returns, Sixteenth Infantry, December 1880.

2. For more about Bode's court-martial see note 14, below.

3. The band would have been the regimental band of the Tenth Cavalry at Fort Concho. Established by the Fourth Cavalry in 1867, at the confluence of the North and South Concho Rivers, Fort Concho served as a key post on the Texas frontier in the heart of the Kiowa and Comanche homelands. An important station on the northern or upper San Antonio– El Paso Road, it also played a role in guarding the Goodnight-Loving Cattle Trail until the post was abandoned in June 1889. J. Evetts Haley, *Fort Concho and the Texas Frontier* (San Angelo, Tex.: San Angelo Standard Times, 1952); National Park Service, *Soldier and Brave,* 320–22; Frazer, *Forts of the West,* 147.

4. Bode's Journal, page 4, identifies this as Grierson Springs, about eleven miles east of Horsehead Crossing of the Pecos River.

5. At that time garrisoned by four companies of the First Infantry and Tenth Cavalry, Fort Stockton was active in the periods 1858–59 and 1867– 86. Rebuilt by the Ninth Cavalry in 1867, after being burned by Confederates, the post served as a station at Comanche Springs at the upper and lower San Antonio–El Paso military road junctions, with the Great Comanche War Trail. By-passed by the railroad, the operational importance of the fort declined by the mid-1880s. Clayton Williams, *Texas' Last Frontier: Fort Stockton and the Trans-Pecos, 1861–1895,* ed. Ernest Wallace

(College Station: Texas A&M University Press, 1982); National Park Service, *Soldier and Brave,* 334–35; Frazer, *Forts of the West,* 162.

6. Part of this description of Leon Spring is from Bode's Journal, page 7.

7. Description of Limpia Canyon is from Bode's Journal, page 9.

8. Companies D, E, and G, Sixteenth Infantry, arrived at Fort Davis on 5 January 1881, joining companies A, C, H, and K of the Tenth Cavalry. This gave the garrison a total of 371 enlisted men and forty-seven officers. The post commander at that time was Major Napoleon B. McLaughlen of the Tenth Cavalry, who commanded until the return of Colonel William R. Shafter in March 1881. On 11 January Company E, Sixteenth Infantry, was dispersed to guard mail stations, a typical task for the infantry. The Eighth Infantry Regiment established Fort Davis in October 1854 to guard the San Antonio-El Paso military road. Named in honor of Secretary of War Jefferson Davis, the post was abandoned by the federal government during the 1861 exodus from Texas. Largely destroyed by Indians during the Civil War, it was slightly relocated and reoccupied by the Ninth Cavalry beginning in July 1867. Fort Davis was the largest and most active post in the trans-Pecos. Abandoned in 1891 the post remains one of the most impressive frontier forts of the National Park Service. Regimental Returns, Sixteenth Infantry, January 1881; Post Returns, Fort Davis, for January 1881, in Post Returns, Fort Davis, Texas, January 1879–June 1891, microfilm no. 617, roll 298, Returns from United States Military Posts, 1800–1916, Adjutant General's Records, NARS (hereinafter cited as Post Returns, Fort Davis); Robert M. Utley, *Fort Davis* (Washington D.C.: National Park Service, 1965); Barry Scobee, *Old Fort Davis* (San Antonio: Naylor Co., 1947); Frazer, *Forts of the West,* 148.

9. On 23 January a detachment of one officer and fifteen enlisted men of the Sixteenth Infantry departed Fort Davis to escort Colonel and Brigadier General of Volunteers Orlando M. Poe to Fort Bliss. Colonel Poe was at this time an aide-de-camp to the general-in-chief of the army, William T. Sherman. Post Returns, Fort Davis, January 1881.

10. These descriptions are extracted from Bode's Journal, pages 12–17. The 1867 army survey of water holes between Fort Davis and El Paso are as follows: Fort Davis, Barrel Springs, El Muerto (Dead Man's Hole), Van Horn's Well, Eagle Springs, Rio Grande, Fort Quitman, Smith's Ranch, Hawkins Station, San Elizario, Fort Bliss. Escal F. Duke, ed., "A Description of the Route from San Antonio to El Paso by Captain Edward S. Meyer," *West Texas Historical Association Year Book* 49 (1973): 128–41.

11. According to the memoirs of Texas Ranger James B. Gillett this occurred the third week in January 1881 and involved Captain George W. Baylor's Texas Ranger Company from Ysleta in pursuit of a small band of Apaches who had robbed a stage and murdered several passengers the week before. Baylor had with him three Pueblo scouts whom Bode mistook for whites dressed as Indians. Baylor's group caught this band a few days

later in the Diablo Mountains and the two groups fought one of the last battles between Rangers and Apaches in Texas. Although having some origins in the period before the Texas Revolution the Texas Rangers were organized in the days of the Texas Republic as a form of militia force. They evolved after annexation into state-controlled federally-funded frontier defense units called Texas Ranging Companies and gradually expanded their powers to general law enforcement as Texas Rangers. James B. Gillett, *Six Years with the Texas Rangers,* Ed. Milo Milton Quaife. (New Haven: Yale University Press, 1925; reprint, Chicago: R. R. Donnelley and Sons Co., 1943), 284–98; Walter Prescott Webb, *The Texas Rangers: A Century of Frontier Defense* (Austin: University of Texas Press, 1965), 402–6.

12. Part of this description is from Bode's Journal, pages 22–23. Established in September 1849 by the Third Infantry, Fort Bliss occupied five different locations across the Rio Grande from El Paso del Norte. Occupied off and on in the antebellum era to protect the southern route to California the post was used briefly by the Confederates during the Civil War. Reclaimed by Union forces in 1862 it was relocated several times in the last half of the nineteenth century. The fort remains an active post in the U.S. Army as the Air Defense Center. Leon C. Metz, *Fort Bliss: An Illustrated History,* (El Paso: Mangan Books, 1981); National Park Service, *Soldier and Brave,* 318–19; Frazer, *Forts of the West,* 143–44.

13. Much of the description of Old El Paso is from Bode's Journal, pages 25–26. Old El Paso, which later became Ciudad Juarez, was an ancient Spanish settlement. In 1598 a colonial expedition headed for New Mexico under Captain General Don Juan de Onate discovered a ford of the Rio Grande that came to be called El Paso del Norte. A small mission was established in 1659 to serve as a station for trains traveling between New Mexico and the interior of Mexico. A larger mission church, Nuestra Señora de Guadalupe de El Paso was built in 1668, and a satellite town grew up in the 1670s. Paul Horgan, *Great River: The Rio Grande in North American History,* 2 vols. (New York: Rinehart and Company, 1954) 1:164–70, 260.

14. Bode was facing a court-martial for being corporal of the guard when a prisoner deserted en route to Fort Davis on the march from Fort Gibson. The court convened in February 1881 at Fort Davis. Captain Nicholas Nolan, Company A, Tenth Cavalry, served as president of the court. Nolan was Lieutenant Henry O. Flipper's company commander at this time. In the larger perspective, for the year 1881 Bode's case was one of 19 general courts-martial for enlisted men in the Sixteenth Infantry Regiment, one of 1,693 for the U.S. Army. During the same period the Army had 8,500 lesser garrison or regimental level courts-martial, an expensive and time-consuming drain on army leadership and a cumbersome legal process until the military justice reforms of the 1890s. Although the records are sketchy it appears that at least 45 percent of all enlisted men faced the peril of court-martial of some form in the post-Civil War era.

It was so common as to not necessarily constitute a stigma or blemish on a soldier's service record, especially as in Bode's case, where he was acquitted. March 1881, index no. 2285, microfilm no. M1105, roll 7, Register of the Records of the Proceedings of the United States Army General Courts-Martial, 1809–1890, vols. 15–16, PP–QQ, 1869–1883, Records of the Office of the Judge Advocate General, RG 153, NARS; "Report of the General of the Army, 10 Nov. 1881," *House Exec. Doc.*, 47th Cong., 1st sess., no. 1, pt. 2, Serial 2010, and "Report of the Judge-Advocate-General, War Department, 1 October 1881," ibid., 73, 208–11; Coffman, *The Old Army*, 378–79; Rickey, *Forty Miles a Day on Beans and Hay*, 141–43.

15. In 1850 Henry Skillman established the first mail run from San Antonio to El Paso. Under contract to George H. Giddings the San Antonio line expanded to Santa Fe in 1853 and to San Diego, California, in 1857. For excellent accounts of the development of the El Paso stage run see Emmie Giddings W. Mahon and Chester V. Kielman, "George H. Giddings and the San Antonio–San Diego Mail Line," *Southwestern Historical Quarterly* 61 (Oct. 1957): 220–39; A. J. Sowell, *The Life of Bigfoot Wallace* (Bandera, Tex.: Frontier Times, 1934), 136–38. For the most detailed account of the trans-Pecos wagon freight development see Roy L. Swift and Leavitt Corning, Jr., *Three Roads to Chihuahua: The Great Wagon Roads That Opened the Southwest, 1823–83* (Austin, Tex.: Eakin Press, 1988).

16. Although Van Horn's Well was not one of his projects, army engineer Captain John Pope, between 1855 and 1858, attempted to dig several artesian wells in the region of the Staked Plains on the Pecos River near the thirty-second parallel. The project was abandoned without success. "Reports of Captain John Pope, Topographical Engineers," *House Exec. Doc.*, 35th Cong., 2d sess., no. 2, Serial 998, 590–608; William H. Goetzmann, *Army Exploration in the American West, 1803–1863* (New Haven: Yale University Press, 1959; reprint, Lincoln: University of Nebraska Press, 1979), 365–68.

17. Fort Quitman was established by the Eighth Infantry in September 1858 to protect the San Antonio-El Paso military road. Occupied by Confederates during 1861 the post came back under federal control for the year 1862–63 with the arrival of the Second California Cavalry. Garrisoned again in January 1868 the post was abandoned in 1877, with the exception of the occasional detachment using the old post during periods of insecurity in the 1880s. Frazer, *Forts of the West*, 157–58.

18. In compliance with Department of Texas Special Orders No. 50, 1 February 1881, Bode's Company D and Company G were transferred to Fort McKavett on 14 March 1881 and arrived there 2 April, but Bode had remained on detached service at Fort Davis, repairing telegraph lines. Regimental Returns, Sixteenth Infantry, March 1881; Post Returns, Fort Davis, March 1881; Post Returns, April 1881, Post Returns, Fort McKavett, Texas, January 1873–June 1883, microfilm no. 617, roll 688, Returns from

United States Military Posts, 1800–1916, Adjutant General's Records, NARS (hereinafter cited as Post Returns, Fort McKavett).

19. Colonel Galusha Pennypacker, the commander of the Sixteenth Infantry, was in command of Fort McKavett at this time. His garrison consisted of D, E, G, I, and K Companies of his regiment and the head-quarters band, composed of twenty-one officers and 256 enlisted men. Established in March 1852 by the Eighth Infantry on the right bank of the San Saba River, Fort McKavett was part of the original line of cordon forts to protect Texas frontier settlements. Abandoned in 1859 the post was used by the Confederates in the Civil War, reoccupied by federal troops in 1868, and later rebuilt by Colonel Ranald S. Mackenzie. Troops from Fort McKavett served in the Red River War and in the Victorio Campaign. By-passed by the railroad and the frontier line, the post was abandoned by the government by 1883. Post Returns, Fort McKavett, April 1881; Martin L. Crimmins, "Fort McKavett, Texas," *Southwestern Historical Quarterly* 38 (July 1934): 28–39; Jerry M. Sullivan, "Fort McKavett: A Texas Frontier Post," *Museum Journal* (West Texas Museum Association, Lubbock 20 (1981): 1–74; Frazer, *Forts of the West*, 154–55.

20. Bode was promoted to sergeant in February 1882, probably in an attempt to persuade him to reenlist. He was one of five men of Company D whose term of service had expired. He declined. This was symptomatic of the retention problem in a frontier infantry regiment. Bode was one of ninety-four men of his regiment whose term of service expired that year. Only six noncommissioned officers reenlisted, again typical of a frontier infantry unit. In the period 1881–82 the regiment had an authorized strength of 550 enlisted men, but had only 392 present for duty (71 percent). It lost 173 through expiration of service, disability, courts-martial, death, desertion, and other causes, a loss of 44 percent. The regiment regained 141 men through recruiting and reenlistment, leaving it in mid-1882 with only 65 percent of its authorized strength. Post Returns, Fort McKavett, March 1881; Regimental Returns, Sixteenth Infantry, March 1882; "Report of the General of the Army, 14 November 1882," *House Exec. Doc.*, 47th Cong., 2d sess., no. 1, pt. 2, Serial 2091, 30–31, 52–54.

ℬ𝒾𝒷𝓁𝒾𝑜𝑔𝓇𝒶𝓅𝒽𝓎

ARCHIVES

Fort Sill Archives, Fort Sill, Oklahoma

Post Returns, Fort Sill, Oklahoma, March 1869–January 1917. microfilm no. NAS-E88-roll 1.

Special Orders, Headquarters, Fort Sill. Vol. 1, no. XD6213763. Special Orders No. 170, 7 Sept. 1877; No. 200, 9 Oct. 1877; No. 129, 16 June 1878; No. 163, 5 Aug. 1879; No. 1, 2 Jan. 1880.

Record of Medical History of Fort Sill, I.T., Feb. 1873–May 1880. No. D62.137.140.

Guard Reports, Fort Sill, I.T., 3 July 1879–29 Nov. 1879. No. D62.137.20.

National Archives and Records Service, Washington, D.C. (NARS)

Records of the United States Army Adjutant General's Office, 1780–1917, Record Group (RG) 94

    Register of Enlistments. vol. 72, 1871–1877, 198 entry 118, Regular Army Muster Rolls, Sixteenth Infantry, Company D, 31 Oct. 1872–Dec. 1902

        Muster Roll for 28 February to 30 April, 1882, box 474

    Returns From United States Military Posts, 1800–1916

        Post Returns, Fort Davis, Texas, January 1879–June 1891, microfilm no. 617, roll 298

        Post Returns, Fort Gibson, Oklahoma, July 1872–October 1897, microfilm no. 617, roll 406

        Post Returns, Fort McKavett, Texas, January 1873–June 1883, microfilm no. 617, roll 688

        Post Returns, Fort Sill, Oklahoma, January 1876–December 1887, microfilm no. 617, roll 1174

    Returns From Regular Army Infantry Regiments, June 1821–December 1916

        Regimental Returns, Sixteenth Infantry, January 1880–December 1889, microfilm no. 665, roll 176

Records of the Office of the Judge Advocate General, RG 153

    Register of the Records of the Proceedings of the United States Army General Courts-Martial 1809–1890, Vols. 15–16, PP–QQ 1869–1883

Letters Received by the Office of Indian Affairs, 1824–1880, RG 75

    Captain H.A. Theaker, Sixteenth Infantry, "Report of Cattle Inspection," Wichita Agency, 24 March 1878, microcopy no. 234, roll 930

Special Collections of the Sterling C. Evans Library, Texas A&M
University, College Station, Texas
  Emil A. Bode Manuscript and Journal. Cataloged as E. A. Baue
  Manuscript. Western box 2, W2.

GOVERNMENT DOCUMENTS

United States Congressional Records
35th Congress, 2d Session.
  House Executive Documents, no. 2, Serial 998 ("Reports of Captain
  John Pope, Topographical Engineers").
44th Congress, 1st Session.
  House Executive Documents, no. 1, pt. 5, Serial 1680 ("Report of the
  Commissioner of Indian Affairs, 1 Nov. 1875").
44th Congress, 2d Session.
  House Executive Documents, no. 1, pt. 2, Serial 1742 ("Report of the
  Secretary of War, 10 Nov. 1876"; "Report of the General of the
  Army, 10 Nov. 1876"; "Report of the Recruiting Service from
  October 1, 1875–October 1, 1876").
45th Congress, 2d Session.
  House Executive Documents, no. 1, pt. 2, Serial 1794 ("Report of the
  Secretary of War, 19 Nov. 1877"; "Report of Brigadier General C. C.
  Augur, Headquarters Department of the Gulf, 12 Oct. 1877";
  "Adjutant General's Report of the Recruiting Service for the Year
  Ending October 1, 1877").
  House Executive Documents, no. 1, pt. 5, Serial 1800 ("Report of the
  Commissioner of Indian Affairs, 1 Nov. 1877").
45th Congress, 3rd Session.
  House Executive Documents, no. 1, pt. 2, Serial 1843 ("Report of the
  Secretary of War, 19 Nov. 1878").
  House Executive Documents, no. 1, pt. 5, Serial 1850 ("Report of the
  Commissioner of Indian Affairs, 1 Nov. 1878").
46th Congress, 2d Session.
  House Executive Documents, no. 1, pt. 2, Serial 1903 ("Report of
  Brigadier General John Pope, Headquarters Department of the
  Missouri, 3 Oct. 1879").
  House Executive Documents, no. 1, pt. 5, Serial 1910 ("Report of the
  Commissioner of Indian Affairs, 1 Nov. 1879").
46th Congress, 3rd Session.
  House Executive Documents, no. 1, pt. 2, Serial 1952 ("Report of
  General John Pope, Headquarters, Department of the Missouri, 22
  September 1880"; "Report of Colonel Edward Hatch, Headquarters,
  District of New Mexico, 5 August 1880").

House Executive Documents, no. 1, pt. 2, Serial 1957 ("Report of the Chief Signal Officer of the Army, 15 Nov. 1880").

47th Congress, 1st Session.

House Executive Documents, no. 1, pt. 2, Serial 2010 ("Report of the General of the Army, 10 Nov. 1881"; "Report of the Judge-Advocate-General, War Department, 1 October 1881"; "Report of the Commissary-General of Subsistence, 10 Oct. 1881"; "Report of the Quartermaster General, 1 Nov. 1881").

47th Congress, 2d Session.

House Executive Documents, no. 1, pt. 2, Serial 2091 ("Report of the General of the Army, 14 November 1882").

BOOKS

Agnew, Brad. *Fort Gibson: Terminal on the Trail of Tears*. Norman: University of Oklahoma Press, 1980.

Albers, Patricia and Beatrice Medicine. *The Hidden Half: Studies of Plains Indian Women*. Washington, D.C.: University Press of America, 1983.

Athearn, Robert G. *William Tecumseh Sherman and the Settlement of the West*. Norman: University of Oklahoma Press, 1956.

Carlson, Paul H. *"Pecos Bill": A Military Biography of William R. Shafter*. College Station: Texas A&M University Press, 1989.

Carter, Robert G. *On the Border with Mackenzie; or, Winning West Texas from the Comanches*. Washington, D.C.: Eynon, 1935. Reprint. New York: Antiquarian Press, 1961.

Chief of Military History. *The Army Lineage Book*. Vol. 2, *Infantry*. Washington, D.C.: GPO, 1953.

Coffman, Edward M. *The Old Army: A Portrait of the American Army in Peacetime, 1784–1898*. New York: Oxford University Press, 1986.

Davidson, Homer K. *Black Jack Davidson: A Cavalry Commander on the Western Frontier*. Glendale, Calif.: Clark, 1974.

Dawson, Joseph G., III. *Army Generals and Reconstruction: Louisiana, 1862–1877*. Baton Rouge: Louisiana State University Press, 1982.

Fairbanks, Charles H. *Cherokee and Creek Indians*. New York: Garland Publishing, 1974.

Flipper, Henry O. *Negro Frontiersman: The Frontier Memoirs of Henry O. Flipper, First Negro Graduate of West Point*. Edited by Theodore Harris. El Paso: Texas Western College Press, 1963.

Fowler, Arlen L. *The Black Infantry in the West, 1869–1891*. Westport, Conn.: Greenwood Press, 1971.

Frazer, Robert W. *Forts of the West*. Norman: University of Oklahoma Press, 1965.

Gibson, Arrell M. *The Chickasaws.* Norman: University of Oklahoma Press, 1971.

Gillett, James B. *Six Years with the Texas Rangers.* Edited by Milo Milton Quaife. New Haven: Yale University Press, 1925. Reprint. Chicago: R. R. Donnelley and Sons Co., 1943.

Goetzmann, William H. *Army Exploration in the American West, 1803–1863.* New Haven: Yale University Press, 1959. Reprint. Lincoln: University of Nebraska Press, 1979.

Hagan, William T. *United States–Comanche Relations: The Reservation Years.* New Haven: Yale University Press, 1976.

Haley, J. Evetts. *Fort Concho and the Texas Frontier.* San Angelo, Tex.: San Angelo Standard Times, 1952.

Hart, Herbert M. *Tour Guide to Old Western Forts.* Fort Collins, Colo.: Old Army Press, 1980.

Heitman, Francis B. *Historical Register and Dictionary of the United States Army.* 2 vols. Washington, D.C.: GPO, 1903.

Horgan, Paul. *Great River: The Rio Grande in North American History.* 2 vols. New York: Rinehart and Company, 1954.

Huntington, Samuel P. *The Soldier and the State: The Theory and Politics of Civil-Military Relations.* New York: Vintage Books, 1957.

Hutton, Paul Andrew. *Phil Sheridan and His Army.* Lincoln: University of Nebraska Press, 1985.

Knight, Oliver. *Life and Manners in the Frontier Army.* Norman: University of Oklahoma Press, 1978.

Lane, Lydia Spencer. *I Married a Soldier; or, Old Days in the Army.* Philadelphia: J. P. Lippincott Co., 1893. Reprint. Albuquerque: University of New Mexico Press, 1987.

Lenny, John J. *Rankers: The Odyssey of the Enlisted Regular Soldier of America and Britain.* New York: Greenburg, 1950.

Leckie, William H. *The Buffalo Soldiers: A Narrative History of the Negro Cavalry in the West.* Norman: University of Oklahoma Press, 1967.

Leckie, William H., and Shirley A. Leckie. *Unlikely Warriors: General Benjamin H. Grierson and His Family.* Norman: University of Oklahoma Press, 1984.

Marcy, Captain Randolph B. *The Prairie Traveler.* New York: Harper & Brothers, 1859.

Metz, Leon C. *Fort Bliss: An Illustrated History.* El Paso: Mangan Books, 1981.

Miller, Darlis A. *Soldiers and Settlers: Military Supply in the Southwest, 1861–1885.* Albuquerque: University of New Mexico Press, 1989.

Millett, Allan R. and Peter Maslowski. *For the Common Defense: A Military History of the United States of America.* New York: Free Press, 1984.

Myres, Sandra L., ed. *Cavalry Wife: The Diary of Eveline M. Alexander, 1866–1867*. College Station: Texas A&M University Press, 1977.

National Park Service. *Soldier and Brave: Historic Places Associated with Indian Affairs and the Indian Wars in the Trans-Mississippi West*. The National Survey of Historic Sites and Buildings. Vol. 12. Edited by Robert G. Ferris. Washington, D.C.: United States Department of the Interior, National Park Service, 1971.

Nye, Captain Wilber S. *Carbine and Lance: The Story of Old Fort Sill*. Norman: University of Oklahoma Press, 1937.

Prucha, Francis Paul. *The Sword of the Republic: The United States Army on the Frontier, 1783–1846*. New York: Macmillan, 1969. Reprint. Bloomington: University of Indiana Press, 1977.

Register of Graduates and Former Cadets, 1802–1964, of the United States Military Academy. West Point, N.Y.: West Point Alumni Foundation, 1964.

Rickey, Don, Jr. *Forty Miles a Day on Beans and Hay: The Enlisted Soldier Fighting the Indian Wars*. Norman: University of Oklahoma Press, 1963.

Schmitt, Martin F., and Dee Brown. *Fighting Indians of the West*. New York: Bonanza Books, 1968.

Scobee, Barry. *Old Fort Davis*. San Antonio: Naylor Co., 1947.

Smith, Sherry L. *The View from Officers' Row: Army Perceptions of Western Indians*. Tucson: University of Arizona Press, 1990.

Sowell, A. J. *The Life of Bigfoot Wallace*. Bandera, Tex.: Frontier Times, 1934.

Spiller, Roger J. and Joseph G. Dawson III, eds. *American Military Leaders*. New York: Praeger, 1989.

Stallard, Patricia Y. *Glittering Misery: Dependents of the Indian Fighting Army*. Fort Collins, Colo.: Old Army Press, 1978.

Stout, Joseph A., Jr. *Apache Lightning: The Last Great Battles of the Ojo Calientes*. New York: Oxford University Press, 1974.

Swift, Roy L. and Leavitt Corning, Jr. *Three Roads to Chihuahua: The Great Wagon Roads That Opened the Southwest, 1823–1883*. Austin, Tex.: Eakin Press, 1988.

Thrapp, Dan L. *Victorio and the Mimbres Apaches*. Norman: University of Oklahoma Press, 1974.

———. *The Conquest of Apacheria*. Norman: University of Oklahoma Press, 1967.

Urwin, Gregory J. W. *Custer Victorious: The Civil War Battles of General George Armstrong Custer*. Reprint. Lincoln: University of Nebraska Press, 1990.

Utley, Robert M. *Frontier Regulars: The United States Army and the Indian, 1866–1891*. New York: Macmillan, 1973.

———. *Fort Davis*. Washington, D.C.: National Park Service, 1965.

————. *Frontiersmen in Blue: The United States Army and the Indian, 1848–1865.* New York: Macmillan, 1967. Reprint. Lincoln: University of Nebraska Press, 1981.

Wallace, Ernest. *Ranald S. MacKenzie on the Texas Frontier.* Lubbock: West Texas Museum Association, 1965.

Webb, Walter Prescott. *The Texas Rangers: A Century of Frontier Defense.* Austin: University of Texas Press, 1965.

Weigley, Russell F. *History of the United States Army.* New York: Macmillan, 1967.

————. *The American Way of War: A History of United States Military Strategy and Policy.* New York: Macmillan, 1973. Reprint. Bloomington: Indiana University Press, 1977.

Williams, Clayton. *Texas' Last Frontier: Fort Stockton and the Trans-Pecos, 1861–1895.* Edited by Ernest Wallace. College Station: Texas A&M University Press, 1982.

Woodward, Grace Steele. *The Cherokees.* Norman: University of Oklahoma Press, 1963.

Wooster, Robert. *Soldiers, Sutlers, and Settlers: Garrison Life on the Texas Frontier.* College Station: Texas A&M University Press, 1987.

————. *The Military and United States Indian Policy, 1865–1903.* New Haven: Yale University Press, 1988.

ARTICLES

Clendenen, Clarence E. "President Hayes' 'Withdrawal' of the Troops: An Enduring Myth." *South Carolina Historical Magazine* 70 (Oct. 1969): 240–50.

Cooper, Jerry M. "The Army's Search for a Mission, 1865–1890." In *Against All Enemies: Interpretations of American Military History from Colonial Times to the Present,* edited by Kenneth J. Hagan and William R. Roberts. Westport, Conn.: Greenwood Press, 1986.

Courtwright, David T. "Opiate Addiction as a Consequence of the Civil War." *Civil War History* 24 (June 1978): 101–11.

Crimmins, Colonel Martin L. "Colonel Buell's Expedition into Mexico in 1880." *New Mexico Historical Review* 10 (April 1935): 133–42.

————. "Fort McKavett, Texas." *Southwestern Historical Quarterly.* 38 (July 1934): 28–39.

Crockett, Bernice Norman. "Health Conditions in the Indian Territory, from the Civil War to 1890." *Chronicles of Oklahoma* 36 (Spring 1958): 21–39.

Dinges, Bruce J. "The Court-Martial of Lieutenant Henry O. Flipper: An Example of Black-White Relations in the Army, 1881." *American West* 9 (Jan. 1972): 12–15.

Duke, Escal F., ed. "A Description of the Route from San Antonio to El Paso by Captain Edward S. Meyer." *West Texas Historical Association Year Book* 49 (1973): 128–41.

Ellis, Richard N. "The Humanitarian Generals." *Western Historical Quarterly* 3 (April 1972): 169–78.

Ellis, Tuffly, ed. "Lieutenant A. W. Greely's Report on the Installation of Military Telegraph Lines in Texas, 1875–1876." *Southwestern Historical Quarterly* 69 (July 1965): 67–87.

Gates, John M. "Indians and Insurrectos: The U.S. Army's Experience with Insurgency." *Parameters: Journal of the U.S. Army War College* 13 (March 1983): 59–68.

Griswold, Gillett. "Old Fort Sill: The First Seven Years." *Chronicles of Oklahoma* 36 (Spring 1958): 2–14.

Hill, Michael D., and Ben Innis, eds. "The Fort Buford Diary of Private Sanford, 1876–1877." *North Dakota History* 52 (Summer 1985): 2–40.

Kreneck, Thomas H. "The North Texas Regiment in the Mexican War." *Military History of Texas and the Southwest* 12, (no. 1 (1975): 109–17.

McClung, Donald R. "Second Lieutenant Henry O. Flipper: A Negro Officer on the West Texas Frontier." *West Texas Historical Association Year Book* 48 (1971): 20–31.

Mahon, Emmie Giddings W., and Chester V. Kielman. "George H. Giddings and the San Antonio–San Diego Mail Line." *Southwestern Historical Quarterly* 61 (Oct. 1957): 220–39.

Miner, H. Craig. "Dennis Bushyhead." In *American Indian Leaders: Studies in Diversity*, edited by R. David Edmunds. Lincoln: University of Nebraska Press, 1980.

Rickey, Don, Jr. "The Enlisted Men of the Indian Wars." *Military Affairs* 23 (1959–60): 91–96.

Simmons, Clyde R. "The Indian Wars and U.S. Military Thought, 1865–1890." *Parameters: Journal of the U.S. Army War College* 22 (Spring 1992): 60–72.

Skelton, William B. "Professionalism in the U.S. Army Officer Corps during the Age of Jackson." *Armed Forces and Society* 1 (Summer 1975): 443–71.

———. "Army Officers' Attitudes toward Indians, 1830–1860." *Pacific Northwest Quarterly* 67 (July 1976): 113–24.

Stewart, Miller J. "Army Laundresses: Ladies of 'Soap Suds Row.'" *Nebraska History* 61 (Winter 1980): 421–36.

———. "A Touch of Civilization: Culture and Education in the Frontier Army." *Nebraska History* 65 (Summer 1984): 257–82.

Sullivan, Jerry M. "Fort McKavett: A Texas Frontier Post." *Museum Journal* (West Texas Museum Association, Lubbock) 20 (1981): 1–74.

Utley, Robert M. "The Frontier and the American Military Tradition." In *Soldiers West: Biographies from the Military Frontier*, edited by

Paul Andrew Hutton. Lincoln: University of Nebraska Press, 1987.

————. "A Chained Dog." *American West.* 10 (July 1973): 18–24, 61.

Walker, Henry P. "The Enlisted Soldier on the Frontier." In *The American Military on the Frontier: The Proceedings of the 7th Military History Symposium, U.S. Air Force Academy, 30 Sept–1 Oct. 1976*, edited by James P. Tate. Washington, D.C.: GPO, 1978.

Wallace, Ernest. "The Comanches on the White Man's Road." *West Texas Historical Association Yearbook* 29 (Oct. 1953): 3–32.

Zimmerman, Jean L. "Colonel Ranald S. Mackenzie at Fort Sill." *Chronicles of Oklahoma* 44 (Spring 1966): 12–21.

Index

Thomas Tyree Smith is a native Texan and a Regular Army Captain of Infantry. He served in Vietnam with the U.S. Navy, earned a B.S. in Ed. Southwest Texas State University, and an MA in History from Texas A&M University. After commanding an infantry company in Germany he is currently on assignment as an assistant professor of military history, United States Military Academy at West Point, New York.